TEACHING SUSTAINABILITY/

TEACHING SUSTAINABLY

TEACHING
SUSTAINABILITY /
TEACHING SUSTAINABLY

Edited by
Kirsten Allen Bartels
and Kelly A. Parker

STERLING, VIRGINIA

Sty/us

COPYRIGHT © 2012 BY
STYLUS PUBLISHING, LLC.

Published by Stylus Publishing, LLC
22883 Quicksilver Drive
Sterling, Virginia 20166-2102

Library of Congress Cataloging-in-Publication-Data
Teaching sustainability, teaching sustainably / edited by
Kirsten Allen Bartels and Kelly A. Parker.
    p.   cm.
Includes bibliographical references and index.
ISBN 978-1-57922-738-8 (cloth : alk. paper)
ISBN 978-1-57922-739-5 (pbk. : alk. paper)
ISBN 978-1-57922-740-1 (library networkable e-edition)
ISBN 978-1-57922-741-8 (consumer e-edition)
1. Environmental education.   2. Sustainable
development.   3. Environmental responsibility—Study and
teaching.   4. Cross-cultural studies.   I. Bartels, Kirsten
Allen, 1968–   II. Parker, Kelly A., 1963–
GE70.T42 2012
338.9′27071—dc23   2011030322

13-digit ISBN: 978-1-57922-738-8 (cloth)
13-digit ISBN: 978-1-57922-739-5 (paper)
13-digit ISBN: 978 1 57922-740-1 (library networkable
e-edition)
13-digit ISBN: 978-1-57922-741-8 (consumer e-edition)

Printed in the United States of America

All first editions printed on acid free paper
that meets the American National Standards Institute
Z39-48 Standard.

Bulk Purchases

Quantity discounts are available for use in workshops
and for staff development.
Call 1-800-232-0223

First Edition, 2012

To our students and colleagues—
past, present, and future—for
continuing to inspire us to strive
for a sustainable future

CONTENTS

vii

INTRODUCTION
Sustainability in Higher Education

Kelly A. Parker

S ustainability is quite literally the way of the future. In the present, though, it remains unclear what exactly the movement toward sustain- ability means for many of us. This is perhaps especially true in higher education: While colleges and universities are often at the forefront of major social changes, and while it is true that academics have contributed a great deal to our overall understanding of the need for sustainability, the commer- cial and public sectors have, in many respects, outrun education in making their day-to-day operations more sustainable. The contributors to *Teaching Sustainability/Teaching Sustainably* are all leaders in sustainable education. Their contributions to this volume report work and discoveries in all aspects of the sustainable education movement. The chapters in Part One provide guidance for rethinking institutional mission, vision, and values in higher education. Part Two shows how faculty members have integrated concepts of sustainability into their disciplines and into the content of their courses, in areas ranging from literary criticism to health-care management to eco- tourism. Part Three features reports on faculty experiments with sustainable teaching practices in the classroom and in campus life. Finally, Part Four presents a variety of ways to train change-making leaders for the future of the sustainability movement. *Teaching Sustainability/Teaching Sustainably* will help and inspire people working in all areas of higher education to move toward sustainability in an effective and responsible way.

This culture shift has been a long time in the making. The current sustainability movement originated with the World Commission on Envi- ronment and Development (more commonly known as the Brundtland

Commission), which was convened by the United Nations in 1983. In their report, *Our Common Future*, the World Commission on Environment and Development defined sustainable development as "development that meets the needs of the present without compromising the ability of future generations to meet their own needs" (1987, p. 43). The commission established the point that what is often regarded simply as *the environmental crisis* is really a complex system of interconnected problems, and that these are primarily caused by human activities that overburden the earth's natural carrying capacity. It is now a commonly known fact that localized problems concerning air quality, water quality, soil depletion, species loss, habitat loss, food production, or energy supply are often related to one another in falling-dominoes fashion. We have increasingly come to understand how physical environmental problems such as these are almost always linked, to a greater or lesser degree, in a vicious spiral with specific social conditions. Economic, political, and cultural factors drive changes to the physical environment and affect the earth's natural systems; changes to those systems in turn force changes—often dramatic and sudden—in the realm of human society. Global climate change, which was still largely a speculative hypothesis at the time of the Brundtland Commission's meetings, has emerged as perhaps the most dramatic and emblematic case of this kind.[1]

Sustainability is a somewhat broader concept than the Brundtland Commission's original *sustainable development* in that it can be applied in many areas beyond those related directly to economic development. Sustainability has emerged as a guiding ideal for understanding and addressing these systematic problems of overburdening. Such problems typically cross not only state and national borders, they also blur the lines between nature and society; between economics and culture; and among various areas of political, professional, and academic expertise. As a *regulatory concept*, sustainability allows us to gauge how destructive any given practice is. If our present use of one kind of fuel does less to diminish future fuel options than does the use of other fuels, for example, the present use of that particular type of fuel is the relatively more sustainable option. As a *guiding ideal*, sustainability provides a way to define target outcomes for alternative ways of doing things. If a farmer wishes to move away from agricultural practices and crops that have become unprofitable, for example, there is an opportunity to introduce methods and crops that are more sustainable in the sense that they do not deplete the soil or require inputs of nonrenewable fuel, fertilizer, or aquifer water. Sustainability can thus function as both a regulatory concept and as a guiding ideal—alongside other factors such as initial cost, long-term expense or profitability, convenience, and effectiveness—in deciding the best way to do anything, from fueling our cars to building hospitals to educating our young people. Because it highlights the outcomes rather than the origins of our practices, sustainability has proven to be a very powerful way to move policy discussions past the limited perspectives often imposed by politics, profession, and geography.

The concept of sustainability, of "going green," has entered firmly into the culture since the 1990s. Governments and politicians have adopted sustainability as an explicit guiding principle. This is evidenced by the emergence of national and regional branches of the Green Party in many places, but the implications of sustainability have so far been most significant at the local level. Frameworks such as The Natural Step (James & Lahti, 2004) have become a standard tool in municipal planning, where sustainability policies can often be adopted most effectively. Businesses ranging from retailers to manufacturers to service companies have committed to sustainability, following the concepts of the *triple bottom line* first proposed by John Elkington (1998) and of *cradle-to-cradle manufacturing* described by William McDonough and Michael Braungart (2002). Triple-bottom-line accountability reports not only on financial profits and losses but also on the social and environmental effects of the organization's activities. Cradle-to-cradle manufacturing advocates designing products and processes so that waste is nearly eliminated through increased efficiency and through careful planning for reuse of both the finished product and intermediate manufacturing materials. Perhaps the most visible manifestation of the sustainability movement in the commercial sector is the Leadership in Energy and Environmental Design (LEED) green building certification system, introduced by the U.S. Green Building Council (USGBC) in 2002. More than 29,000 commercial building projects had been registered worldwide in the LEED directory as of October 2010 (U.S. Green Building Council, 2010). Beyond the political and commercial realms, nonprofits and religious organizations now seek ways to make their activities more sustainable; artists are experimenting with green materials, processes, and concepts; and mainstream media outlets regularly report on sustainability trends and issues. There is hardly a segment of contemporary society, business, or culture that has not been affected by the revolution in awareness represented by the concept of sustainability.

Higher education has not been left out of the green revolution, of course. Driven by the environmental and social awareness on campuses, as well as their own awareness of the sustainability movement in the commercial sector, college administrators and facilities managers have been among the first on our campuses to look seriously into sustainable practices. In 2005, as the number of colleges and universities seeking to introduce sustainable practices in their operations increased, the Association for the Advancement of Sustainability in Higher Education (AASHE) was founded to serve as an information clearinghouse, "to help coordinate and strengthen campus sustainability efforts at regional and national levels, and to serve as the first North American professional association for those interested in advancing campus sustainability" (Advancement of Sustainability in Higher Education, 2011b). One of the first major achievements of AASHE was to launch the American College & University Presidents' Climate Commitment (ACUPCC) in December 2006, with twelve founding signatories; more than 650 institutions had signed the ACUPCC by April 2011 (Advancement of Sustainability in Higher Education, 2011a; Presidents' Climate Commitment, 2011). Another initiative, the College Sustainability Report Card, was established by the Sustainable Endowments Institute in 2007 to provide independent ratings of college and university sustainability efforts (Sustainable Endowments Institute, 2011). The Report Card has become a valuable tool not only for campus administrators and managers but also for students who consider an institution's sustainability rating in deciding which school to attend. Higher education administrators' concern for sustainability is reflected by the many schools that have introduced sustainability as an explicit component of their institutional mission, vision, and values statements or that have established offices for institutional sustainability.[2]

Supported by these on-campus initiatives and by increased public awareness, faculty members have begun to introduce sustainability into the curriculum itself. Business schools, responding to the sustainability movement in the external business community, were among the first to introduce coursework, certificates, and degree programs with a special focus on sustainability.[3] Instructors in biology, natural resource management, engineering, and other ecology-influenced sciences were likewise among the first to include sustainability in the curriculum. Outside these areas, however, incorporation of sustainability themes in the higher education curriculum has been slower and more fragmentary than one might expect, especially when compared to the rapid pace of change in the business and public policy arenas. There are a number of reasons for this, not least of which may be academics' conservative attitude toward the established curriculum: Faculty members are perhaps naturally wary of teaching any concept that has not been refined and developed in the mill of critically reviewed scholarship within their own discipline. With sustainability, another pair of factors is at work. First is the fact that sustainability is a comprehensive concept that functions across many disciplines. Because it does not belong to any one discipline, it is not explicitly relevant to, or validated by, any one discipline.[4] The theater professor may sense that sustainability is in the provenance of the biologists; the chemist may see it as a concern for the engineering and business schools. The second factor is a little more subtle than this tendency to regard sustainability as "somebody else's scholarly problem." As noted above, sustainability functions as a regulative concept and as a guiding ideal for action. That is, sustainability is a *normative* term: It involves a judgment of better or worse, right or wrong. In spite of their considerable expertise at handling complex topics of fact and relationship in their particular fields, many faculty members shy away from teaching or critically assessing anything that looks like a more generalized value judgment about how we ought to live.[5]

It is enormously important for faculty members in higher education to understand and come to terms with the normative implications of sustainability. While any move toward sustainability certainly involves observable and measurable outcomes, the question of what outcomes matter enough to be observed must be determined at the beginning of the process by generalized value judgments. Nothing in the world is *absolutely* sustainable—there is no such thing as a perpetual-motion machine, neither in nature nor in our labs, offices, and classrooms. In any endeavor, resources are depleted, energy is lost, and some things eventually wear out or become so obsolete that they cannot be effectively repaired or reused.[6] Any sustainability initiative requires that an important decision be made at the outset: We must determine *what* is to be sustained. What good thing is to be conserved so that we, and future generations, can continue to meet our needs? What *are* our genuine needs? Some versions of these questions, in certain contexts, do have relatively clear and well-established answers. In business, the economic branch of the triple bottom line most obviously means that a company's profitability, a positive balance sheet, must be sustained; otherwise, the business will cease to exist. The questions of economic sustainability become more complex, however, when we ask whether a particular business should act so as to sustain the broader conditions essential to a healthy economy, one in which that company can flourish. Competition among companies within a market sector is usually regarded as one such condition, for example, but few executives would understand their own corporate commitment to sustainability to mean that they should do much to ensure that their direct competitors remain profitable. Likewise, some environmental goods clearly need to be used in a sustainable manner: Breathable air, drinkable water, and fertile soil are essential for human life to continue. Taken at a general level, this fact is indisputable. The question of environmental sustainability becomes problematic as soon as we move to particular cases, however. Is the appearance of invasive species in Lake Michigan detrimental to "the ability of future generations to meet their own needs"? Is the preservation of the Ogallala Aquifer or the restoration of the Aral Sea essential to future generations of farmers? The loss of these significant natural resources would certainly disrupt life (or make it all but impossible) in the immediate region, but what exactly are we committed to sustain? Should we try to ensure that life can continue as it has been lived recently in the immediate region of the resource, or need we only safeguard prospects for future generations to live *some* kind of good life, perhaps elsewhere and doing something very different?[7] When we turn to the question of social sustainability, matters are immediately murky and conflicted. It is common to assert that fair wages; respect for human rights; minimally safe, secure, and comfortable living conditions; access to education; and opportunity for political participation are key aspects of social sustainability. All of these, and more, may be gathered under the heading of social justice. Yet from the simple standpoint of sustainability as "longevity of a way of life," we may notice that the longest-lived civilizations (ancient Egypt, Rome, China, and India, for example) lacked most or all of these social goods. What the social branch of the triple bottom line typically aims to sustain is not merely some society and way of life that people will accept, but a social order that makes these specific social justice factors central to its value system. It will not do to assert that these values ought to be sustained because they are essential to sustaining a democracy; that is a convincing argument only because it is circular. The autocratic dictator could make the same case for the social values of state supremacy, reeducation programs, censorship, and secret laws that are essential to sustaining a tyranny, after all, and other autocrats would find the argument entirely convincing. Social values need to be justified as worthy of being sustained on their own terms, not because they are essential to maintaining the status quo. Ethics, social and political philosophy, economics, and political science are only the most visible academic disciplines relevant to developing and arguing for a robust notion of social justice. The bad news for advocates of a simple approach to the third bottom line is that these are old, even ancient areas of inquiry that embody very long, very hotly contested debates over what we should even mean by terms such as *justice, fairness, human rights, quality of life, proper education*, and *meaningful political participation*. Attention to sustainability—whether economic, environmental, or social—forces us to decide what exactly is worth sustaining and what is not. Sustainability thus always involves value judgments, and the value judgments we now face concerning environmental and social sustainability in particular are some of the most challenging that anyone has ever had to make.

Sustainability thus organizes our knowledge and directs our activities according to some conception of what is good, of what ought to be sustained. It is unlike the subject matter that most faculty members are accustomed to teaching. Every discipline of course *assumes* its conception of what is good: faculty members in the theater department know it is good to teach people how to create convincing and compelling appearances, physicists know it is good to teach the mathematical and theoretical frameworks that make sense of the physical universe, business faculty members know it is good to teach the importance of profitability and accountability, nursing faculty members know it is good to teach the principles and methods of effective health care, and so on. But few are comfortable with explicitly *developing and criticizing* a general conception of what is good. To introduce a new regulative concept and guiding ideal such as sustainability into any discipline means entering uncharted waters, potentially challenging the way things have always been done.[8] To do so on the basis of a new concept's mere popularity in the nonacademic world may appear, to many faculty members, suspiciously like bending before the winds of a faddish political correctness.

The disciplines that were early to incorporate sustainability into their teaching were those where something like sustainability was already established as a central value. Public policy and business faculty members received a mandate from their nonacademic counterparts that sustainability had arrived in the world and needed to be taught in the classroom. Biology, natural resource management, and the other sciences imbued with ecological thinking had long ago assimilated the implications of finite resources and the limits of natural carrying capacity for other species, and thus saw the extension of these concepts to the human realm as a matter of obvious common sense. With their well-tuned awareness of the value of efficiency in designing and producing things, many engineering faculty members likewise found the concept of sustainability to be a matter of obvious common sense. For faculty members in other disciplines, though, even for those who are personally sympathetic to sustainability as a general social goal, the relevance of this concept for their own discipline may be far from apparent. Attention to sustainability may very well limit what has been done in a discipline with great success, without obviously adding anything to it: It is not clear a priori that sustainable writing instruction, health care, or teacher training will be any better than their familiar (and by perhaps unfair insinuation, unsustainable) current versions.[9] Before leaping into these waters, any sensible faculty member will want an account of what a sustainable version of his or her discipline would be, and an account of why this version would be preferable to what he or she is presently teaching.

The work of providing this account is just beginning. It cannot be imposed from outside, nor can it be developed entirely from within any one of the disciplines. Concepts of sustainability, along with corresponding sustainable practices, must be developed with awareness both of the differing commitments and requirements that are specific to the many disciplines and professions, and of the many dimensions of value that are relevant candidates for being sustained within specific educational fields. There is no template, no stock of proven answers to the questions, "Which aspects of *this* practice can and should be made sustainable?" or "Is this practice so important, at present, that we can justify continuing it even though people in the future will therefore be forced to find a substitute or do without?" Bryan Norton (2005) has noted that a similar lack of ready-made, determinate answers to key questions about sustainability (including even an agreed-upon definition of *sustainability*) exists in the regulatory realm, where science and public policy professionals interact. As Norton puts it, "sustainable outcomes are not definable in advance, but must emerge from a program of active social experimentation and learning" (Norton, 1999, p. 461). Rather than bewailing this situation, or giving in to critics who would suggest that this lack of settled knowledge is a sign that the sustainability emperor has no clothes, Norton suggests that this is what it looks like when significant new organizing concepts are being developed. The task we face is not that of somehow agreeing on some ready-made language for advancing sustainability in higher education, but rather to work together to answer the question, "What language *should* we develop and use for discussing environmental goals, priorities, and policies?" (Norton, 2005, p. 48).[10] The movement toward sustainability in higher education ensures that both conceptual and practical questions will be raised again and again throughout the academy, and that promising answers will be tried by some of the most reflective and well-educated leaders in the various disciplines and professions. *Teaching Sustainability/ Teaching Sustainably* offers a variety of early reports from this emerging interdisciplinary project.

The Organization of This Book

The chapters in *Teaching Sustainability/Teaching Sustainably* are arranged in four parts. Part One, "Sustainability as a Core Value in Education," consists of four chapters that address various ways that the concept of sustainability can function as a thematic focus for courses across the curriculum, and for the college or university as a whole. In "Sustainability for Everyone: Trespassing Disciplinary Boundaries," Douglas Klahr describes an interdisciplinary course he designed to accommodate the realization that sustainability is not just another concept that we might wish to examine, but is rather "the overarching ethos that will govern the lives of this and future generations of students." Klahr outlines the readings he uses to lead students through an appreciation of the importance of sustainability, to a detailed understanding of the key conceptual aspects of sustainability, to a critical perspective on the sustainability movement, and finally to a synoptic vision of the possible future of sustainability as both regulative concept and guiding ideal for our actions. In "Sustainability as a Core Issue in Diversity and Critical Thinking Education," Danielle Lake describes how sustainability—a classic example of what Horst Rittel and Melvin Webber described as "wicked problems"—functions as a central theme in her diversity and critical thinking courses. Wicked problems are not in their nature solvable by appeal to technical expertise; Lake emphasizes the pedagogical potential of the wicked problem of sustainability as the subject for a variety of interdisciplinary and general education courses. In "Sustainable Happiness and Education: Educating Teachers and Students in the 21st Century," Catherine O'Brien describes how courses can employ the concept of *sustainable happiness* as an organizing concept. Happiness studies are central to the positive psychology movement of recent decades, but this approach to understanding the human situation may be traced back to the ancient Greek ethicists, who recognized that education is intended, after all, to help people live better, happier lives. O'Brien argues that the sustainability of our actions and aspirations is itself an essential aspect of whether they indeed result in happiness; conversely, we pursue many unsustainable actions as a result of misguided ideas about what makes for authentic happiness. Finally, Chris Doran makes the case for Christian educators and institutions to embrace the three *E*'s—environmental, economic, and ethical aspects of sustainability—in "A Christian Contribution to Sustainability." Doran shows how these values of the sustainability movement accord with Christian values. He also argues that Christianity's traditional emphasis on social ethics and on responsible stewardship of the earth's resources, which have always been seen as a balance to merely economic motivations, can add depth to our understanding of sustainability.

The eight chapters in Part Two, "Teaching Sustainability in the Academic Disciplines," demonstrate how the theme of sustainability has been incorporated into courses within a wide variety of particular disciplines and programs. In "The Hungry Text: Toward a Sustainable Literary Food Pedagogy," Tom Hertweck and Kyle Bladow make a persuasive case for the integrity and importance of the contributions that literary criticism can make to sustainability studies. While literary critics do not have the same kind of expertise about sustainability issues as scientists, economists, or business-people, literary critics can tell us a great deal about what the experts have written. Hertweck and Bladow illustrate how faculty members and students outside the core areas of sustainability studies can, and should, contribute to the ongoing discourse about sustainability by drawing on their own areas of expertise. In "The Rhetoric of Sustainability: Ecocomposition and Environmental Pragmatism," Kimberly R. Moekle describes her second-year writing course, where sustainability serves as the theme for students' writing assignments. This extended attention to the topic "helps students unpack debates about sustainability and the environment by giving them tools with which to discern the political, social, and moral agendas of those involved, while simultaneously strengthening the effectiveness of their own rhetorical choices." The theme of sustainability, in short, provides students with rich material for their own writing and thinking. George English Brooks relates his use of globalization and consumerism as focal themes for his research writing classes in "Writing Banana Republics and Guano Bonanzas: Consumerism and Globalization in the Composition Classroom." By asking students to research the economic forces that act upon their own lives (forces that often prompt them to engage in unsustainable behaviors), Brooks allows his students to "become personally invested in their own research subjects while learning a great deal about other related topics from their peers." "Sustainably Growing Farmers of the Future: Undergraduate Curriculum in Sustainable Agriculture at the University of Kentucky," by Keiko Tanaka, Mark Williams, Krista Jacobsen, and Michael D. Mullen, describes the process of establishing a new bachelor of science degree program in sustainable agriculture. Their experiences establishing this program in a region where the traditional model of agriculture is undergoing rapid transition will provide valuable guidance for others who wish to introduce similar multidisciplinary agriculture programs. Stacey A. Hawkey, Valdeen Nelsen, and Bruce I. Dvorak describe how their Partners in Pollution Prevention program integrates technical, business, and service-learning education about sustainability in a major college of engineering. "Using a Multilevel Approach to Teach Sustainability to Undergraduates" not only explains the pedagogical approach for an ambitious internship-oriented program, but also presents outcome assessment results that show the effectiveness of such an approach to sustainability education. "Growing Sustainability in Health-Care Management Education," by Carrie R. Rich, J. Knox Singleton, and Seema Wadhwa, describes the structure of a graduate-level course on environmental health care sustainability, which was "the first comprehensive academic course to focus on sustainability in health-care delivery systems." The challenges of institutional change in our health-care systems are daunting, to say the least; Rich, Singleton, and Wadhwa's account of their academic engagement with the triple bottom line in health care is an excellent starting point for what will certainly be a complex and important process of change in the field. In "Teaching Ecotourism in the Backyard of Waikiki, Hawai'i," John Cusick explores the conflict between developing a sustainability framework for tourism in Hawai'i and the fact that mass travel to and from the islands is apparently unsustainable over the long run. Cusick shows how the academic study of sustainability issues can lead students and faculty members alike to rethink an established economic activity that is essential to the region and to begin to think seriously about innovative ways to mitigate this difficult situation. In the final chapter in Part Two, "Who Will Teach the Teachers? Reorienting Teacher Education for the Values of Sustainability," Patrick Howard considers the challenges of teacher training for sustainability in light of the United Nations Educational, Scientific and Cultural Organization's (UNESCO's) call to develop Education for Sustainable Development at the 1992 Earth Summit. Howard emphasizes the necessity for teacher training to include education about the value dimensions of sustainability, and he argues for the legitimacy of such values education.

The four chapters in Part Three, "Education as a Sustainable Practice," each explore efforts to make the logistics of classroom teaching and administration itself more sustainable. In "E-Portfolios in a Liberal Studies Program: An Experiment in Sustainability," P. Sven Arvidson describes the process of initiating paperless student portfolios in a degree program serving 100 students. Each student's portfolio can be 100 pages long, so going paperless represents a significant potential resource savings. As Arvidson relates, however, adopting the e-portfolio format has both benefits and challenges. Justin Pettibone and Kirsten Allen Bartels describe a similar experiment in switching student work to electronic format in "The Paperless Classroom." While they encountered unexpected challenges with the entirely paperless class-room, they also realized unexpected benefits that improved aspects of their teaching. As they report, the experiment led them each to "comprehensively rethink our pedagogical approaches, showing us new ways to communicate to and connect with students." In "Communicating Sustainability: Teaching Sustainable Media Practice," Alex Lockwood, Caroline Mitchell, and Evi Karathanasopoulou describe their experiences introducing sustainable prac-tices as the means, and not just part of the subject matter, of media educa-tion. In their Sparking Sustainability project, "[e]ach encounter (whether in the classroom, the community or the media studio) will begin by asking, Is what we are doing sustainable?" In "Roadblocks to Applied Sustainability," Bart A. Bartels reports on a number of examples of practical sustainability initiatives that have been supported through his university's Sustainable Community Development Initiative Office. These initiatives emphasize the involvement of students, faculty, staff, and university administrators alike. Bartels advocates an experimental, activist approach to implementing sus-tainability initiatives that is attentive to emergent problems such as "green fatigue." He suggests that specific initiatives can be evaluated and refined in light of outcomes, and through this process various parties will develop their own working definitions of sustainability.

Teaching Sustainability/Teaching Sustainably concludes with four chap-ters concerning cultural change toward sustainability in Part Four, "Leader-ship and Reform Strategies for Long-Term Institutional Change." Courtney Quinn and Gina Matkin outline the principles of an emerging area of leader-ship training in their chapter "Teaching Sustainability Leadership." Drawing specific illustrations from the environmental leadership course they teach, Quinn and Matkin show how educators can "help students develop and practice the skills and explore the ideas that will allow them to lead society to a sustainable future." Sarah S. Brophy likewise addresses the training of future decision makers in her chapter "Teaching Sustainability to Future Museum Professionals." Brophy emphasizes the need for institutional change in the world of professional museum management, where some insti-tutions have enthusiastically embraced a vision of sustainability, while others have remained resistant and even skeptical about change. Her chapter out-lines an approach to fostering responsible change in the rising generation of professionals through a combination of course content, fieldwork, and sustainable teaching practices. Tamara Savelyeva addresses the problem of introducing the cross-disciplinary concept of sustainability into the insular academic divisions of a modern university in "Escaping the Structural Trap of Sustainability in Academia Through Global Learning Environments." Savelyeva describes how the mutual, cross-campus effect of the global learning environment strategy introduces sustainability to many interested parties simultaneously, and does so in a variety of contexts that include teaching, service, and research. In the closing chapter of *Teaching Sustainability/ Teaching Sustainably*, Christine Drewel explains the long process by which one university came to be recognized as a leading force in the higher education sustainability movement. Her chapter, "Making Sustainability a Core Value," shows how the university administrators, faculty members, students, and members of the surrounding community have all been brought into an ongoing effort to make sustainability an asserted value *and* an actual guiding force in the way the institution goes about its work.

Notes

1. Measurements of atmospheric carbon dioxide began in the 1950s; in 1967, computer modeling suggested that global temperatures could increase by as much as 4 degrees Fahrenheit ("A History of Climate Change," 2011). Beginning in 1974, study of Antarctic ice core samples allowed us to begin to chart atmospheric carbon dioxide levels from the distant past. More definitive evidence of a correlation between carbon dioxide levels and global temperatures was finally established from ice core samples taken in the mid-1990s (Quiroz, 2008).

2. See the chapters by Bart Bartels (chapter 16) and Christine Drewel (chapter 20) in this volume for accounts of initiatives like the one at Grand Valley State University, which has been recognized as a leader in the campus sustainability movement.

3. Aquinas College, in Grand Rapids, Michigan, introduced a BS in Sustainable Business in 2003, through its Center for Sustainability. This is believed to be the first degree program of its kind in the United States (Center for Sustainability, 2011).

4. Tamara Savelyeva discusses the "structural trap" that this situation creates in her contribution to this volume (chapter 19).

5. Many contributors to this volume emphasize aspects of value thinking in sustainability initiatives. See especially the chapters by Chris Doran (chapter 4); Tom Hertweck and Kyle Bladow (chapter 5); Patrick Howard (chapter 12); Alex Lockwood, Caroline Mitchell, and Evi Karathanasopolou (chapter 15); and Christine Drewel (chapter 20).

6. At the extreme end of this line of thought, astronomers assure us that even the sun itself, the ultimate source of all the usable energy on our planet, will eventually burn out. A gloomy thought, but this will not occur for some 5 billion years, so it is not a problem we need to address any time soon.

7. This question raises the important distinction between *weak* and *strong* sustainability, which arises from the unresolved debate over the degree to which *substitution* of human-made resources for natural resources is permissible in the effort to achieve

sustainability. Suppose, for example, that we reasonably expect to develop a genetically modified corn that will require less water in order to produce the same yield as our present corn varieties. Weak sustainability would allow the expected new crop to substitute for a certain amount of water in our sustainability considerations, and we would not be obligated to ensure that present amounts of water will be available to future corn farmers, who will have the new seed. Essentially, the idea is that we may substitute human capital, ingenuity, or technology for natural resources that will not be available in the future. Strong sustainability rules such substitution of resources out of consideration. Advocates of strong sustainability argue that substitution opens the door to excessive speculation in planning, and in particular that it invites an irresponsible degree of technological optimism and even self-deception in our calculations. Extended discussions of strong and weak sustainability are provided by Gowdy, Van Den Bergh, and Ayres (2001) and by Neumayer (2003).

Beyond the substitution problem lies another concern, wherein we begin to speculate not only about what natural resources people of the future will require to meet their needs, but what their needs will even be. For all we know, people seven generations from now might all live on spaceships, preferring and enjoying a world of plastic trees and virtual reality, all powered by a nearly cost-free cold fusion technology that we imagine someone will soon discover. If we convince ourselves of something along these lines, our present concerns about sustainability become very quaint indeed—something like the pride our great-grandfathers took in passing along their indispensable knowledge of horsemanship.

8. See John Cusick's contribution to this volume (chapter 11) for one example of such a fundamental challenge to the field of tourism studies.

9. It is not yet even clear to what degree sustainable business practices actually improve a company's performance, though it seems reasonable to expect a variety of outcomes. A recent analysis of company performance by Human Impact + Profit (HIP) did find that the top performance indicators, beyond the balance sheet, were "customer satisfaction, employee satisfaction and retention, low greenhouse gas emissions per unit of revenue, gender and ethnic diversity among executives and board members, and transparency. HIP took the Standard & Poor's 100 Index and reweighted the companies using measures of social responsibility. The HIP 100 has beaten the Standard & Poor's 100 by more than 4 percentage points in its first 18 months of existence" (Rosenberg, 2011). A reliable 4 percent advantage will make investors very wealthy indeed, but this kind of discovery is just now emerging, after a large number of companies have been explicitly committed to sustainability for many years. Needless to say, there is no comparable index for measuring the success of sustainable practices in mathematics education, teacher training, or any other area of the higher education curriculum.

10. Bart Bartels provides examples of this experimental, practical approach to refining the meaning of sustainability in his contribution to this volume (chapter 16).

References

Association for the Advancement of Sustainability in Higher Education. (2011a). ACUPCC reporting system. *Association for the Advancement of Sustainability in Higher Education*. Retrieved from http://acupcc.aashe.org/

Association for the Advancement of Sustainability in Higher Education. (2011b). Frequently asked questions. *Association for the Advancement of Sustainability in Higher Education.* Retrieved from http://www.aashe.org/about/faq

Center for Sustainability. (2011). *Aquinas College.* Retrieved April 11, 2011, from http://www.centerforsustainability.org/resources.php?category = 79

Elkington, J. (1998). *Cannibals with forks: The triple bottom line of 21st century business.* Stony Creek, CT: New Society Publishers.

Gowdy, J. M., Van Den Bergh, J. C. J. M., & Ayres, R. U. (2001). Strong versus weak sustainability: Economics, natural sciences, and consilience. *Environmental Ethics, 23*(2), 155–168.

History of Climate Change, A. (2011). *Directgov.* United Kingdom. Retrieved from http://www.direct.gov.uk/en/Environmentandgreenerliving/Thewiderenviron ment/Climatechange/DG_072901

James, S., & Lahti, T. (2004). *The natural step for communities: How cities and towns can change to sustainable practices.* Gabriola Island, BC: New Society Publishers.

McDonough, W., & Braungart, M. (2002). *Cradle to cradle: Remaking the way we make things.* New York: North Point Press.

Neumayer, E. (2003). *Weak versus strong sustainability: Exploring the limits of two opposing paradigms.* Cheltenham, UK: Edward Elgar.

Norton, B. (1999). Pragmatism, adaptive management, and sustainability. *Environmental Values, 8*(4), 451–466.

Norton, B. (2005). *Sustainability: A philosophy of adaptive ecosystem management.* Chicago: University of Chicago Press.

Presidents' Climate Commitment. (2011). Mission and history. *American College & University Presidents' Climate Commitment.* Retrieved from http://www.presidents climatecommitment.org/about/mission-history

Quiroz, E. (2008). Temperature and CO_2 correlations found in ice core records. *Angles/2008.* Massachusetts Institute of Technology. Retrieved from http://web .mit.edu/angles2008/angles_Emmanuel_Quiroz.html

Rosenberg, T. (2011, April 14). Ethical businesses with a better bottom line. *Opinionator. The New York Times.* Retrieved from http://opinionator.blogs.nytimes .com/2011/04/14/ethical-businesses-with-a-better-bottom-line/

Sustainable Endowments Institute. (2011). About us. *The College Sustainability Report Card.* Retrieved from http://www.greenreportcard.org/about/

U.S. Green Building Council. (2010). About LEED [PowerPoint slides]. *U. S. Green Building Council.* Retrieved from http://www.usgbc.org/DisplayPage.aspx?CMS PageID = 1720

World Commission on Environment and Development. (1987). *Our common future.* New York: Oxford University Press.

PART ONE

SUSTAINABILITY AS A CORE VALUE IN EDUCATION

SUSTAINABILITY FOR EVERYONE

Trespassing Disciplinary Boundaries

Douglas Klahr

I t can be said without hyperbole that sustainability is the quintessential interdisciplinary topic of study. Over the course of the next few decades, every academic discipline will have to respond to the paradigm of more sustainable life practices. I state this not as a solemn pronouncement but merely as an observation of a very real equation: As our students make their way through this emerging world, they will encounter challenges springing forth from this paradigm shift, and they will demand that every academic discipline demonstrate substantial relevance to these challenges. Indeed, any academic discipline that fails in this regard may find itself ultimately unsustainable. If you consider such a scenario unlikely, recall that a critical mass of students is and will remain the lifeblood of any discipline. If a discipline fails to attract sufficient numbers of students, it will sink into obscurity. Thus sustainability, *in its deepest and most expansive sense*, is perhaps the pivotal factor, not in preserving academia as we know it, but rather in enabling it to undergo a paradigm shift. If you welcome this change, however radically it may transform your life as an educator, then you "get it." If you fear it, then you will find adapting to what is coming our way all the more difficult.

A true paradigm shift means that, within a realm of life, *everything* is subject to change, and this encompasses change that is often unforeseen and unimaginable at the outset of the shift. That is why phrases such as *thinking outside the box* cannot begin to describe the degree of fluidity, transmutability, and rapidity that will characterize those individuals who adapt successfully in the coming decades. Once again, my goal is not to issue a somber prognostication but merely to reflect an essential aspect of sustainability that frequently is not acknowledged. *Sustainability is not a goal, but an endless process of constant implementation, assessment, and readjustment.* There are two reasons for this inconvenient reality. First, the degree of damage and peril that humanity has inflicted upon our planet precludes any end "goal" of sustainability because the efforts of many future generations will merely be to slow the pace of damage. Second and more important is perhaps the hardest fact for people to comprehend, especially well-intentioned individuals: *Every decision regarding sustainable life practices is a compromise, not a solution.* I am not speaking of an individual-centric notion of compromise in terms of what one must give up, but rather from the simple truth that the daily actions of almost 7 billion human beings will always contain components that are detrimental to our planet: such is the inescapable impact of the human race. These two factors—the temporal and the substantive—are the signposts of sustainability.

Integrating into a discipline-specific course a component of sustainability begins when an educator asks a simple question: In the coming decades, as humanity faces unprecedented challenges in terms of resources and climate change, what can my discipline or area of research contribute toward a better understanding of these issues? The discipline need not be future-oriented. An archaeologist, for instance, could incorporate into a course some aspects of sustainable archaeological practices in areas threatened by rapid climate change, as well as examples of sustainable or unsustainable ways of living practiced by members of the long-gone society under investigation. Another example is the study of French, which has seen well-publicized declines across American campuses, yet the language can be repositioned as one that is necessary for any scientist, engineer, or doctor seeking to work in the vast regions of Africa where French remains the official language. In that case, the sustainability of the discipline might appear to outweigh sustainability as a topic of study, but such a dichotomous assessment is illustrative of precisely the type of antiquated thinking that will not serve our students and our careers well. Rather, teaching sustainability and teaching sustainably—to the point where both might mean the survival of a program of study at a school—are symbiotic. Will every discipline or area of research be able to transform itself to flourish in the emerging age of sustainability? The answer depends on how well its practitioners comprehend this symbiotic relationship and embrace it.

Courses about sustainability or courses that feature components of sustainability are found within many academic disciplines, and such disciplinary-specific approaches are necessary. But what we also need are courses about sustainability that shatter and smash through disciplinary boundaries, not merely because trans- and interdisciplinary approaches are in vogue, but because our students require them to thrive in the multiple careers most of them will face. Once again, we need to face the fact that we are in a student-driven profession, although this reality is often obscured within the discipline-specific halls of academia. In the next few decades, any institution of higher education that neglects to equip students with the mental flexibility to segue between disciplines will fail in the broadest sense regarding its responsibilities toward its students. If the "nobility" of such an education-based argument does not sway you, then perhaps a blunt economic one will: Within the competitive academic landscape of the United States, colleges and universities that fail to truly inculcate trans- and interdisciplinary mentalities within their students will lose market share to those academic institutions that do.

Akin to gently separating the layers of an onion with a surgeon's scalpel, the richness and expansiveness of sustainability now begin to come into focus. Sustainability is not merely a buzz word of the moment or an academic fad, although it may be treated by some as such. *Rather it is the overarching ethos that will govern the lives of this and future generations of students.* We—and our students—have no choice: The present evidence suggests that we have no alternative. If this is the case, then we are speaking of making sustainable living practices the guiding force in our lives, and this reality trumps any geographical, political, economic, societal, cultural, or disciplinary identities that we have assumed. Thus, sustainability is both a topic and a way of life that exceeds any other categorization in the breadth and depth of its dimensions. As a professor, I find the expansive, discipline-busting essence of sustainability—and the challenge it poses to our academic institutions—not threatening but exhilarating. It will transform academia in ways that we can only begin to imagine, and it was within this frame of mind that I set out in 2009 to create a course that would respond to this challenge.

The course was designed to answer one simple question: Because the subject of sustainability sprawls across disciplinary boundaries, shouldn't a course about the topic do the same thing? In other words, if we are truly going to understand how integral sustainability will become in all of our lives—regardless of whether we care about it or not—don't we have to understand the big issues that comprise sustainability and how they are inter-related? An examination of the economic, environmental, philosophical, and societal aspects of sustainability therefore comprised the content of the course. Although I teach architectural theory and history within the School of Architecture, I designed the course as an upper-level elective that was marketed to all colleges and schools at the University of Texas at Arlington. Architectural issues were not examined unless they arose within the readings in a most general way because I wanted to attract all students, not just those studying architecture. Students within the school of architecture are required to take a senior-year course that deals specifically with sustainable building practices, so my course was designed as a separate and distinctive interdisciplinary venue.

This was an intensive reading course that brought together a wide variety of sources. After reading through 2,500 pages of source material, I assembled a reading list for undergraduates of approximately 1,000 pages (graduate students had an additional book to read). More important, however, was the *progression* of the readings. I tend to think like a choreographer, carefully positioning course material not only with regard to logical sequence but also with regard for intellectual and even emotional impact, regardless of whether I am working with images or readings. The implications of this approach will become clear a bit later. The issue is the variety and sequence of readings, not so much the readings themselves, for by the time you read this essay, I will have updated the list of readings. My purpose is to demonstrate how I created a challenging interdisciplinary course about sustainability.

Pertinent at this point is that student interest in what was supposed to be a seminar limited to 20 participants resulted in a course enrollment of 77, underscoring the appeal of a truly interdisciplinary approach to sustainability. With such a large class, discussions on the intimate scale of a true seminar obviously were not possible, yet the course functioned as the discussion venue I envisioned. As is my practice, I believe that the benefits accrued by having open enrollment in my upper-level courses outweigh the adjustments in class dynamics and procedures. After all, I am in this profession *to teach*, and if many students want to take a course with me, I am honored and feel beholden to admit them.

Books or documents read in their entirely included the following:

1. *The Bridge at the Edge of the World: Capitalism, the Environment, and Crossing from Crisis to Sustainability* by James Gustave Speth (2008)

2. *The Ethics of Climate Change: Right or Wrong in a Warming World* by James Garvey (2008)
3. *Cradle to Cradle: Remaking the Way We Make Things* by William McDonough and Michael Braungart (2002)
4. *Transition to Sustainability: Towards a Humane and Diverse World* by W. M. Adams and S. J. Jeanrenaud of the International Union for Conservation and Nature (IUCN) (2008)

Chapters from the following books were also required reading:

1. *The Long Emergency: Surviving the Converging Catastrophes of the Twenty-First Century* by James Howard Kunstler (2005)
2. *Introduction to Sustainability: Road to a Better Future* by Nolberto Munier (2005)
3. *Deep Economy: The Wealth of Communities and the Durable Future* by Bill McKibben (2007)
4. *What's the Worst That Could Happen? A Rational Response to the Climate Change Debate* by Greg Craven (2009)
5. *Heat: How to Stop the Planet from Burning* by George Monbiot (2006)
6. *Six Degrees: Our Future on a Hotter Planet* by Mark Lynas (2008)
7. *Cool It: The Skeptical Environmentalist's Guide to Global Warming* by Bjørn Lomborg (2008)

Graduate students were required to read Adrian Parr's *Hijacking Sustainability* (2009) and take a special reading essay exam about the book, in addition to the essay reading exams that all students took. Finally, all students were encouraged, although not required, to purchase *Ready, Set, Green: Eight Weeks to Modern Eco-Living* by Graham Hill and Meaghan O'Neill (2008).

Readings from James Howard Kunstler's *The Long Emergency* served as bookends for the course because they provided a clear picture of how unsustainable our current American way of life has become. Kunstler possesses a gift for tying together the disparate strands of modern life so that the reader understands interconnections, which is the essence of sustainability. I felt it crucial that students first be exposed to Kunstler's graphic narrative of future life in the United States before delving into the components of sustainability, and the initial reading from his book accomplished that purpose: Students were staring at the unvarnished reality of their future. By the end of the first week, students were so immersed in the topic that they expressed feelings of depression, which I took as a sign of success. The previous spring, I had introduced an equally intense course, Slum Housing in the Developing World, whose initial reading likewise plunged students into a graphic narrative about the topic. Based on that earlier success (56 students enrolled in that course) I patterned the start of my interdisciplinary course about sustainability in the same manner.

We now had a clear grasp of how unsustainable our current way of life is, and the time had come to define the word *sustainability*, which occurred in the second week. For this, we turned to Nolberto Munier's *Introduction to Sustainability*. Far better than many other texts, Munier clearly yet comprehensively defines the parameters of sustainability. More important, however, is his discussion about weak versus strong sustainability; sustainable development versus economic growth; an ecological footprint versus an ecological rucksack; "emergy" accounting; externalities; the notion of resilience; and three types of capital: human, natural, and cultural. I found that securing a sound understanding of these concepts *early* in the course was essential toward having my students grasp the paradoxical relation between *individual* lifestyle decisions and their *collective* global impact.

Nolberto Munier's dense but important chapter about sustainability permitted the class to segue back toward a narrative text, this time Bill McKibben's *Deep Economy*. His chapter entitled "After Growth" served as the balancing act after Kunstler's passionate vision of the future and Munier's workmanlike tour through definitions. McKibben draws from many sources to construct his smooth, flowing text, integrating figures while questioning notions such as "more," "better," "happiness," and "satisfaction." I was aware that McKibben's masterful demolition of the equation "more = better" might receive a quizzical, if not hostile, reaction within the milieu of Texas that celebrates such a model of achievement. Yet because McKibben writes with a tone of studied concern and not anger, I felt that McKibben would be a diplomatic messenger of the unsustainable nature of "more = better." Students eagerly discussed the reading in class because it resonated with a uniquely temporal and local context: the $1.3 billion (Dallas) Cowboys Stadium, a symbol of excess on a global scale, had just opened less than one mile away.

This fortuitous confluence highlights what I regard as a crucial component of success when teaching sustainability, whether discipline-specific or interdisciplinary. Interconnections define sustainability, so any *local* example that can be placed within a *global* context will help students understand on a deeper, more personal level this interconnectedness. The new stadium offered an excellent example: Challenging its appropriateness as a 21st-century symbol of local and state pride forced students to consider it in a new light. No longer would they view the world's longest truss arches merely as an engineering achievement; now they saw that importing the steel from Luxembourg to build a statement of such monumental architectural machismo meant that an oversized carbon footprint forever would be part of the stadium's legacy. Because students now had a firm grasp of carbon footprints, they could mentally envision the exponential growth of that over the years due to the fact that the gleaming hulk, alone among the world's greatest stadiums, could be reached by private vehicle—only. The citizens of Arlington, Texas, the nation's largest city with no mass transit of any sort, had once again voted against diminishing the monolithic sanctity of the automobile within their city limits. Perhaps not every educator will be blessed with such a stark example regarding issues of sustainability, but within every community, some local example should be located and discussed because it offers an emotional connection for students that is of great value.

The environmental aspect is the one that the public—students included—most readily associate with sustainability, and to grasp this complex component, we next turned to Greg Craven's *What's the Worst That Could Happen?* Craven's book is a fluid, user-friendly explanation of climate change, the overarching environmental issue related to sustainability. His presentation of a "spectrum of credibility" was perhaps the most crucial notion covered in my course because it provided students with a method of evaluating and assessing information long after the course's conclusion. Craven demonstrates how to create a scale of credibility based on not only an individual's professional credentials but also on his or her professional associations. Thus, a scientist who is an active member of a professional society has a higher degree of credibility than a lone scientist. The important lesson for students was that, in this sound-bite era of political polarization and spin, an informed citizen always needs to ask two questions: Who is doing the talking and writing? Is the person truly qualified to deliver an assessment, as opposed to merely offering an opinion?

Of similar utility was Craven's decision grid, an adaptation of the grid that medical personnel have used for years to identify different patients' outcomes based on the strength or weakness of a pathogen versus the strength or weakness of the host body. In his version, Craven positions the variables of global warming being true or false against the options of doing significant or little to no action about it now. Craven merely displays the possible outcomes of all four options on the grid, creating a simple yet powerful visual tool that helps analyze the issue from a standpoint of rational deliberation, devoid of political subtexts. Armed with both a spectrum of credibility and a decision grid, my students were now ready to confront the dire predictions regarding climate change, and selections from George Monbiot's *Heat* and Mark Lynas's *Six Degrees* provided explicit and dramatic narratives. Whereas the earlier selections from *The Long Emergency* and *Deep Economy* had supplied overarching narratives of unsustainable practices, these chapters on climate change helped students focus on this component. Because climate change is the most publicized aspect of sustainability, I felt it equally important to transition quickly into the connection between this environmental issue and economics.

Part One of James Gustave Speth's *The Bridge at the Edge of the World* is entitled "System Failure," and it admirably fulfilled making this very connection. Speth's integrity is anchored in his experience as an environmental activist; his recognition of the movement's failures; and his clear, razor-sharp assessment of the economic systems that have brought the planet to potential collapse. In this first third of his book, he turns an unflinchingly critical eye not only toward our society but also toward himself. When he combines this with simple graphics, the result is not only powerful but also serves as an excellent example of how intertwined environmental, economic, and philosophical issues are within sustainability.

Part One of IUCN's *Transition to Sustainability*—"The Challenge of Sustainability"—was our next reading, and this functioned as a global overview of issues, akin to documents published by the United Nations. It served as a respite of sorts, summarizing matters before students faced their first essay exam. Following the exam, we examined the philosophical aspect of sustainability by reading chapter 3, "All for One, or One for All," of *Deep Economy*. McKibben discusses big-box retailing, affluenza, recent studies about happiness in relation to material possessions, and the advent of hyperindividualism and its unsustainable nature in terms of depleting the earth's resources. Nothing that McKibben states is new to researchers, but to students, this chapter presented perhaps the clearest challenge to how they envision their lives. In this regard, I felt that it helped prepare them for delving directly into ethical concerns, which we did by reading James Garvey's *The Ethics of Climate Change*.

After an opening chapter entitled "A Warmer World," Garvey examines the issues of responsibility and right versus wrong. Perhaps the most valuable concepts from this portion of Garvey's book were spatial and temporal complexities related to the notion of responsibility: In other words, what spatial and temporal contexts frame a decision regarding ethics that confronts one? The child drowning in the pond across the road offers dramatically different spatial and temporal parameters than the child dying from contaminated water in some far-distant slum. Once we had tackled the first portion of James Garvey's book, it was time to read the second half, which consisted of three chapters: "Doing Nothing," "Doing Something," and "Individual Choices." If my students had not yet studied Craven's decision grid, they might not have been as well prepared to delve into the difficult matters that Garvey discusses. With an ethical framework now in sight, I felt it was the right moment for us to read the second chapter of William McDonough and Michael Braungart's seminal volume, *Cradle to Cradle*: "Why Being 'Less Bad' Is No Good." The chapter served a dual function: It reminded students that decisions often have unforeseen consequences, and it also challenged them to develop trains of thought that pushed the sequence of possible consequences as far as possible.

The readings from *The Ethics of Climate Change* and *Cradle to Cradle* set the stage for one of the most important readings in the course: Bjørn Lomborg's *Cool It*. At this moment, I felt the interdisciplinary strands of the course coming together most vividly, with the controversial nature of Lomborg's book being a catalyst. In essence, the series of readings to this point was carefully crafted to bring students on a journey and then metaphorically drop them off a cliff with *Cool It*. The result was precisely what I expected: Students were flustered, upset, fascinated, angry, and incredulous—but most of all, deeply involved. Many stated that the reading had disturbed them, not merely because of Lomborg's stance but also because it came as a shock. Perhaps an ethical question might be raised regarding how my sequence of readings manipulated students' emotions. Students were deeply engaged with the material, both in and out of class, and in my assessment, that counts as a success.

After the explosive discussion about *Cool It*, we needed to return to a writer of equal lucidity who would serve as an answer to Lomborg, so we delved into the second part of James Gustave Speth's *The Bridge at the Edge of the World*. In this clear-eyed, hard-hitting, yet dispassionate examination of capitalism's benefits and deficiencies, Speth provided an outline of possible solutions that he labeled "The Great Transformation." This was challenging reading that deserved more class time than I had allotted. When I teach this course again, I will position the second part of Speth's book a bit later in the course. Grouping it within the course material for the second exam, which immediately followed it, was a bit too ambitious on my part. The students were exhausted from our examination of ethical and philosophical issues, and it would have been better to have given them the second exam immediately after *Cool It* and start a new portion of the course with Speth's demanding reading.

The remaining chapters of *Cradle to Cradle* came next: "Eco-Effectiveness," "Waste Equals Food," "Respect Diversity," and "Putting Eco-Effectiveness into Practice." Many students already were familiar with *Cradle to Cradle*, but rereading these portions of the book within an interdisciplinary course apparently brought forth new insights during our discussion. Students had encountered the book previously within a strictly architectural context, but now they were being challenged to connect it to the wide variety of readings we had studied. The intensity of McDonough and Braungart's text was paired with the remainder of the IUCN's *Transition to Sustainability*, which continued the document's global stance. Some chapter headings from *Transition to Sustainability* were "Decarbonize the World Economy," "Commit to Justice and Equity," and "Build the Wider Architecture of Change." By now students had developed a critical eye toward the diplomat-speak that is a hallmark of the IUCN document. As I had hoped in the course called Slum Housing in the Developing World, I wanted students to understand the aspirations and limitations of documents produced by global organizations such as the IUCN and the United Nations.

To complement the IUCN's document, the concluding segment of *The Bridge at the Edge of the World* came next, "Seedbeds of Transformation." James Gustave Speth is perhaps the antithesis of the diplomat-writer, often fearlessly stating what diplomats do not. Yet this final reading from his book served a more important purpose: It showed students how even an author as astute as Speth can stumble at times. "Seedbeds of Transformation" is the weakest part of Speth's book because he attempts to conclude his analysis of a dire planetary situation on a positive note, casting hopeful glances at what he regards as the faint stirrings of a global movement by people, as opposed to governments, to seek a more sustainable way of life. In this final segment, Speth lapses into diplomat-speak, and I wanted students to witness this immediately after our dissection of the IUCN document.

The final two readings, "Living in the Long Emergency," by James Howard Kunstler, and "Two Degrees" from Mark Lynas's *Six Degrees*, brought students back to vivid narratives. Both readings offer probable, as opposed to possible, scenarios of the future, which I felt was important because these readings helped the course conclude on a somber but not sensationalist note. It was crucial for my students to leave the course understanding the reality of the present and the probability of the future in a measured, reasoned fashion. It also was critical to expose my students to Kunstler's observations and predictions about how different regions in the United States will respond and react to the seismic changes that will occur as the fossil fuel age comes to a close. Many students did not know about the different civic structures in different national regions, and this chapter was an eye-opener for them. It helped them begin to grasp that, even though issues of sustainability are global, a region's response to the challenges ahead will be determined, to a great extent, by local frames of reference.

One year later, my interdisciplinary course, "Sustainability for Everyone," has achieved some "street cred" within the School of Architecture as a course to take. I get questions and requests from students every few weeks regarding when it will be on the schedule, and although I did not achieve the cross-campus enrollment that I initially desired, I am pleased that the course is now viewed as a complement to the mandatory one specifically concerned with architectural issues that all students within the School of Architecture must take. Students continue to express how appreciative they are that someone gave them the broad contexts that exist within sustainability, a holistic approach, if you will. The challenge remains, to attract more non-architecture students the next time I offer the course. In these days of reduced degree program hours—a reality dictated by the Texas Legislature—students also face reduced hours set aside for electives. Despite an extensive, campuswide marketing campaign and extensive coverage by the student newspaper prior to course registration, it became evident that students were reluctant to take an elective that would appear as "Architecture" on a transcript. This reality underscores a paradox: While students need to gain expertise within a field in order to successfully compete once they leave academia, their jobs increasingly will require them to reach out across disciplines. It is academia—and the push to get into graduate school—that is not responding rapidly enough to the changing reality of the workplace, a point with which I commenced this essay.

The conventions and pretensions of academia and college professors too often preclude offering an interdisciplinary and integrative course such as the one that I developed. Ingrained attitudes and disciplinary territorialism want to dismiss such an endeavor as "dumbed down." I hope that I have demonstrated that a demanding course can be created and that such attitudes should be thrown into the dustbin of history. Such attitudes underscore how ineffectual and irrelevant academia can become if it does not adjust itself rapidly to fast-changing realities. Students are ready for such integrative courses, and we need to cast off personal or departmental timidity and respond to their needs.

References

Adams, W. M., & Jeanrenaud, S. J. (2008). *Transition to sustainability: Towards a humane and diverse world.* Gland, Switzerland: IUCN.

Craven, G. (2009). *What's the worst that could happen? A rational response to the climate change debate.* New York: Penguin.

Garvey, J. (2008). *The ethics of climate change: Right or wrong in a warming world.* New York: Continuum.

Hill, G., & O'Neill, M. (2008). *Ready, set, green: Eight weeks to modern eco-living.* New York: Villard.

Kunstler, J. H. (2005). *The long emergency. Surviving the converging catastrophes of the twenty-first century.* New York: Atlantic Monthly Press.

Lomborg, B. (2008). *Cool it: The skeptical environmentalist's guide to global warming.* New York: Vintage.

Lynas, M. (2008). *Six degrees: Our future on a hotter planet.* Washington, DC: National Geographic Society.

McDonough, W., & Braungart, M. (2002). *Cradle to cradle: Remaking the way we make things.* New York: North Point.

McKibben, B. (2007). *Deep economy: The wealth of communities and the durable future.* New York: Times Books.

Monbiot, G. (2006). *Heat: How to stop the planet from burning.* New York: Penguin.

Munier, N. (2005). *Introduction to sustainability: Road to a better future.* New York: Springer.

Parr, A. (2009). *Hijacking sustainability.* Cambridge, MA: Massachusetts Institute of Technology.

Speth, J. G. (2008). *The bridge at the edge of the world: Capitalism, the environment, and crossing from crisis to sustainability.* New Haven, CT: Yale University Press.

2

SUSTAINABILITY AS A CORE ISSUE IN DIVERSITY AND CRITICAL THINKING EDUCATION

Danielle Lake

A s educators, we recognize that teaching sustainability is not something that needs to be limited to environmental studies and business courses. I suggest that the integration of sustainability into diversity courses is not only appropriate, but necessary. Understanding sustainability as a *wicked problem*, and recognizing how an *egoist ethic* otherizes the environment and is thus in large part responsible for the abuses that have led to a number of current environmental and social problems, are central to the resolution of this pressing situation. While it is certainly the case that most general education courses have something valuable to say about the issues surrounding sustainability, I focus here on the learning outcomes of integrating sustainability into diversity education. This smaller scope reflects both the limits of time and space here and my own experience teaching diversity issues as connected to issues of sustainability.

Sustainability as Characteristic of Our Time

What makes the issue of sustainability particularly characteristic of our time in history? While a full-scale argument is not provided here, a few key points should illustrate the central role sustainability plays in our present and imminent future. First, we must acknowledge that, given our swift technological advances, our ability to make a huge impact on our environment has never been greater; however, we often lack the will to examine possible long-term outcomes and the desire to make changes. In his book *Sustainability*, Bryan Norton (2005) warns us that "human actions, enhanced by technological prowess, can change nature irreversibly, quickly, and pervasively" (p. 455). To counteract this tendency, he proposes we take hold of Aldo Leopold's suggestion that we think like a mountain to consider the impact of our choices far beyond our local or temporal lives: "Coming to think like a mountain is accepting responsibility for both the short-term and local scales and also for long-term and larger-scale, ecological impacts" (Norton, 2005, pp. 455–456). Our technology has also given us the means to consume more of the world's resources than ever before. A consumerist ethos has sold us the idea that to enjoy, we must possess. While this ethos is not new, it is rampant today and, combined with globalization and the increased ability to consume even more, leads us into dangerously unsustainable territory. As I will focus on later, this ethos also encourages highly individualistic life-styles, promoting a focus on self over and above a focus on community. Higher education must do more to respond to these pressing environmental and social issues.

Interdisciplinary Research and Teaching as a Means to Diminishing Lag in Higher Education

In general, higher education institutions have been responding to the need for change by working to become more environmentally sustainable as insti-tutions and by offering courses in sustainability. I argue that we also need to focus on incorporating sustainability into more of our core courses and on building dialogue between and among the disciplines so that successful inter-disciplinary research and teaching can occur. Dialogue between the disciplines is essential for providing an opportunity for transformational knowledge. By bringing together various interest groups, we can begin to build common knowledge and thus a foundation from which to work when confronting sustainability as an open problem with multiple facets. To the extent that different groups tend to work with different mental models, such organiza-tions have the ability to create communal models from which the commu-nity can act.

On the other hand, many of our higher education communities have not reacted intelligently to the sustainability problems they are facing. We must acknowledge that many of the problems our institutions faced in their creation are no longer problems today, and that some of the issues now crying out for a resolution were not yet understood as problems during the formation of these institutions. *Sustainability*—as the word is used today—is a fairly modern, politically charged, and forward-looking term. The university, as a centuries-old social institution, can and often has adjusted, of course; but the complaint levied here is about the lag between an initial recognition of the problem and subsequent adjustments.

Interdisciplinary opportunities at the university level, along with the integration of sustainability as an important topic in many core or general education courses, leads to the creation of what Bryan Norton refers to as *bridge concepts*. These bridge concepts "serve to link the various scientific disciplines and to relate environmental science with social values in the search for rational policies" (Norton, 2005, p. x). We already have such bridge terms in the health field: Norton mentions the term *obesity*, for example. *Obesity* as a term is defined by both its scientific, measurable description and by the social values it invokes (Norton, 2005, p. 39). With bridge terms, science becomes a useful tool in deciding what option a community should seek when addressing a complex problem.

Conversely, Norton's reference to *towering* highlights how interdisciplinary work is stymied. Towering here refers to the creation and maintenance of a sharp distinction between science and values, as well as the desire to pursue scientific studies prior to discussing desired outcomes or values. While Norton discusses the issue of towering in relation to public policy decisions, I see this issue as also central to the divide between the disciplines. Insights from outside the individual disciplines (towers) have no impact; all information is built up from within the discipline.[1]

When various disciplines do come together to discuss the issue of sustainability, the likelihood of miscommunication is high. For instance, economics and ethics have—since the early 1970s—been the two major fields dealing most rigorously with sustainability, but these two disciplines rarely interact. Both fields have built up completely separate models for dealing with environmental issues. On rare occasions when professionals do communicate, they are often accused of talking past one another (Norton, 2005, chapter 1).

In the end, towering creates *blind spots* and prevents or—at the very least—makes true learning difficult (Norton, 2005, pp. 33–34). The assumption that science *is* the answer to our problems or that science yields certain answers is, in part, responsible for the lack of a multidirectional flow of information. While we certainly need to look to the most current and most respected scientific studies to inform our discussions, it is a mistake to rely on science alone. As educators, we need to acknowledge that interdisciplinary research and teaching require us to learn new things and to step outside our areas of expertise and our comfort zones. In general, more interdisciplinary work presents itself as a cost, both in time and effort. Thus, we need to remove the barriers that make the work of integrating sustainability across the disciplines more difficult to accomplish. Understanding that many of our core communal problems today are not going to be solved through the insights of one discipline, nor by the application of any one theory, is a good starting point toward needed integration.

Sustainability as a Wicked Problem

Wicked problems can be defined at least partially as those not capable of being solved by one discipline alone. Generally speaking, professors can be so specialized they forget the value of interdisciplinarity and integration to their students. Horst Rittel and Melvin Webber develop the concept of wicked problems in contrast to tame problems in a 1973 article entitled "Dilemmas in a General Theory of Planning." The authors describe tame or benign problems as easily identifiable and solvable by professionals; wicked problems are characterized as "tricky" and "malicious" (1973, p. 161). The mistaken assumption is that such problems can be solved by relying on experts, that is, scientists; while science may sometimes tell us how to solve certain problems, like how to treat our water supply, it is evident that science cannot alone solve most of the communal problems we face today. Even coming to a consensus on what the problem *is* proves to be controversial. In fact, controversy and gridlock over the issue of sustainability—how to define it; where to locate the problem; and what, if any, solutions are needed—can be seen here as a failure to recognize sustainability as a wicked problem.

In complex and open systems, it is difficult if not impossible to locate *the root* of a wicked problem. This difficulty stems from the fact that there is most often no single root problem; instead, when looking at the issue from multiple angles, we tend to find both that multiple factors feed into the problem and that this problem is linked to other various communal problems. While we do not want to content ourselves with inaccurately viewing a symptom as a cause, neither do we want to oversimplify the problem.

In a diverse society, these problems are understood through very different lenses and values, and these varying perspectives lead us into contentious debates and gridlock. Because we define the problem differently, it is no surprise that we also often seek out and call for different solutions. If, instead, we approach such complex problems with the aim of working together to integrate various disciplinary insights, consensus on potential ameliorative actions becomes far more likely.

Adequately preparing our students for contemporary life means we need to ensure that they are capable of applying critical and integrative thinking to complex situations, engaging in dialogue that is productive, and returning to and revising prior decisions in light of the consequences of previous policy decisions. General education, when it is done well, develops such skills, and general education, with a focus on developing the skills of integration as well as critical and creative thinking, is the foundation of liberal education. Thus, the best approach toward addressing the various issues of sustainability is found in the process of liberal education. As a process, liberal education also stands out as key in adequately responding to issues of sustainability because any actions we take to resolve wicked problems such as sustainability yield waves of consequences over time.

These problems are set within a matrix of open, variable, and interacting systems, so any changes we seek to apply to the problem will result in numerous and often unforeseen consequences both at the locus of application and further out. Thus, the work of addressing wicked problems must be continuous; we need to be aware of changing circumstances, watchful of the consequences of our choices, and prepared to make adjustments in our thinking. Even seemingly minor environmental concerns can cause tremendous problems when change is rapid and we find the responsible parties resistant or alarmingly unprepared to address the issue.

Wicked problems are also interwoven with each other and must be viewed together so that work on one does not hinder work on another. Wicked problems are never truly solved. Any cessation of work here is due to a lack of time, funds, or effort, or else reflects the need to pause and reflect. Any attempt to "solve" the problem will, we hope, meliorate it, but there is no final resolution for all of the various reasons given in this chapter. As a wicked problem, sustainability must always be understood in context. What it means for a system to be sustainable depends on the time at which, and the perspective from which, one is examining the system.

Diversity and Sustainability

While I have argued that most general education courses can fairly easily link the issue of sustainability to material from the course as originally designed, I now move to focus more specifically on how this is done in courses focusing on diversity. While a central goal of my diversity course is to examine how identity is affected by race, education, gender, class, and sexual orientation, I argue it is also key to this diversity course to examine how identity is affected by one's relationship with the environment. Val Plumwood, in particular, offers those teaching courses in diversity a conceptual bridge for doing just this in her article, "Paths Beyond Human-Centeredness." Plumwood begins by describing an egoistic ethic; this ethic is the means by which one can, without remorse, use others who do not reside within the ethical framework because it is limited (Plumwood, 1999, p. 70). This egoistic ethic often leads us to the abuse and even the destruction of those seen as separate from ourselves. The ethic manifests itself in the use of our natural, nonhuman world without the attachment of any ethical import. The egoistic ethic says that anything that does not fall within the ethical world can be used and abused, owned and destroyed at will; owners have that right under the egoistic ethic, within some loose limits. Nature under this ethic is understood as dead and mechanical, for instrumental use alone. We see that categorizing something as other, as radically different from oneself, can lead to its possession. When land is a commodity, its abuse is a private matter and such abuse inspires no guilt and little concern beyond that of self. In his proposal for a land ethic, Leopold (1949) suggests that if we instead begin to "see land as a community to which we belong, we may begin to use it with love and respect" (p. viii). Land as community instead of commodity enriches the picture under examination here and has roots in our agricultural history.

Our current focus on technology, our ever-increasing specialization, and our mass exodus to the suburbs and cities have led to lives far removed from the agrarian traditions that informed Leopold's thought. There is no going back to these old farming communities, even if we desired to do so, but understanding what values and habits such a life encouraged may lead us to consider how to address the problems, especially the problem of sustainability, that today's communities face. Scrutinizing our past to better understand our present is, in fact, another central goal of almost any diversity course and, in fact, of liberal education more broadly. While there are very important environmental consequences to the way in which we approach diversity, there are also environmental reasons for the historical and social consequences we examine in class. For instance, dependency on and respect for the land were central to farming life in the past. Paul Thompson, author of

The Agrarian Vision (2010), says that such virtues can be found today, at least in part, in art and literature about farming; taught in schools and churches; and reappropriated in trips to the local farmer's market, working vacations, or camps focused on sustainable farming communities, and even in the way we approach food (p. 229).

Whereas such an ethic encourages community, the egoistic ethic ignores many of the categories of our identity that are shared with and by the other. We are not, in reality, simply human, but also mammal, and also, Anthony Weston (1999) reminds us, an *earth being* (p. 5). That is, the whole story of who we are cannot be told by concentrating on our species alone, nor by focusing on our race or sex or country of origin. Our desire to simplify the complexities of our identity mirrors our desire to oversimplify the dynamic and complex problems we face. In opposition to this egoistic ethic, Martha Nussbaum (2004) advises us that what we truly need is a *world ethic* (pp. 42–47). This world ethic depends on obtaining accurate information about our world, on our ability to critically examine our own lives, and on what she calls the *compassionate imagination*. Nussbaum's compassionate imagination is not so different from Plumwood's call for us to move beyond our own self-centeredness. Central to both suggestions is the need to see difference not as a lack, but as a bounty and to become aware of how dependent we all are.[2] The focus on recognizing our dependency and thus on broadening perspectives here makes sense at least partially because of what Bryan Norton (2009) calls *convergence* (p. 46). A self-enclosure ethic prevents us from seeing beyond our own immediate welfare to the welfare of others, just as towering prevented effective communication. There is a failure not only to look into and appreciate the welfare of distant others, but also to appreciate the long-term effects of our choices. Recognition of this interdependency in all its forms motivates the move to approach sustainability through various general education courses and justifies the need for liberal education.

Thompson (2010) also reminds us that successful social movements were "effective *because* they were not understood strictly in terms of a narrow or clearly specified set of norms" (p. 258). Sustainability is not simply about the environmental impact of our lifestyles today. If we consider "sustainability as a banner that can encompass a number of causes" there exists an even greater need for working together and through this, a better chance for success (Thompson, 2010, p. 261).

Along these lines, both Nussbaum (2004) and Plumwood (1999) also encourage us to appreciate the diverse understandings of nature across the world. Through exploring how others have come to conceptualize and inter-act with nature we recognize not all cultures have so abused the land or otherized nature. Thompson (2010) and Nussbaum (2004) both point out how our increasing specialization has made it far more difficult to see the larger whole in which we live. Thompson (2010) warns that

> the fragmentation of contemporary life corresponds to a vision of human beings as "choice-makers" who move from transaction to transaction, eval-uating options in atomistic terms, as if choices and the people and places in which they live and work did not form a larger, more integrated whole. (p. 38)

Coming to see our interactions with nature as meaningful is part of develop-ing the ability to see "a larger, more integrated whole" (Thompson, 2010, p. 38).

While Nussbaum proposes a *world ethic*, Aldo Leopold advocates for a *land ethic*. A land ethic defines community more broadly. Community encompasses not simply the people and social institutions one is surrounded by, but also the animals, plants, and even the soil and water of one's environ-ment. "A land ethic changes the role of *homo sapiens* from conqueror of the land-community to plain member and citizen of it. It implies respect for his fellow-members, and also respect for the community as such" (Leopold, 1949, p. 204). Leopold further suggests that we not understand nature as a simple balancing act, but instead understand it as a biotic pyramid where land is the foundation for all life upon it; this dependency begins with the sun and the soil, the roots, the plants, insects, and rodents, and continues to move upward toward larger animals (p. 215). To subsist, every layer depends on the one below it. As Leopold warned, our lack of daily connection to the land is reflected in our failure to recognize that breakfast does not simply come from the store, nor heat from the furnace. A land ethic promotes a perception of our environment as something other than a threat to be con-trolled and more than a resource to be consumed. Recognizing our depen-dency is a key step toward moving forward in every one of the ethics already described, whether the focus is Thompson's agrarian vision, Nussbaum's global community, or Plumwood's move beyond human centeredness. While this recognition is an important step toward sustainability, it is, of course, insufficient.

Conclusions

Thus, we arrive at a number of key conclusions: (1) The refusal to see beyond human concerns is simply another manifestation of the resistance to seeing beyond oneself or one's immediate community. These issues manifest themselves when we examine many different categories, including race, sex, social class, religion, country of origin, and nature. (2) The desire for tame problems subject to clear and direct resolution generates resistance toward recognizing how complex and how interdependent we all truly are. (3) In working to broaden student perspectives, we should recognize these enclosed views and help students not only to see the human community more broadly but also to see beyond our own human community. That is, we should be expanding perspectives here not only to various cultures but also to the natural world in general, a world to which we are intimately bound and on which we depend. (4) In doing so, we should be identifying complexity, interdependence, and the various perspectives from which we can view the problem. This is precisely what a liberal education is designed to do.

Integrative education is needed to help students see sustainability as a wicked problem and thus recognize its connections to diversity. The development of critical and creative thinking exposes the complexity of the problems we face. Many students do not see the abuse of others, the racism, and other pervasive social ills until they are *exposed* to them in a diversity course. Given the separation of our daily lives from nature, many are not fully aware of the abuse of animals or of the land occurring around them. Abuse stops when we develop an ethical relationship with the other—whether this is nature or humans. These forms of engagement become far more likely when we, as educators, work to engage our students from multiple disciplines and in multiple formats, bridging boundaries and working with them to co-create a vision for a sustainable future.

Notes

1. For instance, the editors of *Environmental Pragmatism*, Andrew Light and Eric Katz, rightly complain that environmental philosophers have had little to no impact on environmental science or policy and argue that we all need to work together to find "workable solutions to environmental problems now" (Light & Katz, 1996, p. 4). But in reality we see that an intense focus on specialization, discord from within the discipline, and a failure to see eye to eye on deep philosophical issues stymies possible progress on the political front even when agreement here could be found.

2. In Nussbaum's case, this dependency is focused on the human community, while in Plumwood's case, this dependency is focused on nature more broadly. We are certainly highly dependent on each other in today's globalized world as well as dependent on nature.

References

Leopold, A. (1949). *A Sand County almanac*. New York: Oxford University Press.

Light, A., & Katz, E. (1996). Introduction. In A. Light & E. Katz (Eds.), *Environmental pragmatism* (pp. 1–20). New York: Routledge.

Norton, B. (2005). *Sustainability: A philosophy of adaptive ecosystem management*. Chicago, IL: University of Chicago Press.

Norton, B. (2009). "Convergence and contextualism: Some clarifications and a reply to Steverson." In B. Minteer (Ed.), *Nature in common? Environmental ethics and the contested foundations of environmental policy* (pp. 36–48). Philadelphia, PA: Temple University Press.

Nussbaum, M. (2004). Liberal education and global community. *Liberal Education, 90*(1), 42–47.

Plumwood, V. (1999). Paths beyond human centeredness. In A. Weston (Ed.), *An invitation to environmental philosophy* (pp. 69–106). New York: Oxford University Press.

Rittel, H. W. J., & Webber, M. M. (1973). Dilemmas in a general theory of planning. *Policy Sciences, 4*(2), 155–169.

Thompson, P. (2010). *The agrarian vision: Sustainability and environmental ethics*. Lexington: University Press of Kentucky.

Weston, A. (1999). Is it too late? In A. Weston (Ed.), *An invitation to environmental philosophy* (pp. 1–15). New York: Oxford University Press.

3

SUSTAINABLE HAPPINESS
AND EDUCATION

Educating Teachers and Students in the 21st Century

Catherine O'Brien

Sustainable happiness is happiness that contributes to individual, community, and/or global well-being without exploiting other people, the environment, or future generations.

(O'Brien, 2005)

Who or what teaches us about happiness? What are they teaching? What could this possibly have to do with sustainability education? Why is sustainable happiness relevant to education in the 21st century? The short answer to these questions is that lessons from happiness studies and understanding sustainable happiness can assist educators and students to enhance their own well-being while also helping them make more sustainable choices. The rest of the chapter gives the longer answer!

In a survey of current education practices, a United Nations (UN) report questioned whether education is contributing to sustainability or detracting from it. "At current levels of unsustainable practice and over consumption it could be concluded that education is part of the problem. If education is the solution, then it requires a deeper critique and a broader vision for the future" (United Nations Education, Scientific, and Cultural Organization [UNESCO], 2005, p. 59). Despite many exemplary initiatives worldwide, sustainable development and sustainability are not well understood by many educators, regardless of whether we are referring to elementary, secondary, or postsecondary levels of education (UNESCO, 2005).

This chapter introduces the concept of sustainable happiness and outlines a university course in sustainable happiness that is assisting students to embrace opportunities to live and work more sustainably. A new curriculum supplement that links sustainable happiness with health education outcomes offers students and classroom teachers similar opportunities.

Happiness, Health, and Sustainability

A considerable challenge for sustainability education is to move beyond raising individual awareness and toward fostering sustainable behavior. This is particularly difficult in many industrialized countries, where students and educators live in the social and cultural milieu of the consumer society. An antidote may be found, however, in positive psychology, which offers some intriguing opportunities for sustainability education.

Positive psychology emerged over the last decade as a new field within psychology. It takes the refreshing view that understanding what contributes to and sustains happiness and life satisfaction can be applied to enhance individual well-being. Seligman (2002) sees positive psychology as the study of positive emotions, positive traits, and positive institutions. We are learning that happiness skills can be taught and that this has implications for emotional, physical, and spiritual well-being (Seligman, 2002).

Happiness and Health

Happiness is defined by Veenhoven (2008) as *"the overall appreciation of one's life-as-a-whole*, in short, how much one likes the life one lives" (p. 2). This is often measured through tests of subjective well-being and life satisfaction. While definitions of happiness may vary, researchers have demonstrated that positive experiences of subjective well-being correspond with numerous positive health outcomes (Seligman, 2002; Steptoe, Wardle, & Marmot, 2005), including lower blood pressure, the inclination to seek out and act on health information, and more robust immune systems than those of less happy people. Research published in the *European Heart Journal* followed more than 1,700 Nova Scotians over 10 years and found that those who had experienced and expressed positive emotions at the outset of the study had reduced incidence of heart disease. Participants who had scored highest in terms of positive emotions were also less likely to be smokers (Davidson, Mostofsky, & Whang, 2010). Veenhoven (2008) completed an extensive survey of studies regarding the relationship between happiness and physical and mental well-being. He concluded that the evidence "implies that we can make people healthier by making them happier" (p. 6).

Happiness and Sustainability

In a world where global warming has begun (Intergovernmental Panel on Climate Change [IPCC], 2007) and climate scientists are investigating both mitigation measures and adaptation measures, where human suffering has reached almost unfathomable levels, a focus on happiness could appear to be a diversion from the hard issues of sustainability. On the contrary, there is a natural connection between sustainability and positive psychology. Happiness is at the heart of who we are and what we do, but in a consumer society, where consumption and happiness are believed by many to be inextricably linked, individuals confuse the "path to the 'good life' as the 'goods life'" (Kasser, 2006, p. 200). Our unbridled pursuit of happiness is often at the expense of other people and the natural environment. Happiness research also suggests that this unsustainable pursuit of happiness is flawed and that *authentic happiness* is derived through relationships with family, friends, meaningful work, and engagement in our community rather than through a relentless striving for material possessions (Seligman, 2002).

There is also evidence that once basic needs are met, substantial increases in income do not translate into substantial increases in happiness (Diener & Seligman, 2004; Stutz, 2006). It seems that the overconsumption common in consumer societies is neither the ultimate path to authentic happiness nor the path to sustainability.

In short, we have a consumer society whose default informal education process tends to reinforce individual lifestyles that are unsustainable *and* less likely to lead to authentic happiness. We have education systems that have not fully embraced education for sustainable development (ESD), educators who are not well informed about sustainability (and possibly not very interested in the concept), and educational institutions that are often not models of sustainability. It would seem that the education sector has a compelling rationale to become part of the solution. Incorporating sustainable happiness into education curricula may contribute to protective factors that enhance student well-being.

Sustainable Happiness

The concept of sustainable happiness was developed by O'Brien (2008) to draw attention to the consequences, both positive and negative, of how individuals, communities, and nations pursue happiness. In a globalized world, everyone's actions have repercussions on distant lands and people. Some are immediate and short term, while some endure indefinitely. Thus, further aims of combining the two terms are to link happiness to sustainability, now and into the future; to emphasize our mutual interdependence; and to generate discussion regarding the potential for making substantial contributions to sustainability efforts through research from happiness studies.

Sustainable happiness is a concept that can be used by individuals to guide their actions and decisions on a daily basis. Consider, for example, the momentary pleasure of drinking a cup of coffee. Benefits of attending to and being mindful of our sensory experience have been discussed by Brown and Kasser (2005) and Kabat-Zinn (2005). Viewed through the lens of sustainable happiness, this momentary pleasure can be placed in a wider context. Individuals can also attend to whether they are drinking fair trade coffee, which means that workers in the coffee plantation have been paid fairly and the coffee was grown with regard for the environment. It is important to reflect on whether the positive emotion derived from the coffee (or anything else for that matter) has come at the expense of other people or the natural environment. The conditions under which clothes are manufactured, how far our food is transported, or how we transport ourselves and relate to one another represent daily decisions through which we can contribute to, or detract from, individual, community, and global well-being.

Sustainable happiness reinforces the fact that we are interconnected and interdependent with all life on the planet, even life that is yet to be born. It can also be used to foster sustainable behavior. Our natural desire for happiness can become the entry point for discovering that our well-being is inextricably linked to the well-being of others and the natural environment. It can also dispel a common misconception that living sustainably will lower our quality of life. Brown and Kasser (2005) suggest that "as long as environmentally responsible behavior is framed in self-sacrificial terms, individuals will be faced with tough choices about how to act" (p. 349) because such behavior is assumed to detract from happiness. Sustainable happiness offers a fresh approach that invites reflection on sustainability issues coupled with opportunities to enhance our quality of life *and contribute to individual, community, and global well-being.* Through an exploration of sustainable happiness we can unlink happiness from consumption and discover ongoing opportunities to enhance well-being *and* sustainability.

Thus, sustainable happiness is a superb approach for introducing sustainability to teachers, motivating teachers to become models of sustainability, and exciting them to integrate sustainable happiness into their teaching practice.

Sustainable Happiness and Teacher Education

Sustainable happiness is an elective course in Cape Breton University's Bachelor of Education program (Nova Scotia, Canada). Weekly activities prompt students to examine the relationship between their daily life and the impact (positive or negative) on themselves, other people, and the natural environment. Some of these activities include the completion of a baseline chart, reflections on genuine wealth, reducing consumption of nonrenewable resources, drawing an interdependence map, expressions of gratitude, happiness literacy, and a sustainable happiness project.

Baseline Chart

Using the *baseline chart* in figure 3.1, students monitor their behavior and experience for one day and indicate what impact their activities had for themselves personally, for other people, and for the natural environment. They are also prompted to consider what opportunities exist for making different choices that may improve their own well-being, community well-being, and the well-being of the natural environment. This helps to demonstrate that some of their activities (drinking coffee that isn't fair-trade coffee) may bring a fleeting experience of pleasure but has adverse consequences for others. It also becomes evident that behaviors that contribute to their own well-being (e.g., physical activity) may have additional benefits, such as reducing use of a motorized vehicle, motivating them to spend time with a family member, or reducing stress so that they relate to others in a more balanced way. The following student comment on her behavior change during the sustainable happiness course suggests the effect of the baseline chart exercise on student behavior:

> I am trying very hard to purchase locally grown produce when possible and I have also started buying my coffee from the Bean Bank Café in Sydney more often than Tim Horton's because it serves fair-trade coffee and Tim Horton's does not. I have started to incorporate more physical activity into my days and, although this is a hard thing to get used to, I have succeeded in walking about three times per week after supper and

FIGURE 3.1
Baseline Chart

Choose one day this week to create your own log of activities, and fill in as much detail as you can. This chart gives you a sample of what you might write. You may complete the chart for more than one day if you wish. Remember to answer the question below the blank chart, too.

Sample Baseline Chart

Date: _____

Time	Activity	Emotional Experience	Impact on Self	Impact on Others	Impact on Natural Envonment
8:00	Breakfast: coffee, toast, cereal	Rushed, distracted, thinking about day	Didn't taste the food, fairly healthy meal, could have chosen whole wheat bread	Coffee was fair-trade coffee so positive for coffee workers; bread from farmer's market, good for local producers; cereal, not sure	Fair-trade coffee, care taken for environment; bread is made locally so not transported very far; cereal is highly processed and transported a long way
8:30	Carpooled to class/work	Enjoyed talking with friends	Less expensive; less stress than driving alone; feel good about it	Pretty good regarding air quality but would be better to be able to cycle or walk	Better than driving alone, but it is still my best option given where I live

Your Baseline Chart

Date: _____

Time	Activity	Emotional Experience	Impact on Self	Impact on Others	Impact on Natural Environment

Do I see any areas where I could improve my own well-being, the well-being of others, and/or the natural environment?

doing some strength training on the alternate nights. . . . I am trying to do more self-less acts for people. . . . Overall, there are aspects of my life that have changed for the better since the onset of this course, such as my physical activity levels, my eagerness to purchase local and fair-trade products, and my outlook on life and the well-being of others.

Genuine Wealth and Reduced Consumption

The topic of genuine wealth (Anielski, 2007) assists students to explore the nonmaterial wealth that comes from relationships, the beauty of their natural environment, trusting neighbors, and meaningful engagement with their studies. Students identify their own genuine wealth and opportunities to increase it and/or to reduce their consumption of nonrenewable resources. The effect of this exercise is suggested in the following student comment about completing the genuine wealth activity:

I must admit that I have lain in bed a few Sunday mornings wondering what life would be like if I won the 649 [lottery]! I thought about paying off all our debt, buying a new home, giving money to my family and those in need, and traveling. After reading our articles this week, I think that "day dream" would play out differently now. My measure of true happiness is ensuring I sustain solid relationships with my husband and children and maintain my health. Material items have been displaced further down the list.

Interdependence Map

An *interdependence map*, like the one in figure 3.2, is used to chart the web of interconnection between the student, other people, her or his natural environment, the resources used, as well as historical and cultural events that have shaped who the student is today. A simple way to imagine an interdependence map is to consider all the factors that influenced the existence of a piece of paper. If the paper was made from wood pulp, the map would include natural resources such as the sun, wind, soil, and water, as well as inventions that affected our use of paper (printing presses); machines that were created to harvest trees, transport logs, and convert the wood into paper; and the human resources along all the stages of creating and transporting the paper to the place where it was purchased and used. This interdependence map for paper is tiny in comparison to the web that students create. The assignment helps them to realize that their life touches and is touched by others both near and far on a daily basis. Changing one thing in that map, therefore, can have far-reaching results.

Gratitude and Appreciation

Gratitude and appreciation are associated with positive well-being. There may be many reasons for this. Happy people tend to be grateful, and grateful people are more prosocial, which contributes to healthy relationships—which in turn are associated with happiness and life satisfaction (McCullough, Emmons, & Tsang, 2002; Watkins, 2004). Students discover that simple actions, such as writing a letter to express appreciation, making a point of thanking people for simple things, counting blessings, or an artistic expression of appreciation, can have unanticipated positive benefits.

Happiness Literacy

One unit of the course explores the social and cultural influences on our view of happiness. We consider who or what teaches us about happiness and

FIGURE 3.2

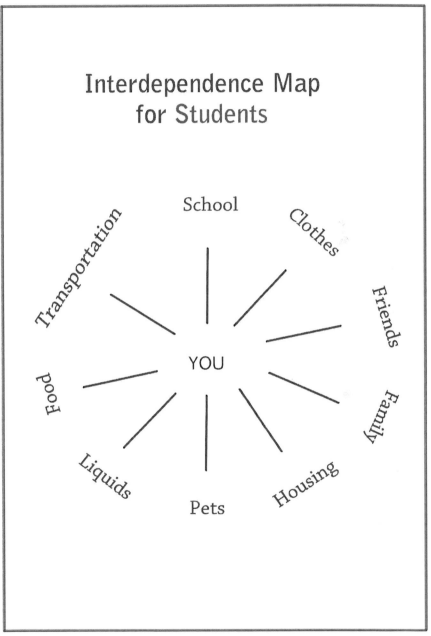

Interdependence Map
for Students

what we are learning. Students interview the happiest person they know to discover what contributes to that person's happiness, how he or she has dealt with adversity, and what lessons the student may draw from this. Students also analyze a television commercial, magazine advertisement, or popular song that portrays happiness to determine the overt and underlying messages about what brings happiness.

Sustainable Happiness Project

Each student is required to complete a sustainable happiness project that contributes to personal well-being, community well-being, and/or environmental well-being. Projects have ranged from reducing the use of plastic water bottles by utilizing a reusable water bottle (the student calculated her personal savings would amount to more than $800 per year); shifting to sustainable modes of transportation such as walking, cycling, public transit, and carpooling; organizing neighborhood clean-ups; initiating workplace recycling; and changing from disposable to cloth diapers. One woman involved her children and members of the community, all girls, and decided that they would be Girls Against Garbage (GAG).

Lessons Learned

The sustainable happiness course exemplifies transformational learning. Student comments suggest that they feel motivated to leave a legacy of sustainable happiness because they understand and appreciate that their well-being is inextricably linked to the well-being of other people and the natural environment. It would be reasonable to wonder if these sentiments and behaviors would persist beyond the course. A survey was sent to students one year following the completion of the course. There was a 50% response rate (16 students of 32 responded). Healthful, sustainable behavior had not only been sustained, it had increased over the intervening time. It is possible that the students who were most committed to sustainability were the ones who responded. Even if this is the case, shifting the behavior of 50% of a class through an online course is compelling and suggests that further investigation is warranted.

One of the most surprising and unanticipated outcomes of the sustainable happiness course was that students elected to engage in healthy lifestyles without a great deal of information on the benefits of doing so. It seemed that by exploring readings on happiness and sustainability, they became motivated to take greater care of themselves, their family and friends, and the natural environment. Perhaps the most compelling and gratifying aspect of this course is that most students voice the realization that an individual's actions *can* and *do* make a difference.

In the fall of 2010, a new curriculum resource was developed for Grades K–6 that links sustainable happiness with the health education curriculum outcomes for every Canadian province. Integrating sustainable happiness with health education provides another resource for fostering healthy, sustainable lifestyles for students and teachers and may contribute toward more sustainable schools. Future work will track the results of the new resource.

Concluding Thoughts

Sustainable happiness has the capacity to attract the attention of individuals who might never consider themselves to be environmentalists. It also has the capacity to forge a transformational shift for students who internalize the realization that we are interdependent.

Education in the 21st century can continue to evolve at a comfortable pace that is entirely out of step with the leadership that is needed to embrace sustainability education—or we can engage in a "deeper critique and broader vision for the future" (UNESCO, 2005, p. 59). Sustainable happiness provides a concept and process for doing the latter. Our experience with student teachers is that sustainable happiness inspires *them* to become part of the solution.

References

Anielski, M. (2007). *Economics of happiness: Building genuine wealth.* Gabriola Island: New Society Publishers.

Brown, K., & Kasser, T. (2005). Are psychological and ecological well-being compatible? The role of values, mindfulness and lifestyle. *Social Indicators Research, 74,* 349–368.

Davidson, K. W., Mostofsky, E., & Whang, W. (2010, February) Don't worry, be happy: Positive affect and reduced 10-year incident coronary heart disease: The Canadian Nova Scotia Health Survey. *European Heart Journal, 31*(9),1065–1070.

Diener, E., & Seligman, M. (2004). Beyond money: Toward an economy of well-being. *Psychological Science in the Public Interest, 5*(1), 1–31.

Intergovernmental Panel on Climate Change. (2007). *Climate change 2007: The physical science basis.* IPCC Secretariat. C.P.N. No. 2300. Retrieved March 20, 2008, from http://www.ipcc.ch/ipccreports/ar4-wg1.htm

Kabat-Zinn, J. (2005). *Coming to our senses: Healing ourselves and the world through mindfulness.* New York: Hyperion.

Kasser, T. (2006). Materialism and its alternatives. In M. Csikszentmihalyi & I. Csikszentmihalyi (Eds.), *A life worth living: Contributions to positive psychology* (pp. 200–214). Toronto: Oxford University Press.

McCullough, M., Emmons, R., & Tsang, J. (2002). The grateful disposition: A conceptual and empirical topography. *Journal of Personality and Social Psychology, 82,* 112–127.

O'Brien, C. (2005). Planning for sustainable happiness: Harmonizing our internal and external landscapes. Paper prepared for the *2nd International Conference on Gross National Happiness,* Nova Scotia, Canada.

O'Brien, C. (2008). Sustainable happiness: How happiness studies can contribute to a more sustainable future. *Canadian Psychology, 49*(4), 289–295.

Seligman, M. (2002). *Authentic happiness.* Toronto: Free Press.

Steptoe, A., Wardle, J., & Marmot, M. (2005). Positive affect and health-related neuroendocrine, cardiovascular, and inflammatory process. *Proceedings of the National Academy of Sciences,* USA *102,* 6508–6512.

Stutz, J. (2006). *The role of well-being in a great transition.* GTI Paper Series No. 10, Tellus Institute. Retrieved November 26, 2007, from https://www.gtinitiative .org/documents/PDFFINALS/10WellBeing.pdf

UNESCO. (2005). *Guidelines and recommendations for reorienting teacher education to address sustainability.* Education for sustainable development in action. Technical paper No. 2. Retrieved September 4, 2009, from http://unesdoc.unesco.org/ images/0014/001433/143370E.pdf

Veenhoven, R. (2008). Healthy happiness: Effects of happiness on physical health and the consequences for preventive health care. *Journal of Happiness Studies, 9*(3), 449–469.

Watkins, P. (2004). Gratitude and subjective well-being. In R. A. Emmons & M. E. McCullough (Eds.) *The psychology of gratitude* (pp. 167–192). New York: Oxford University Press.

4

A CHRISTIAN CONTRIBUTION
TO SUSTAINABILITY

Chris Doran

I n its most basic sense, sustainability can be defined simply as the
capacity to endure into the future, hopefully indefinitely. This rather
uncomplicated concept has become intertwined with, if not outright
substituted by, the much more perplexing, and sometimes downright con-
voluted, term *sustainable development*. The latter comes from the 1987
Brundtland Commission report, *Our Common Future*, in which sustainable development is defined as "development that meets the needs of the
present without compromising the ability of future generations to meet
their own needs." (Brundtland Commission, 1987) Throughout the report,
the commission referred frequently to environmental, economic, and ethical components that would constitute truly sustainable development.
These three components have often been referred to by many as the three
*E*s of sustainability, or sustainability's triple bottom line.[1]

While the Brundtland report must be commended for trying to accomplish many virtuous things at the same time, not the least of which was
extending the idea of distributive justice into the future, its definition of
sustainable development has not been the panacea that many believed it
would be. Most notably, the replacement of *sustainability* with *sustainable
development*, as it has been interpreted almost ubiquitously by developed
world nations, has more to do with economics than it does with either the
environment or ethics. Sustainable development has become more synony-
mous with economic growth than it has with a genuine triple bottom line.

Nonetheless, this should not come as a shock to developed world citizens. As sociologist Daniel Bell (1996) once profoundly stated, economic

growth has become "the secular religion of the advanced industrial societies" (pp. 237–238). This could not be a more fitting description of our present society, where the ups and downs of the stock market are routinely the leading story of the evening news. From my perspective as a Christian theologian, economic growth has become a primary idol of both the developed world and developing world. Consider for a moment what we believe economic growth will provide for us if we make the appropriate sacrifices: a higher standard of living, more participatory democracies, significant amelioration of world poverty, and environmental protection. And yet we often hide the fact that the sacrifices this idol demands have been undeniably dire: dignity of human labor, health of employees, sovereign political democracies, and ecosystem vigor and stability, to name a few. When the priests of this idol tell us that growth has actually occurred despite the gap between the haves and have-nots continuing to increase spectacularly, it is suggested that more economic growth is needed, and subsequently more sacrifices, not a wholesale reassessment of whether our idol is actually making good on its promises. We, as a society, could not be farther away from anything resembling sustainable development.

This situation has led Mary Evelyn Tucker (2008) to assert, "Thus, in discussing the topic of sustainability we may need a broader basis than simply sustainable development. That is because sustainable development may still be viewed too narrowly as measured by economic indicators of growth" (p. 118). Furthermore, Lloyd Sandelands and Andrew Hoffman (2008) contend, "Economic calls to sustainability fail because they do not speak to that part of being that is fully human, to that part of us beyond nature, to that part of us that hungers for meaning, and for the transcendent absolute" (p. 136). This critique, however, is not new. In the middle of the 20th century, U.S. conservationist Aldo Leopold (2001) found the economic basis for conservation equally troublesome: "No important change in ethics was ever accomplished without an internal change in our intellectual emphasis, loyalties, affections, and convictions. The proof that conservation has not yet touched these foundations of conduct lies in the fact that philosophy and religion have not yet heard of it. In our attempt to make conservation easy, we have made it trivial" (p. 168). It seems to me that Leopold's "conservation" can easily be replaced by "sustainable development" or "sustainability" now. How many times have advertisers tried to persuade us that merely purchasing that latest eco-device will transform us into the sustainable society we long for? Yet, as we have seen, particularly over the last decade, merely buying an energy-efficient appliance or a hybrid car has not placed societies on more sustainable pathways. Something else altogether is needed if we are to become sustainable. Perhaps Michael Nelson and John Vucetich (2009) have put it most aptly, "True sustainability needs an ethical revolution."

I maintain these thinkers are exactly correct: We need a novel way to talk about sustainability because the present discussion, dominated by our worship of economic growth, is benefiting very few humans and even fewer nonhuman creatures. If Sandelands and Hoffman are right and sustainability needs to connect to the human hunger for meaning and transcendence in order to be meaningful, then Christianity has much to contribute. Christianity can speak to all three *E*s and, therefore, I think, offer a compelling starting point for the needed revolution.

While Christian churches will undoubtedly play a significant role in such a revolution by asking people to think and act differently, another institution may be of equal importance: Christian higher education. Christian colleges and universities are poised to be serious players in the global discussion about sustainability not only because they are shaping the minds of the next generation of leaders, but they are doing so by asking different sorts of questions than many public universities. If Christian colleges and universities are willing to allow sustainability issues to permeate their curricula and their institutional missions, they could, in a sense, become the home base of operations that every revolution needs.

Christianity as a Starting Place for Environmental Care

In the wake of Lynn White Jr.'s (1967) infamous hypothesis, some wonder what Christianity can really contribute to the discussion about environmental care. More specifically, there has been much debate about how the Bible can actually be helpful in providing a cornerstone for effectual environmental ethics. While there is no doubt that professing Christians and specific interpretations of scripture have been literally damaging to the environment throughout history, I believe that Christianity in general—and biblically based Christianity in particular—can be especially advantageous in our present endeavor to create a more meaningful and thus transformative concept of sustainability. Let us briefly examine a few of those concerns, and I shall suggest which Christian ideas might be especially consequential to this discussion.

One of the central charges against the Bible being used in environmental ethics is that the Bible is anthropocentric and hence has little, if anything, to say about the intrinsic value of nonhuman creatures. Yet, as John Cobb notes, there are two chief problems with this assertion. First, he argues that the Bible is not anthropocentric, but rather theocentric. The biblical focus on human beings is in fact derived from its way of describing and comprehending God. "It is because God made us in God's image, because God cares for us, because God sent Jesus to suffer for us, that we are to appreciate our own worth and care for one another. When we shift from this theocentric vision to an anthropocentric one that takes human value and importance as its starting point, we have abandoned the biblical perspective" (Cobb, 1992, p. 93). Second, considering the Bible's theocentric emphasis, he turns the tables on those who believe that the Bible is anthropocentric and states that they have the burden of proof to show that only *Homo sapiens* have intrinsic value (Cobb, 1992, p. 95).

The very opening chapters of the first book of the Bible actually set the stage for a wide-ranging way to view environmental care. As the story goes in Genesis 1, God creates the universe and everything in it, both human and nonhuman creatures, by merely speaking them into existence. From a theological perspective, Christians conclude that everything God creates shares a common characteristic: a radical dependence on God for their very existence. This kinship among all creatures is symbolized further in the creation narrative of Genesis 2. In this account, all living creatures are made out of the same "earth," which suggests that any anthropocentric viewpoint should be tempered by the fact that we came out of the same ground as everything else God created.

Returning to Genesis 1, God not only creates each and every creature that fills the world, but God says that each of these creatures is "good" and when God finishes creating, God proclaims that all of it is "very good." We should note that this divine declaration is equivalent to saying that every creature, both human and nonhuman, has intrinsic worth. The dignity of each creature is bestowed upon it by divine affirmation, not by human assessment of its possible instrumental value.

While many Christians will concede that the dignity of nonhuman creatures is established by God in these stories, those same Christians often will not grant that God has included those creatures—not just humans—within the divine plan of redemption for the universe. The Bible consistently references God's plan for the consummation of the entire universe (e.g., Isaiah, 11, 6–9; 65, 17, 25; Colossians 1, 14–20; 1 Corinthians, 15, 28; Ephesians 1, 10;

Romans, 8, 19–22; Jonah, 3, 16–17). What many Christians do not seem to realize is that if God does not redeem everything that God creates and said in the beginning was very good, then, as James Nash (1991) states most succinctly, "Both the intrinsic value of creatures and the moral character of God are jeopardized" (p. 130). For Christians then, God's promise to redeem the entire universe means that all creatures are loved by God and all creatures, not just *Homo sapiens*, have a role to play in God's plan for creation.

God's bestowal of worth on members of creation and the kinship of all members of creation are not the only themes that the Bible might be able to contribute to a grander idea of sustainability. Recent scholarship has illuminated how the biblical prophets are also extremely relevant to this discussion. Hilary Marlow (2009) asserts persuasively that Amos, Hosea, and Isaiah all rely on a worldview that that sees an explicit interdependency among God, humanity, and nonhuman creation. For example, in Amos, the prophet proposes that nonhuman creation sides with God in the divine response to the Israelites forsaking the covenant. In Hosea, the prophet castigates the Israelites for breaking the covenant, but tells them that God has given them the hope of restoring the created order by engaging in ethical behavior. Finally, in the first half of Isaiah, the prophet tells the Israelites that justice, righteousness, and peace are not only conditions that mark the health of human relationships, but also the health of relationships between human and nonhuman creation. Michael Northcott (2007) finds a similar theme in the prophet Jeremiah, as he maintains, "The biblical narrative of justice suggests that it is ecologically situated and not just a human value" (p. 161). He concludes that Jeremiah believed the exile from Israel during his time was brought upon them because of their injustice, that is, by the Israelites polluting the land in a quest for power and wealth rather than living by the covenant of God that included justice for the poor in conjunction with proper care of the land.

Nick Spencer et al. (Spencer, White, & Vroblesky, 2009) argue that in the vision depicted in the latter half of Isaiah, the prophet presents an image of God's plan for creation or the "right order of things" (pp. 104ff). This order of things relies on the underlying recognition of the interdependency of all creatures and their shared dependency on their creator. Isaiah seems to believe that there is no discernible distinction between what we might call social and environmental sustainability. Spencer et al. contend, "Instead, the message is that environmental regeneration is not to be understood in isolation from social redemption, just as neither can be understood separately from the spiritual dimension of humanity's relationship with God" (p. 106).

The profound insight of Isaiah, according to Spencer et al., is that the divine right order of things is a moral order and thus implies moral obligations, for example, care for the poor or protection of threatened species.

Thinking about Technology

While the idol of economic growth trades on the promise that technology can get humans out of even the stickiest of situations without any major changes in behavior, Christianity has a much more sober assessment of the human condition. In Genesis 11, the narrator tells the infamous Tower of Babel story. This account strongly insists that our ability to create technology makes us think that we are, in fact, comparable to the divine, as we give into our delusions of grandeur. While human ingenuity and any resulting technology from that imagination will undoubtedly play a role in sustainability efforts now and in the future, there is no question that we have quite a love affair with technology. Whether it is talk about the next wave of energy-efficient devices that will help solve our addiction to oil, or geo-engineering that will dramatically slow down climate change until we have better technology to solve our energy problems, we have the amazing ability to rationalize away our past technological failures and focus solely on our technological triumphs. This is hubris of the worst sort. Instead, we must remember that technology does not make us more godlike because, in fact, the history of technological achievements is much more ambiguous than we care to acknowledge. For every advancement in our understanding of the atom that has been used to create nuclear energy, which many would argue is beneficial to human civilization, the same knowledge has been used to create nuclear weapons, which have the ability to destroy humanity.

The biblical story of Noah and his ark is equally illustrative, but from a slightly different perspective. Against the sort of technological hubris that often dominates the current sustainability discussion, Michael Northcott (2007) argues, "[T]he Noah saga suggests that turning away from the ecologically destructive path on which humanity is headed requires humility and a preparedness to change direction in response to the clear signs of impending danger" (p. 79). He goes on to maintain that this story not only reminds us of how highly God views nonhuman creatures (remember Genesis 1) by including them in the ark, but also Noah's demonstration of care for the nonhuman creatures that God sent to him is representative of the important vocation that humans have in God's plan for the universe. Interpreting this story theologically for our situation, we see that technology (building the ark) must work alongside the behavioral change needed to react successfully to an oncoming crisis. One could not exist without the other if Noah and the other creatures were to survive.

Frugality as Economic Justice

That the rhetoric of economic development has heretofore dominated the discussion about sustainability does not mean that this considerable part of the triple bottom line has been decided. While Christianity has much to contribute to a public discussion concerning the role of economics in modern society, I must presently confine the examination to one aspect of the participation of an individual moral agent in our political economy. To do this, let us turn to an exploration of a virtue that rarely finds its way seriously into conversations in the United States today, and even less so into conversations about sustainability: the virtue of frugality. This, I believe, is a serious oversight because frugality is a critical way of conceiving of our involvement in an economic system that can often be devoid of love and justice.

Frugality should bring to mind thoughts like moderation or temperance or a general satisfaction with material sufficiency. In our present situation, we might add cost-effectiveness or the efficient use of natural resources. For Christians, however, frugality should be about more than just clipping coupons or using the latest energy-saving electronic device. According to James Nash (1994), frugality is primarily about sacrifice for the sake of love. "Frugality . . . is an expression of love—seeking the good or well-being of others in response to their needs and to the God who is love. The source of the sacrificial dimension in frugality is love of neighbor, for love always entails giving up at least some of our self-interests for the sake of the welfare of others in communal relationships" (p. 56). While advertisers attempt to convince us that being frugal means sacrificing the highest quality of living that is our American birthright, as Nash defines it, frugality is really about living an abundant life. This life, however, is about being more rather than having more; it is about qualitative rather than quantitative enrichment (p. 55). Being frugal then forces one to distinguish between the needs and wants in one's life and to ask questions such as: Is clean air a need or a want? Is biodiversity conservation a necessity or a luxury?

Frugality is not about cutting back one's consumption in order to hoard goods or to be miserly, but rather it is a commitment to consume less in order that one's neighbors, especially those in developing nations, might have the opportunity to consume at a level that we believe reflects a dignified human existence. By consuming what one needs and not indulging in one's every want, this virtue is not only an extension of love to one's neighbor but also allows one to do justice because frugality is an individual's participation in distributive justice. Choosing to be frugal allows more resources to be left available for our neighbors in the developing world, and it creates the space for us to be in solidarity with the world's poor as they live "frugally" as a means of survival rather than a voluntary virtuous act. For Christians, living frugally will get us closer to an economic system that is at least a pale reflection of the kingdom of God (McFague, 2008).

Nash (1994) is undoubtedly correct: In today's society, frugality is ultimately a "subversive" virtue (pp. 50–51). It is subversive because it strikes at the heart of economic growth as it disputes our cultural belief in the idol's innate goodness and ability to deliver on its many promises. Frugality is subversive because it rejects the primary assumption of advertising and the culture of consumption: that human happiness is defined by an unrelenting commitment to material accumulation. Frugality is subversive because it refuses the temptation to always go after bigger, better, faster, newer, more attractive, or state-of-the-art products. For these reasons, the priests of economic growth have resisted including this virtue in the discussion about sustainability.

A Different Kind of Hope

As one peers out onto the horizon of global problems that cry out for significant sustainable solutions, one wonders whether it is reasonable to be hopeful about the future. Take climate change, for example. Is it reasonable to imagine that the world's governments will come together, and very soon at that, to provide the simultaneous international cooperation that is needed to grapple with the myriad political and economic issues that are needed to address climate change? To me, it seems unreasonable to hope that governmental agencies will be able to reorient their mindsets to think sustainably, and then subsequently create, implement, and enforce consequential policies that can tackle an issue such as climate change. It seems equally unreasonable to me merely to hope that technology will come through in the end, as if it were the messiah that will swoop in and solve all of our environmental problems. So, then, where does this leave us? If we become paralyzed due to a lack of hope in the significance of our actions, then sustainable solutions really will remain out of reach.

For Christians, the concept of hope deals with two questions: (1) What does hope mean? and (2) In whom or what do we actually place our hope? In today's society, when someone says, "I hope X will happen," one generally is connoting an emotional state of desire for something to occur that is not necessarily based on any sensible consideration or reflection on past experience. The biblical notion of hope, however, means something entirely different. The Greek word for hope (*elpis*) denotes expectation, especially an expectation related to a divine promise. Therefore, in the best sense of the word, when a Christian hopes for something, she confidently expects it to happen because she has placed her hope in the one who has demonstrated in the past the power to deliver on previous promises, specifically the one who had the power to raise Jesus from the grave.

Conclusion

Let me not be misunderstood. Technological advancements will be essential to sustainability. International political cooperation that leads to sustainable policy formation will also be necessary to meet the needs of our most pressing global problems. My hope, though, is not in those things. My hope is in the one who has created a universe that has a "right order of things," wherein social redemption and ecological restoration are intrinsically linked to each other because this order reflects the character of the creator. There is much work to be done on the sustainability front, and Christians have much to contribute precisely because we understand the creative and redemptive power of God as well as humanity's true place in the universe. John Cobb (1992) once said, "Apart from the transformative power of grace, there would be no grounds for hope. We would have to resign ourselves to the inevitable or seek release from an unendurable world in mystical transcendence. Because of grace, resignation and release are not acceptable choices for Christians. We know that we are not masters of history, but neither are we mere victims" (p. 11). Being frugal then can be seen as a symbol of Christian hope. One individual exercising frugal means will obviously not crush the idol of economic growth overnight, but economic sacrifice for the sake of the neighbor is an actual expression of the fact that living according to the "right order of things" is possible and even transformative.

If true sustainability requires an ethical revolution, then Christianity can provide a clear and compelling case for what that moral vision must include.

We must begin to acknowledge that humans are part of an interdependent web of existence that includes nonhuman creatures. We must begin to consider genuinely the intrinsic value of species other than *Homo sapiens* as we search for sustainable solutions. We must recognize that technology will not be the messiah that the idol of economic growth and its priests in the developed world have proclaimed it to be for decades. We must understand that any sort of sustainable future will necessitate frugal sacrifice on the part of the citizens of the developed world. In doing this, we will not only be able to find true moments of solidarity with the world's poor, but we will also discover a qualitatively enriched and abundant life for ourselves. Finally, we must ask ourselves sincerely and consistently, "Where does our hope lay?" By confronting these issues honestly, we might be able to navigate the road between mastery and victimhood that leads toward a sustainable future and that includes consideration for ethics, the environment, and economics. And what better place to engage in this sort of honest reflection than in Christian institutions of higher education? Christian colleges and universities that decide to take a leading role in the discussion about sustainability will be able to shape the minds of a generation of global citizens who will be equipped to participate in not only defining the various facets of sustainability from a unique viewpoint, but who will be able to contribute meaningfully in the construction of actual sustainable solutions to the world's most pressing issues.

Note

1. While the Brundtland Report may have set the terms for the global discussion about sustainability, it is worth noting that in 1974 the World Council of Churches (WCC) put forward a definition of a "sustainable society." The WCC contended that four factors would define a sustainable society: (1) only the equitable distribution of scarce resources and highly participatory forms of government would allow for social stability; (2) the need for food must be below our ability to supply it and levels of pollution must be below the capacity of the earth to absorb them; (3) the use of nonrenewable resources must not exceed our ability to increase resource efficiency through technology; (4) a society cannot be sustainable if it is continually disrupted by variations in planetary events caused by climate change (World Council of Churches, 1974).

References

Bell, D. (1996). *The cultural contradictions of capitalism* (20th ed.). New York: Basic Books.

Brundtland Commission. (1987). *Our common future.* Retrieved from http://www.un-documents.net/ocf-02.htm#

Cobb, Jr., J. B. (1992). *Sustainability: Economics, ecology, and justice.* Maryknoll, NY: Orbis Books.

Leopold, A. (2001). *A Sand County almanac: With essays on conservation.* New York: Oxford University Press.

Marlow, H. (2009). *Biblical prophets & contemporary environmental ethics: Re-reading Amos, Hosea, and First Isaiah.* Oxford, Eng.: Oxford University Press.

McFague, S. (2008). *A new climate for theology: God, the world, and global warming.* Minneapolis, MN: Fortress Press.

Nash, J. (1991). *Loving nature: Ecological integrity and Christian responsibility.* Nashville, TN: Abingdon Press.

Nash, J. (1994). Ethics and the economics-ecology dilemma: Toward a just, sustainable, and frugal future. *Theology & Public Policy, 6,* 33–63.

Nelson, M., & Vucetich, J. (2009). True sustainability needs an ethical revolution. *Ecologist.* Retrieved from http://www.theecologist.org/blogs_and_comments/commentators/other_comments/383966/true_sustainability_needs_an_ethical_revolution.html

Northcott, M. (2007). *A moral climate: The ethics of global warming.* Maryknoll, NY: Orbis Books.

Sandelands, L., & Hoffman, A. (2008). Sustainability, faith, and the market. *Worldviews, 12,* 129–145.

Spencer, N., White, R., & Vroblesky, V. (2009). *Christianity, climate change, and sustainable living.* Peabody, MA: Hendrickson Publishers.

Tucker, M. E. (2008). World religions, the earth charter, and sustainability. *Worldviews 12,* 115–128.

White, L. (1967). The historical roots of our ecologic crisis. *Science, 155,* 1203–1207.

World Council of Churches. (1974). The theme of humanity and creation in the ecumenical movement. Retrieved from http://www.jaysquare.com/resources/growthdocs/grow10b.htm

PART TWO

TEACHING SUSTAINABILITY IN THE ACADEMIC DISCIPLINES

5

THE HUNGRY TEXT

Toward a Sustainable Literary Food Pedagogy

Tom Hertweck and Kyle Bladow

I n 2009, James E. McWilliams ignited something of a firestorm in food and culture communities when he released his *Just Food: Where Locavores Get It Wrong and How We Can Truly Eat Responsibly*. Despite the subtitle (which was likely an addition of an overzealous publisher), McWilliams sets his task not as dismantling food localism but as exposing the inherent ambiguities within food activism generally, a movement he rightly describes as often simple-minded and without a capacity for self-criticism. The book covered a rich terrain fraught with danger—eating locally, food miles, organic, genetically modified (GM) crops, meat, aquaculture, and agricultural subsidies—and responses to the book were deeply mixed. On the one hand, popular review outlets hailed the book's lucidity and ability to inform readers in a lively style. On the other hand, some in the food movement took deep offense and suggested the ways in which McWilliams's research was incomplete or compromised by his funding sources, and that the author had a star-grabbing agenda.[1]

Literature and Ethical Practice: Reading Food Sustainably

Well-intentioned though it may be, the skill set of literary critics simply does not lend itself to exposing the errors in food research like McWilliams's. Put another way, deconstruction, as the critical theory that seeks to expose the shadows of meaning that our speech acts carry with them, tells us little about fair-trade practices. Historicism, as a mode of exploring language and power structures, has little to say about whether a given consumer ought to be buying conventional or organic apples next time he or she is at the grocery store. Narratology, as the practice of charting and describing movements of plot and character development, simply cannot expose the hidden risks of pesticide use. Reader response criticism, as the investigations of each reader constructs the meaning of works while engaged in the act of reading, tells us little to nothing about water rights and irrigation issues. How could they, or any of the countless other methodological praxes? No literary critical project can because these are theories of texts and culture, not of food, nutrition, or environmentalism.

Instead of despairing about this position, we find that there is much to celebrate. In the first place, there is something appealing about being reminded that those in the ivory tower of the humanities are just like everyone else, making decisions in a world of missing or incomplete information. But more than this, it should come as a relief to those working in the humanities to be absolved, to a degree, of having to sort out problems that are, properly speaking, simply out of the realm of our departments or even college. Not to mention influence: Who would ever seek out a literature professor for advice on, say, Starbucks' fair-trade practices? (To be sure, notable exceptions exist—for example, Simon [2009] has a book on this very topic worth looking at.[2]) But at base, one wonders: What do earnest scholars of Milton have to tell us about mercury and bioaccumulation? What does *The Joy Luck Club* instruct us in the health of pan-Asian cuisine for ecosystems? Instead, why not involve ourselves in debates about sustainability out of those skills that we have spent so much time and effort developing, like close reading, contextualization, poetic analysis, and cultural and historical study? In this way, we will legitimate our contributions to food sustainability along a number of vectors.

First, literary food pedagogy provides a basis for the reading of texts— broadly construed, from fiction to nonfiction, music to film—in ways that interrogate the systems of value that they encode. Take as an example perhaps the most famous passage on food in American literature, Ralph Ellison's (1952) *Invisible Man*'s five-page internal dialogue on hot buttered yams. Here, the summary capitulation—"I yam what I am!" (p. 266)— encapsulates the complexities of race-thinking, as the invisible man considers consumption, identity, and taste: "Why, you could cause us the greatest humiliation simply by confronting us with something we loved" (p. 264). These thoughts merge with class and regional issues: The sense of loving something figured as base or undignified as yams or chitterlings would cause a so-called enlightened urban black (like the invisible man or the teacher Bledsoe) to "revert to field-niggerism" (p. 265), a supposedly lesser position of southern agrarian blackness. As the case illustrates, food issues extend from personal food choices out into questions of consumption, but also into the world of political thought—thought that must be considered before the invisible man can make his food choice.[3] Through discursive analysis, then, steeped in the historical and cultural development of the positions texts express, literary food pedagogy takes seriously diverse and complex positions on food and its place in the world.

Second, literary scholars will provide a sorely needed perspective on the particular modes of discourse utilized by writers on subjects as diverse as labor practices and risk policy, especially as they narrate how these subjects attain social value. For example, Ruth Ozeki's (2003) *All Over Creation* tells the story of an aging couple's Idaho farm threatened by an influx of genetically modified products, and narrates a host of positions bearing directly on sustainability issues. The couple sees it as a biblical directive to save seeds and sell them through their homespun catalog to a loose national network of other seed traders. An agriproducts multinational corporation sends their public relations man to meddle, and a roaming band of food-justice anarchists come into town to disrupt the scene. Meanwhile, other local farmers just want to turn a profit in the difficult financial climate of modern agribusiness, a sketchy promise made by the GM spuds. And, finally, the couple's estranged daughter, the protagonist, has returned home in the midst of the struggle to sort out her past and future on the farm. The story is compelling because, for too long, we believe, food sustainability studies generally have been led by specialized technical communication and research meant to instruct people on better and worse ways of engaging the world. While we do not discount the value of such research—it is, after all, essential to changing world systems—technically driven work often remains blind to the potentially authoritarian tone it takes, risking sinking ideas before they are even able to get off the drawing board. But more than this, Ozeki's novel ably illustrates, without drawing simplistic conclusions, that technical rationality is certainly not the only view, and it comes into contest with any number of differing value systems. Literary study, therefore, provides a way to negotiate these competing values by exploring the various subject positions of interested parties, taking care to understand that these positions do not emerge out of wholesale irrationality, but out of simply incompatible or incommensurable rationalities.[4]

Finally, and perhaps most importantly, by using the tools of the literary humanities openly and with the skill and professionalism we bring to all literary study, literary critics will legitimate our own sustainability practice: In doing what we know best, we act ethically by trying not to do someone else's job. Building on our own existent professional integrity, we may come to understand our greater service to sustainability in a more robust and nuanced way. Instead of casting our critical attention toward those disciplines to which we are strangers, our time will be better spent "locally," in our own intellectual territory, strengthening our knowledge of the roles that language and literature play in sustainability issues. From this praxis, we draw strength by using our extant expertise, all the while maintaining our credibility with our fellow disciplines and thereby solidifying a foundation from which we might continue to engage and trouble the world of sustainability discourse. Rethinking literary practice in this way, through the lens of sustainability and food, tests our conceptions of ecology by understanding that how we translate value through language has an effect on the world—and this is a test worth taking seriously.

Envisioning Literary Food Pedagogy: Assigning Food and Writing

Some will assume that the narrowness of this subject matter will somehow limit students in their creativity as they work on their own projects. Not so, especially after students are exposed to lively introductions to food and food writing such as Tobin (2003, 2009), Bloom (2008), Willard (2002), and Kaufman (2008), which demonstrate writing as a practice that locates how we think about the value of food, its production, consumption, and place in our world.

Student papers will astound in both their range of textual reference and their seemingly limitless creativity, as a sampling of our students' own papers demonstrate. What are the political appeals and aesthetic perils of so-called compromised art—works that develop a heavy-handed message, as in Upton Sinclair's food and labor justice classic *The Jungle*? What does a writer's invocation of a well-known plot structure, like that of Chaucer's *Canterbury Tales* in Maria Lewycka's novel *Strawberry Fields*, add to a story of migrant labor injustice? How do traditional foods expose fissures in the way we think about gender and sexuality, as in Margie Norris's moving poem "Tortillas," that invokes the title's Chicano slang term for lesbians? Is it possible that works about a single product (like Mark Kurlansky's bestseller *Salt*), what Bruce Robbins (2005) calls "commodity histories" (p. 454), can be more than just capitalist propaganda? How do writers trouble our mental images of farmers, as Don Kurtz does in his immensely sad and haunting novel *South of the Big Four*? By using the example of Psyche Williams-Forson (2006) and her work connecting African American racism and food stereotypes, how does literature show characters reclaiming and recuperating cultural identity? What does the relentless use of food simile and metaphor in Helena María Viramontes's novel *Under the Feet of Jesus* tell us about the environmental justice struggles of immigrant farm workers? How does the poetic richness of food imagery in Ray Gonzalez's "Praise the Tortilla, Praise the Menudo, Praise the Chorizo" explore ideas of family, memory, and loss? How does Scott Hamilton Kennedy's documentary *The Garden* explore urban food issues amid debates about the use of public space? How do films like Edgar Wright's *Scott Pilgrim vs. the World* humorously depict a vegan diet and vegetarianism? Each student paper explores some aspect of food while connecting it to bigger issues about representation and cultural value. Just as in any literature class, a combination of close reading skills and an attention to research will help students dig into the particularities of a specific food or food issue, and thereby push students to decode the complex narratives that foods, their movements through the world, and their broader cultural import. Taken in aggregate, these impetuses emerge as a vision of sustainability that takes seriously the interconnectedness of food choices and food discourses.

Student activities or assignments, however, need not end with the research paper, especially in lower-level survey courses or special topics electives meant to reach a broad range of students or programmatic outcomes. Because much food discourse hinges on particular terminology, from the fuzziness and seeming free-for-all of advertising language ("fresh," "natural," or "healthy") to the specialized discourse of federally regulated commercial speech ("diet," "organic," or "free-range"), students can easily engage their research writing skills by crafting a Raymond Williams–like keyword glossary or essay in which they work through the historical development of these vocabularies, how the various discourse communities that invoke them might harness or blur meanings, or what cultural phenomena coalesce around such seemingly banal language. Students will become both horrified and delighted, for example, to learn that *natural* has effectively no meaning whatsoever, while *diet* means not just bad-tasting (a cultural value), but something very particular, governed not by cultural assumptions, but by the Food and Drug Administration (FDA), which is a legal value.

In a similar vein, students encountering a range of foods and foodways in literary texts are eager to dig deeper into the attitudes and practices that inform what they read, making a food discourse portfolio a deeply satisfying exercise in research and presentation. Here, students are asked to pick a single food (say, eggplant) or food practice or issue (Brazilian barbecue, perhaps) and research the wide and varied terrain in which these foods or subject matters appear. More than just producing a Wikipedia entry, students work over the course of a semester to find out not just factual information about a favorite food, but to locate as many textual reference points (drawn from written texts, songs, movies, advocacy groups' websites, and the like) for their subject matter here. The portfolio, then, includes an annotated bibliography, appropriate illustrations, a short reflective essay about a relevant and related food experience, and a summary report that draws larger conclusions about the cultural artifacts collected and what ways they traffic in a multiplicity of valuations about food. Students should be encouraged to draw conclusions about their subject, and they should be given the leeway to make tentative "arguments" based on their materials, answering big questions: What is the validity of the stories we tell about animal welfare in confined animal feeding operations (CAFOs)? Where does the majority of our information about milk come from? Who are the interested parties involved in the global banana trade? Who governs information about diet claims, and how can we identify slippery assertions in product copy? In this, instructors have as much to gain as the students. Indeed, who could ever be an expert on every single food product? Presentations, alternative genre assignments, website design, or short film productions are a must because a collective model of learning in the food and literature classroom serves all students.

In all of these assignments, students develop the critical literacy skills necessary to meet the needs of most, if not all, literature courses, by digging into texts and their plurality of significations and exploring how history and culture are complicit in literary production. But more than this, by appealing to their natural interest in the foods they eat, students are drawn into the larger discursive practices of writing in an academic world in ways that for many of the uninitiated can seem highly artificial. Food choices matter; students already know this. What they do *not* know, however, is the extent to which literary technique is implicated in their own knowledge and in how they interact with others in the world, and how being taught to be a critical, skeptical reader (the goal of all good English professors, one hopes) can affect this most fundamental of aspect of their lives.

The rewards of literary food pedagogy, even in the traditional research paper, then, are great both for the students as well as for the teacher. They not only solve the problem of the student's tired complaint, "I don't know what to write about," but they also appeal to the basic sense of the world that students already know by tapping into an area of intuitive expertise they have developed over a lifetime of eating. The troubles here are good ones: getting students to question received knowledge, identifying blind spots in argumentative strategy, and encouraging research into the differing (and often conflicting) views that writers ably and creatively express.

Worry not: Invariably, many good projects undertaken by thoughtful students will engage with sustainability issues directly. However, it remains the case that, because the evaluation of texts interrogates the ways they traffic in value, sustainability issues will work their way into all projects. Sustainability already requires an attunement to broader ecological and social-systemic implications. Food literature always implies some sense of consumption (or its negation, in the rejection of certain foods), whether of money, time, resources, labor, or simply goodwill. Because the literatures of food are best understood as trafficking in cultural capital, of value generally, an understanding of all facets of their discursive elements can only help us understand better how we can translate knowledge about sustainability and how people figure it—literally, as figures of speech—in the world at large. To know how sustainability speaks to its various and fractious constituencies is the as-yet-undescribed world that we as scholars have an obligation to understand both for ourselves and for our students.

Finally, a note of encouragement: It will not be difficult to find texts to think about. In fact, seeking out food in literature is a little like hunting mushrooms: Once one has his or her mind attenuated to literary food, one sees the embarrassment of riches creative writers have put out into the world. What *will* remain a challenge, however, will be to remember that thinking about food sustainability through literature is not simply a matter of cherry-picking texts that assert a specific food justice agenda. To do this would simply commit the sin of indoctrination so many critics of higher education levy against academia already, not to mention risk exposing literary critics to charges of dilettantism, dabbling in, say, nutrition science or agricultural economics without the specialist training required to do so meaningfully. And no one (one hopes) wants to perpetuate the same old sloganeering that those like McWilliams have spent considerable time debunking. Leave the technical matters to the researchers in their appropriate fields to reach consensus. Better that the literary humanist's time be spent considering how we encode that information in narrative and public opinion; the ways in which we transmit notions of value; and how the vicissitudes of language reveal and conceal the machinations of power, work, race, home, class, gender, and the like. And, what is more, to engage students along these lines seems an appropriate ethical commitment, inasmuch as giving them these tools allows them the ability to self-critique, to draw into question a whole host of positions they themselves might wish to engage as they see the issues that are important to them refracted through the prism of language.

This may come as a disappointment to those who want to teach literature classes and somehow influence students' food choices. Stanley Fish (2008) would rightly call this immediate influence not just a non sequitur (teaching food choice would simply not follow from the realm of expertise of literary scholars) but a dereliction of one's professorial duty to pass along specialized knowledge and skills, a giving up of one's job for some other politically motivated activity in the classroom, a practice that leads to all manner of problems he outlines eloquently. Rather, by using the particular training of textual scholarship, literary thinkers are poised to plumb perhaps the greatest depths of food and sustainability: how language expresses, covertly and not so covertly, what matters. And while not the banner-waving, bumper-sticker-generating activism some would want, narrative and rhetorical techniques and the brand of inquiry they engender nonetheless remain essential to sustainability's future, if only because they envelop every person, every food, and every utterance, every single time we attempt to tell someone some piece of information about the things we eat. In this way, what more far-reaching and important work could one ask for?

Notes

1. For a typical positive popular review, see Sullum (2009); for a typical vitriolic review, see Trueman (2009).

2. It should be acknowledged that Simon, a professor of American studies, isn't an English professor but a historian at Temple University.

3. Instructors taking up Ellison's yam passage would benefit from the work of Witt (1999), Opie (2008), and Hertweck (forthcoming).

4. See also Ozeki's (1999) *My Year of Meats* for a novel about the challenging subject of meat consumption and media, as well as Ozeki's (2006) short story "The Death of the Last White Male," about food and disease, available on her website, www.ruthozeki.com.

References

Bloom, L. Z. (2008). Consuming prose: The delectable rhetoric of food writing. *College English, 70*, 346–362.

Ellison, R. (1952/1995). *Invisible man.* New York: Vintage.

Fish, S. (2008). *Save the world on your own time.* New York: Oxford University Press.

Hertweck, T. (forthcoming). Hungering for oppression? Soul food and the urban black novel.

Kaufman, F. (2008). *A short history of the American stomach.* New York: Houghton Mifflin.

McWilliams, J. E. (2009). *Just food: Where locavores get it wrong and how we can truly eat responsibly.* New York: Little, Brown.

Opie, F. D. (2008). *Hog and hominy: Soul food from Africa to America.* New York: Columbia University Press.

Ozeki, R. (1999). *My year of meats.* New York: Viking.

Ozeki, R. (2003). *All over creation.* New York: Viking.

Ozeki, R. (2006). The death of the last white male. *Configurations, 14*(1), 61–68.

Robbins, B. (2005). Commodity histories. *PMLA, 120*, 454–463.

Simon, B. (2009). *Everything but the coffee: Learning about America from Starbucks.* Berkeley: University of California Press.

Sullum, J. (2009, August 22). Recipes for virtuous dining. *Wall Street Journal.* Retrieved from http://online.wsj.com/article/SB10001424052970204683204574355241010631018.html

Tobin, F. (2003). Booking the cooks: Literature and gastronomy in Molière. *Literary Imagination: The Review of the Association of Literary Scholars and Critics, 5*(1), 125–136.

Tobin, F. (2009, May 4). *Thought for food: Literature and gastronomy.* [Audio podcast]. Retrieved from iTunes U/UCTV Podcasts

Trueman, K. (2009). Inflammatory new book attacking local food movement has one grain of truth buried under heaps of manure. *AlterNet: Environment.* Retrieved from http://www.alternet.org/environment/142202/

Willard, B. E. (2002). The American story of meat: Discursive influences on cultural eating practice. *Journal of Popular Culture, 36*, 105–118.

Williams-Forson, P. (2006). *Building houses out of chicken legs: Black women, food, and power.* Chapel Hill: University of North Carolina Press.

Witt, D. (1999). *Black hunger: Food and the politics of U.S. identity.* New York: Oxford University Press.

6

THE RHETORIC OF SUSTAINABILITY

Ecocomposition and Environmental Pragmatism

Kimberly R. Moekle

Fifteen years ago, Cheryl Glotfelty accurately proclaimed, "If your knowledge of the outside world were limited to what you could infer from the major publications of the literary profession, you would quickly discern that race, class, and gender were the hot topics . . . but you would never suspect that the earth's life support systems were under stress. Indeed, you might never know that there was an earth at all" (Glotfelty & Fromm, 1996, p. xvi).[1] Since then, publications in the field of literary studies as a whole have increasingly engaged with issues of sustainability. As Owens (2001, p. 3) indicates, these texts cover a range of specializations, including environmental rhetoric (Bruner & Oelschlaeger, 1994; Herndl & Brown, 1996), ecofeminism (McAndrew, 1996), the rhetoric of sustainability (Killingsworth & Palmer, 1992), environmental discourse and communication (Cantrill & Oravec, 1996), nature writing and composition (Roorda, 1998), postcolonialism and environmental pedagogy (Brown, 2000), and ecocomposition (Dobrin & Weisser, 2001, 2002). Despite this body of work, however, some scholars argue that the field remains far behind other disciplines in considering our research and teaching in light of environmental pressures.

The word *sustainability* is indeed more frequently associated with ecology, environmental studies, earth systems, ecological economics, and urban planning, for example. But our responsibility to address this topic across the disciplines is more critical than ever. As Derek Owens asserts in his text entitled *Composition and Sustainability: Teaching for a Threatened Generation*, "as it becomes increasingly impossible to ignore our escalating local and global environmental crises . . . educators in a number of fields will have to make room for sustainability in their teaching and their research" (Owens, 2001, p. 1). Although much has changed over the past decade, I agree with scholars such as Owens and others that the fields of literary studies, rhetoric, and composition must recognize that sustainability is "not only equal in importance to race, class, and gender but also entails many of the concerns associated with these rubrics" (Owens, 2001, p. xiii). In spite of the political frameworks that have historically marginalized the place of composition programs within the academic ecosystem, writing studies is an ideal disciplinary arena for engaging undergraduates in conversations about sustainability. First- and second-year composition courses, in particular, can offer college students a preliminary way to connect with sustainability-based thinking, both throughout and beyond their academic careers.

In this chapter, I describe a second-year writing course I teach entitled "A Planet on Edge: The Rhetoric of Sustainable Energy."[2] I explain why I find this rhetoric so important and share examples of how former students have brought their research and learning to bear on the world. By analyzing the discourse surrounding energy controversies in a composition class, students discover how diverse publics perceive environmental issues and policies, and how rhetoric in a particular context frames social realities. In this way, I argue, the course illustrates how composition specialists can encourage students to explore matters of sustainability using the lens of rhetoric, that is, the study of the most effective means of persuasion as well as of how competing expressions shape our thoughts and actions. In other words, rhetorical analysis can help students unpack debates about sustainability and the environment by giving them tools with which to discern the political, social, and moral agendas of those involved, while simultaneously strengthening the effectiveness of their own rhetorical choices.[3]

For their projects in my class, students select a controversial local, national, or international sustainable energy topic, such as the viability of building a green dorm on campus as a living laboratory for sustainability, or the development of a geothermal power plant in Newberry National Park in Oregon, or the proposed Severn tidal barrage between the English and Welsh coasts. Some students find creative ways to dovetail their own academic interests with topics related to sustainable energy; among these are a plant biologist who studied the viability of cellulosic ethanol and a civil engineer who studied the difficulties of achieving Leadership in Energy and Environmental Design (LEED) certification.[4] Through completing the required assignment sequence (which consists of a research proposal, a written research-based argument, an oral delivery of research, and a research reflection essay over the 10-week quarter), students develop an increasingly complex approach to constructing successful arguments. Their projects focus not only on the technical aspects of the controversies they've chosen, but these projects also consider the rhetoric that students encounter in both academic and popular media sources about those topics.

While conducting their research, students frequently reflect on the pessimism and optimism that surround debates over the development and use of sustainable energy. They consider the issues from a variety of perspectives—social, economic, scientific, and political—as they analyze news coverage, press releases, websites, television commercials, scholarly articles about rhetoric and the environment, and writings by scientists. As concerned citizens, we all face a variety of conflicting viewpoints about the environment from sources we feel we should trust, but it's hard to sort out the complexities and consequences of such rhetoric. It's a playing field in which the media, politics, and science collide on a regular basis. As a result, the discourse of energy is particularly useful in the composition classroom, precisely because it so clearly exemplifies rhetorical issues such as audience, persuasion, evidence, facts, anecdote, narrative, and plot. Students quickly begin to notice rhetorical patterns, such as various appeals to reason and emotion, figurative language, and metaphors, used by different stakeholders with varying objectives. They evaluate the rhetoric that characterizes the debates, analyzing the ways in which language and diction shape public perception and policy outcomes. In their papers, they propose a solution to the problem or a new way of thinking about the controversy at hand. One student, for example, investigated the implementation of sustainable fuel sources for cooking in small villages in Ghana. She reframed the issue, however, as one of gender inequality as much as an environmental crisis because the pollution and health problems associated with the collecting and inefficient burning of biofuel in confined spaces largely affect the women and young girls of such communities. Another student studying congestion pricing in New York City reframed her topic to include issues of socioeconomic inequality because some argue that congestion pricing directly targets low-income motorists with inadequate access to alternative means of transportation.

By evaluating the discourse of sustainable energy and the policy related to its development and implementation, students examine how rhetoric helps determine the way science is received by the general public and how it ultimately contributes to policy outcomes. At minimum, such rhetorical analysis can reveal positions and conflicts that may otherwise go unquestioned or unnoticed. At best, this heightened awareness becomes most useful when students apply their research in more concrete ways. Some students, for example, report that their research into the rhetoric of sustainable energy has an unexpected impact on personal behavior, such as the small decisions they make in the daily business of living, or the weightier decisions they make as voters. Others use their research as a platform to apply for internships with organizations such as the Environmental Defense Fund, the United Nations Foundation, or the National Resources Defense Council. Some find projects that dovetail with their academic disciplines, while others use the course as an opportunity to explore material that would otherwise fall outside the scope of their customary schoolwork. Most notable perhaps are those who bring important insights and change back to their academic disciplines and to the communities in which they were raised.

One student experienced a revelation at the end of the quarter regarding the intermittent failure of the scientific community to share its research findings about sustainable energy with the public in effective ways. As a plant biologist, the student had already been well indoctrinated in the conventions of her discipline. She knew how to communicate her findings in an exact and idiomatic way, under the assumption that accurate data and a proper scientific tone always get the job done. What she learned was that those conventions worked only with other scientists in her field. She initially struggled to find a less technical but still academic voice. By the end of the term, she finally found successful ways to share knowledge about the production of cellulosic ethanol to an audience of non-plant-biologist classmates. She explained this process in her end-quarter reflection:

> I have come to understand that any scientific discovery must be paired with effective rhetoric if it is to have real-world impacts. Not only do appropriate rhetorical choices allow scientists to communicate their work clearly, but they also facilitate the adoption of new technologies by the public. These insights have made me more aware of my own use of rhetoric, and have contributed to my development as a writer, speaker, and thinker in this course. (Abrash, 2007)

In this case, by studying the rhetoric surrounding her topic in addition to the science of it, the student became more aware of her opportunity—and responsibility—to communicate her own research effectively, not only within the scope of her own academic discipline, but in other rhetorical situations, too. She recognized that developing the rhetorical skill to communicate clearly to laypeople would be crucial to her future success, as well as to her ability to contribute in meaningful ways, both within and outside her field.

While some students apply their new rhetorical understanding to their own academic work, other students take their awareness back to their communities. About 3 years ago, a student of mine from Kenya researched the viability of small, off-grid solar arrays in African villages. His project considered the inherent effects of limited fuel resources on the cultural, physical, and economic well-being of African women in particular, highlighting the impact that simply having enough electricity with which to cook and heat water could have on these women and their families. His research in my course was a springboard to securing a summer internship in Africa with a solar start-up company. From there, he refined his paper and presentation, and he eventually participated in securing the necessary funding and technology to bring electricity to a variety of villages for the first time.

In a similar case 2 years ago, a Native American student of mine conducted research regarding the ongoing inequities surrounding energy resources and distribution on Native American reservations. His project consisted of a variety of case studies in which various tribes succeeded in gaining some measure of energy security and independence through the production of sustainable energy on their land, rather than through the exploitation of fossil fuel resources. He looked particularly at the successful Rosebud Wind Turbine, which was installed in 2003 on the Rosebud Sioux Indian Reservation in South Dakota. Much like the plant biologist mentioned earlier, this Native American student came to realize the necessity of conveying his research findings in different ways to different audiences. By the end of the course, he determined that the voice he used to speak to his classmates would not be effective in communicating his findings to the elders of his tribal council at home because his class presentation, crafted for an audience of sympathetic college students, would not be as convincing to the men of the Cochiti Pueblo. In other words, he found that his research and writing were more than an isolated academic act in the context of a particular course; they were also social activities with real-world potential that could vary depending on his audience.

These brief examples of student work in a required writing class reveal how a proper sense of audience enhances a student's ability to translate her or his research into practice. They demonstrate the fate of words, facts, evidence, and ideas in different political and institutional settings. And they show how students learn to implement words effectively in different communities. This experience has shown me that, if a writing course is designed around important themes in students' lives, even a required writing course can offer a specific context in which to develop rhetorical skill. A sharp focus makes it easier for students to recognize that knowing their audience is essential to persuasive writing and speaking. When students care about a topic, they are eager to participate in the discussions that characterize that field of study, and they want to have an impact on their audience.

As instructors think about how best to approach the writing process in a class such as the one I've described briefly here, it can be helpful to think of writing in ecological ways, that is, as a social versus an isolated act of communication. Over the past decade, ecology has become a significant area within the field of composition studies. In 1998, Randall Roorda, Lee Smith, and Michael McDowell used the term *ecocomposition* during a panel at the Conference on College Composition and Communication in Chicago (Dobrin & Weisser, 2002, p. 7). Three years later, Sidney Dobrin and Christian Weisser defined ecocomposition as

> an area of study which, at its core, places ecological thinking and composition in dialogue with one another in order to both consider the ecological properties of written discourse and the ways in which ecologies, environments, locations, places, and natures are discursively affected. That is to say, ecocomposition is about relationships; it is about the coconstituitive existence of writing and environment . . . it is about the production of written discourse and the relationship of that discourse to the places it encounters. (Dobrin & Weisser, 2001, p. 2)

This definition is notable because it emphasizes that ecocomposition focuses on more than the "natural" world, or simply the interpretation of environmental literature or news. In teaching the course that I describe in this chapter, I employ a form of ecocomposition pedagogy that Dobrin and Weisser classify as *discursive ecology*. This form of pedagogy examines the relationships of various acts and forms of discourse, "asks students to see writing as an ecological process . . . and to explore writing and writing processes as systems of interaction, economy, and interconnectedness" (Dobrin & Weisser, 2002, p. 116). Although students engage with environmental texts and write about issues of sustainability, the course itself emphasizes writing and discourse. Ecocomposition courses may have begun by emphasizing, as Terrell Dixon (1999) notes, "reading and writing about nature and the environment" (p. 77), but I agree with Dobrin and Weisser that this field of study must include writing and the production of discourse. Language and texts are not simply the means by which *individuals* discover and communicate information, but are instead *social* activities dependent on shared structures, both in their interpretation and production (Cooper, 1986, p. 366).[5] Here, the field of environmental ethics, particularly the methodology of *environmental pragmatism*, provides a useful model in the continuing development and re-envisioning of ecocomposition courses.

In his essay, "Pragmatism and Environmental Thought," Kelly Parker (1996) presents a brief overview of the fundamental ideas of American pragmatism and their relationship to the central concerns of environmental philosophy. For Parker, environmental pragmatism stresses that humans, as well as other organisms, are embedded in a particular environment, so that knowledge and value are the result of transactions or interactions with the world. Pragmatic value theory focuses on what's good for a particular organism in its environment, thus acknowledging a multiplicity of values. Parker is critical of the notion that an "environment" exists distinct from human activity and experience, as well as the idea that nonanthropocentric and intrinsic values can be the basis of environmental ethics. According to Parker, the central concepts for environmental pragmatists include "the observations that the human sphere is embedded at every point in the broader natural sphere, that each inevitably affects the other in ways that are often impossible to predict, and that values emerge in the ongoing transactions between humans and the environment" (p. 21).

Parker's observations regarding environmental pragmatism are useful to the area of ecocomposition, especially as instructors think about the teaching of writing. For example, the concept that we're all embedded in a particular environment, with knowledge and values resulting from our sense of experience in that environment, applies equally to our students' writing. When students view their research and writing as a process that involves transactions with a variety of environments, they become aware of how discourse shapes those environments. Framing the writing process as one that connects students to the world around them and is grasped by active experience—rather than as an isolated act that occurs in the solitude of their home, dorm room, or library—those same students realize that every point in their research and writing process unfolds in a larger system. A rhetorical and pragmatic approach to ecocomposition thus teaches students that writing is itself an environment in which experience occurs. Ecocomposition courses can also encourage students to take their research into a broader social area by lobbying for reform, participating in internships, or simply learning to communicate more effectively with a wide variety of audiences.

Bringing sustainability into the undergraduate experience through courses in rhetoric and composition is valuable precisely because the many challenges of sustainability will be solved not only through science and policy, but through writing studies that focus on communicative acts among various audiences. Such courses can help young writers combine their specific environmental interests with rhetorically effective ways of analyzing, framing, and communicating their work. Focusing on issues of sustainability in the composition classroom can also provide students with a variety of opportunities to navigate the complexities of a planet on edge. By strengthening their abilities to state a problem and craft possible solutions, students learn that, through their research and writing, they can help communities adjust to changing environmental conditions. They can also see how effective writing can change habits and attitudes toward the environment.

The time is right for our conversations in the writing classroom to address sustainability. The field of writing studies creates an ideal context in which students can explore this subject as a shared, human concern, whatever their academic interests and specializations may be. By generating discussion about the intersections between rhetoric and sustainability, we offer students a space in which to make connections that transcend disciplinary boundaries and enable them to collaborate for a better future.

Notes

1. Cheryl Glotfelty was one of the founding members of the Association for the Study of Literature and the Environment (ASLE), and was hired by the University of Nevada, Reno, in 1990 as the nation's first professor of Literature and Environment. Glotfelty's first book, *The Ecocriticism Reader: Landmarks in Literary Ecology* (Glotfelty & Fromm, 1996), co-edited with Harold Fromm, showcased the work of dozens of literary scholars who had published books and articles on literature and landscape, literature and ecology, and literature and the environment, but had rarely cited each other's work. Glotfelty and Fromm proposed the term *ecocriticism* (coined in 1978 by William Rueckert) to name the field.

2. One example of student work from my writing course, as well as the connection between ecocomposition and environmental pragmatism, originally appeared in Moekle (2010).

3. I am fortunate to work in a writing program that gives individual instructors the freedom to select a specific theme as an occasion for the study of writing. At many institutions, regularized composition syllabi are necessary to deliver consistency across large numbers of sections, taught largely by graduate students, part-time lecturers, and adjuncts. Students are often reluctant to take required writing

courses, but if we can give them the chance to work on rhetorical skills in a variety of interesting frameworks, teaching theme-based composition courses can be a significant advantage.

4. Created by the United States Green Building Council (USGBC), LEED is an international building certification system that provides, among other things, "third-party verification that a building or community was designed and built using strategies aimed at improving performance across all the metrics that matter most: energy savings, water efficiency, CO_2 emissions reduction, improved indoor environmental quality, and stewardship of resources and sensitivity to their impacts" (United States Green Building Council, 2010).

5. It is beyond the scope of this essay to examine the history of ecocomposition as a field. For an excellent overview of ecocomposition pedagogy and the specific branches of "ecological literacy" and "discursive ecology," see Dobrin and Weisser's (2002) chapter 5, "Ecocomposition Pedagogy" (pp. 115–151).

References

Abrash, Emily. (2007, Winter). A planet on edge: The rhetoric of sustainable energy. End-quarter reflection essay, Stanford University.

Brown, S. (2000). *Words in the wilderness: Critical literacy in the borderlands*. Albany: State University of New York Press.

Bruner, M., & Oelschlaeger, M. (1994). Rhetoric, environmentalism, and environmental ethics. In C. Wadell (Ed.), *Landmark essays on rhetoric and the environment* (pp. 209–225). Mahwah, NJ: Hermagoras Press.

Cantrill, J. G., & Oravec, C. L. (Eds.). (1996). *The symbolic earth: Discourse and our creation of the environment*. Lexington: University Press of Kentucky.

Cooper, M. (1986). The ecology of writing. *College English, 48,* 364–375.

Dixon, T. (1999). Inculcating wildness: Ecocomposition, nature writing, and the regreening of the American suburb. In M. Bennett & D. W. Teague (Eds.), *The nature of cities: Ecocriticism and urban environments* (pp. 77–90). Tucson: University of Arizona Press.

Dobrin, S. I., & Weisser, C. R. (Eds.). (2001). *Ecocomposition: Theoretical and pedagogical approaches*. Albany: State University of New York Press.

Dobrin, S. I., & Weisser, C. R. (2002). *Natural discourse: Toward ecocomposition*. Albany: State University of New York Press.

Glotfelty, C., & Fromm, H. (Eds.) (1996). *The ecocriticism reader: Landmarks in literary ecology*. Athens: University of Georgia Press.

Herndl, C. G., & Brown, S. C. (Eds.). (1996). *Green culture: Environmental rhetoric in contemporary America*. Madison: University of Wisconsin Press.

Killingsworth, M. J., & Palmer, J. S. (1992). *Ecospeak: Rhetoric and environmental politics in America*. Carbondale: Southern Illinois University Press.

McAndrew, D. A. (1996). Ecofeminism and the teaching of literacy. *College Composition and Communication, 47,* 367–382.

Moekle, K. R. (2010). Rhetoric, environmental pragmatism, and the ecology of writing. *Transformations: Teaching Earth, 21,* 36–46.

Owens, D. (2001). *Composition and sustainability: Teaching for a threatened generation.* Urbana, IL: The National Council of Teachers of English.

Parker, K. A. (1996). Pragmatism and environmental thought. In A. Light & E. Katz (Eds.), *Environmental pragmatism* (pp. 21–37). New York: Routledge.

Roorda, R. (1998). *Dramas of solitude: Narratives of retreat in American nature writing.* Albany: State University of New York Press.

United States Green Building Council (USBGC). (2010). Intro—What LEED is. *USGBC Home Page: LEED.* Retrieved from http://www.usgbc.org/DisplayPage .aspx?CMSPageID = 1988

7

WRITING BANANA REPUBLICS AND GUANO BONANZAS

Consumerism and Globalization in the Composition Classroom

George English Brooks

Fed by the products of their soil, dressed in their
fabrics . . . why would we neglect to understand
. . . these nations?

  (Voltaire, 1784, quoted in Appiah, 2006, p. xv)

The social and environmental effects that our consumer decisions have in other parts of the world can be tremendously difficult to trace, imagine, and control. Having recently left high school and often their parents' homes, undergraduate college students are beginning to come to terms with their own emergent status as agents, citizens, thinkers, consumers, and participants in this larger world. As a place where most undergraduates will spend at least one semester, the research writing classroom can be an ideal venue for students to pursue their own curiosities while learning how the decisions they make as consumers affect both local and remote people and ecologies.

Local and bioregional approaches to composition pedagogy have long provided and continue to offer a valuable awareness of the meanings of sustainability and how it can be practiced in different places. But a more global approach is also critical for students who, for better and certainly for worse, are inheriting an increasingly globalized world. With iPods and other electronics composed of parts made in several sites in China and Taiwan; jeans and other clothing manufactured anywhere from Mexico to Lesotho;

and lunch (for those students still packing their lunches) most likely grown at least several counties away, if not in another latitude or hemisphere, the average undergraduate enters the college classroom a walking manifestation of globalized consumption patterns. And if we instructors are to be honest with ourselves, so do we, to similar degrees. How aware are our students that the free promotional T-shirts handed out at the student union each require hundreds of gallons of water to produce? Do they know that whenever they turn on a computer, somewhere in the world a mountain is turned inside out to produce the computer's component metals and the electricity to power it?

Our students also enter the classroom with various levels of knowledge of and interest in their consumer relationships with the world around them, something we can identify as a key aspect of ecological literacy. In the preface to his book *Composition and Sustainability: Teaching for a Threatened Generation*, Derek Owens (2001) begins his definition of sustainability with the similar objective of "recognizing the short- and long-term environmental, social, psychological, and economic impact of our conspicuous consumption" (p. xi). John Barry (2006) likewise proposes the consumer as integral, not antithetical, to notions of environmental citizenship. Barry argues that the issue

> of consumption is not simply to condemn and reject it out of hand as normatively (as well as ecologically) flawed and blameworthy. Rather, the issue is to attempt to cultivate and support mindful as opposed to mindless consumption . . . not to reject consumption and the consumer identity in favor of a citizen one. . . . Such simplistic dualisms do not capture the full range of possibilities open to green citizenship. Put simply, there are ecological virtues available as consumer, parent/householder, and producer/worker. (p. 38)

As students come to better comprehend their status as global consumers, they are more prepared to appreciate the material basis of their global citizenship and its ethical implications.

But what makes all of these concerns the business of the research writing classroom? In their article "Breaking Ground in Ecocomposition: Exploring Relationships between Discourse and Environment," Sidney I. Dobrin and Christian R. Weisser (2002) affirm their conviction "that the writing instructor's first duty is to teach writing." However, they go on to assert that "learning more about a particular subject—whether that subject is the natural environment, the political struggles involved in environmental debates, or any other subject of importance—is inseparable from learning to write effectively and well. Learning about our global, national, and local environments is perhaps the most important subject of study today" (p. 584). And Ursula Heise (2008) observes that "if studying local plants is valuable . . ., so is exploring where the bananas one buys come from and under what conditions they were grown; under what circumstances and with what waste products one's TV set was put together; or how the shipping out of waste from one's own city might affect the community where it will be deposited" (p. 56). In an increasingly corporate and still largely specialized academic landscape, it can be difficult to imagine where such lines of inquiry might fit into a general curriculum. Perhaps more important, how might we frame such inquiry in ways that engage student interest without narrowly limiting their curiosity within a single discipline?

As Owens (2001) notes, composition teachers and students can "orchestrate zones of inquiry that juxtapose eclectic webs of information, inspiration, and provocation, the likes of which can't easily be generated elsewhere in academe." Owens also recognizes that "the inherently cross-disciplinary composition course can serve as an introductory arena where students begin to view their personal and academic needs and desires through the lens of sustainability" (pp. 5–6). Taking on such diverse and specialized topics may at first appear daunting to writing instructors, let alone to many undergraduate writing students. As composition teachers, our formal background in global trade patterns and their specific social and ecological ramifications is likely uneven at best.

But lecturing in an area of expertise and then assigning student writing that responds to that material has never been the point of the undergraduate research writing class. Rather, if one can arrange a specific but flexible framework for the course, beginning with some of the fundamental premises and reasons for research (curiosity, justice, advocacy, progress), then introducing students to different models of how this research can be communicated (journalism, analysis, exploratory essay, argument), and then promoting independent student inquiry, the result can be a powerful exercise wherein students become personally invested in their own research subjects while learning a great deal about other related topics from their peers. Last but not least, such an egalitarian dynamic can level the playing field, empowering students to become class experts on their topics and to collaborate with their classmates as their lines of research occasionally intersect.

In this chapter, I discuss one example of how such a course can be approached, structured, and perhaps improved upon. Before choosing to build a composition course around globalization and consumerism, I had experimented earlier with service learning arrangements; oral history transcriptions; and field trips to canyons, political gatherings, and a local meat-packing plant, all with mixed results. I had also, in less focused ways, encouraged interested students to pursue investigations of clothing, electronics, energy, fast food, and other commodities. But lacking a more coherent framework for such research, it was often difficult to stimulate student collaboration and take advantage of the collective momentum that comes with a more thematically unified course.

Settling on an inter-American approach to consumer patterns and relationships was, for me, a matter of both personal interest and recognition of where my largely Nevadan and Californian students are coming from. Currently and historically, Nevada and the Sierra of northern California share certain parallels with the oil sands regions of Canada; the bauxite, silver, and copper mines of Central and South America; the mountain top, coal removal sites of Appalachia; and the guano extraction sites of South America and the Pacific Islands. Anyone who has lived in or done much traveling through Nevada—and surely other regions, too—has seen a bumper sticker that reads, "If it can't be grown, it has to be mined." Apparently an expression of mining pride and boosterism, the statement articulates equally well the absolute material origins of everything we consume: food and ore, textiles and plastics, timber and coal.

Once I was able to settle on this hemispheric approach, the models of the banana republic and the guano bonanza seemed to offer especially helpful ways for students to conceptualize transregional relationships between sites of production and consumption, and to locate themselves within these networks. Although some students may be familiar with the imperial origins of the term *banana republic*, to others it means little more than a chic clothing retailer. For our purposes in the course, both meanings are useful starting points for considering how what we eat and wear connects us materially, ecologically, socially, and politically with other places.

The guano bonanza also serves as a paradigm for the ways in which capitalist growth imperatives have influenced and continue to drive U.S. foreign policy, often to the social and ecological detriment of other locales, in the case of guano, Peru and several Pacific islands. Metaphorically, the term *guano bonanza* also offers a colorful ingress for analyzing the batshit-crazy rhetoric often used to legitimize such commodity exchanges involving the manipulation, occupation, and even annexation of other remote lands where the United States maintains economic interests. Although I was careful not to frame the course within any explicitly postcolonial program, beginning with readings that covered several of these examples helped students recognize unsustainable patterns in the global "free market" economy that have persisted, since colonial times, into neoliberal capitalism.

But depending on where, geographically, students are learning, there are certainly equally or perhaps more effective organizing metaphors than banana republics and guano bonanzas: the network, the watershed, borders, supply chains and food chains, the notions of downstream or downwind, and so on. To begin with a region like "the Americas" artificially circumscribes these discussions as much as it focuses them. However, once we had covered a set of common readings over the first half of the semester, students were then given more autonomy to find ways of applying these research questions to their own topics of interest, which, as it turned out, spanned the globe. Having first read and discussed several specific cases of unsustainable practices, students brought to their research a keener sense of what sustainability means, its complexity, and its many stakeholders. In other words, one effective way for students to understand sustainability is by recognizing what sustainability is not: coercive manipulation of other sovereign nations for control of their commodities, environmentally and socially destructive resource extraction, and a credulous consuming public that is uncritical of the political and corporate discourses perpetuating these exploitive systems.

This does not mean, however, that all or even most of these introductory readings must be negative examples of dysfunction. On the contrary, I tried to offer texts that represented a wide and useful spectrum of experiences, perspectives, positions, and genres in order to prepare students not only to formulate meaningful research questions but also to work with different kinds of texts they will likely encounter in their research, and to choose a presentation style that they can fit appropriately to their analysis. The following are several examples of texts that were either assigned reading in the first half of the semester or provided as options for the students to work with later as they began to develop their own research projects.

The students spend the first 3 weeks of the course working mainly with their two required texts: the research guide (I use Ballenger's *The Curious Researcher* [2009]) and the course reader (for this most recent course I used Hallowell and Levy's *Listening to Earth* [2004]). The latter provides a balance of readings ranging from place-based writing and personal reflections, to considerations of environmental justice and biocentrism. Some of the more applicable readings we covered were Aldo Leopold's "The Land Ethic," Tara Hullen's "Dispatch from Toxic Town," Rachel Carson's "The Human Price,"

Terry Tempest Williams's "The Clan of One-Breasted Women," Darcy Frey's "How Green Is BP?," and E. O. Wilson's "The Environmental Ethic."

Most of the available texts covering guano bonanzas are largely academic and, honestly, somewhat dry to most undergraduate readers. Such readings can get students accustomed, however, to forms of scholarly discourse that they would likely struggle with if left to work though them on their own. So our class discussions of these texts (excerpts placed on electronic reserve) touch not only on content but also on audience, style, and methods for approaching and accessing such material for their individual research purposes. Hollett and Mathew's *More Precious than Gold: The Story of the Peruvian Guano Trade* (2008) and Skaggs's *The Great Guano Rush* (1995) discuss the mid-nineteenth-century decline in U.S. agricultural productivity that led to the mining and importation of guano for fertilizer, the booming industry that arose, and the exploitation and various absurdities that attended this monumental case of destruction and shortsightedness.

A very engaging 30-minute radio documentary detailing the natural, colonial, and more recent political history of the remote Pacific island of Nauru—including its guano exploitation—is Jack Hitt's "No Island Is an Island," produced for the *This American Life* program (2003). The same episode opens with a discussion of the great Pacific marine trash vortices. Another *This American Life* episode of interest is Rachel Louise Snyder's 30-minute "Dreams of Distant Factories," about sweatshop clothing production and Cambodia's recent attempts to implement more fair labor practices (2005).

When it comes to natural, cultural, and political histories of bananas, there is a lot of material to choose from, perhaps the most outstanding of which is John Soluri's work in several recent books, including *Banana Cultures* (2005). Chapter fifteen from Gabriel García Márquez's *One Hundred Years of Solitude* (2008), even taken out of the context of the rest of the novel, is poignant as a fictionalized narrative treatment of the Colombia banana massacre of 1928. It also provides a chance to discuss how, when handled appropriately in the research and writing process, fiction and other nonscholarly sources can illustrate ideas powerfully and in ways unavailable through more academic writing. Dan Koeppel's recent book *Banana: The Fate of the Fruit That Changed the World* (2008) is accessible and provides students with one model for how they might interpret their research from more scholarly sources for a popular audience. One chapter of particular interest is where Koeppel describes his personal response to reading García Márquez's novel, relating this to his overall project of tracking the banana's history and meaning. Two other literary sources that still raise relevant questions about sustainability, environmental justice, and free trade are Pablo Neruda's 1950 poem "La United Fruit Co./The United Fruit Co." and Augusto Monter-roso's 1959 short story "Mister Taylor." The latter story, about opening a U.S. market for shrunken heads, is a poignant fable of colonialism told with the dark humor typical of this Guatemalan writer, and it turned out to be a favorite in both of the classes where I assigned it.[1]

Finally, Taylor and Scharlin's *Smart Alliance: How Global Corporations and Environmental Activists Transformed a Tarnished Brand* (2004) provides an overview of one encouraging instance of a partnership between Chiquita Bananas (United Fruit Company's successor) and The Rainforest Alliance, showing how informed "consumers can be transformed from passive victims of corporate spin into a legitimate political force" (p. 3). Although sometimes hard to come by, such stories bring a much-needed countercurrent of hope to what would otherwise be a heavy and dispiriting discussion. This is definitely not to say that consumer awareness alone will solve these problems. There is no universal agreement on the value of or direct traction gained in matters of sustainability through a solely consumer-oriented approach, as opposed to one of policy work, political advocacy, and activism. Derrick Jensen (2009) has argued compellingly that simply reigning in our individual consumption is not a powerful political act, that "personal change doesn't equal social change," and that "consumer culture and the capitalist mindset have taught us to substitute acts of personal consumption (or enlightenment) for organized political resistance" (p. 18).

Perhaps, in this way, the primary objectives of the course are modest ones, meeting undergraduates where they already are, as consumers. Students in the class chose to research and write on topics as diverse as energy production (coal, nuclear power, wind, and other alternatives); Chilean copper mining; water issues in Nevada and Nepal; oil in the United States and the Niger Delta; factory farming; logging, lumber, and sustainable forestry; Disney marketing; Nike and sweatshop manufacturing; prostitution and human trafficking; blood diamonds; and a range of other commodities such as chocolate, cocaine, ivory, and coffee. Many students collaborated with classmates, and all had opportunities to share their findings with the class, formally and informally. In the process, one of their research assignments was to write a rhetorical analysis of a text relating to their topic, responding critically to what they identified as the author's intent, use of language, word choice, appeals, evidence, and reasoning.[2] Through this and other research and writing activities, students are invited to consider alternatives, not just to consumption and passive acceptance of marketing, propaganda, and other rhetoric, but alternatives to the research paper itself.

At the end of the semester, once the final, formal research papers have been collected, the students' last assignment is to revise their work, presenting it in an alternative genre. Revision options include a "proposal for change" letter (to an elected representative, other policymaker, or newspaper editor), a children's book, a poster, a flyer, or other kind of document. Those with multimedia capabilities might also encourage students to compose audio or video public service announcements for airing on community radio or posting on the Internet.[3] These alternative genre revisions can be an empowering way for the students to decide what their new command of this recently acquired knowledge means to them. Once students have demonstrated to themselves and to each other that these globalized consumption patterns, although complicated and often challenging to understand, are knowable, this final revision is a way for students to determine how to reconcile their new understanding with the world around them.

As Jensen (2009) contends, if we simply accept the redefinition of citizens as consumers, "we reduce our potential forms of resistance to consuming and not consuming." However, if we can connect our location as consumers to global and environmental citizenship, we "have a much wider range of available resistance tactics, including voting, not voting, running for office, pamphleting, boycotting, organizing, lobbying, [and] protesting" (p. 19). Although it may not fall to us to organize our students in the streets, as committed citizens, teachers, and, yes, consumers, it is our responsibility to prepare our students to research and write well about the world around them, and to help them develop the practices that will make that knowledge and writing matter in their world.

Notes

1. Although space constraints do not allow a more complete description of materials students worked with in the course, brief descriptions of a few additional texts may prove helpful for those who are interested.

- Vicky Funari and Sergio De La Torre's documentary *Maquiliapolis: City of Factories* (Funari & De La Torre, 2006) depicts the lives and struggles of several women working in Tijuana *maquiladoras* (factories). The film raises questions of labor rights and environmental justice.
- In a series of interview trips to China and New Orleans, David Redmon's documentary *Mardi Gras: Made in China* (Redmon, 2006) follows Mardi Gras beads from their manufacture, to the festivities, to the morning after as they're scrubbed out of the gutters by street sweeper trucks.

- Science journalist and author Charles C. Mann's recent article in Orion Magazine, *The Dawn of the Homogenocene: Tracing Globalization Back to Its Roots* (May/June 2011), engagingly discusses the early biological implications of globalization, drawing heavily from Alfred Crosby's concept of ecological imperialism.
- First published in 1978, Salman Rushdie's *The Jaguar Smile* is a short, firsthand account of his visit to Nicaragua in the wake of the Sandinista revolution. It includes his observations on Central American relations with the United States.
- The *New American Dream* website (2010) has a wealth of resources to help "Americans consume responsibly to protect the environment, enhance quality of life, and promote social justice."
- The *Story of Stuff* website features several short, effective cartoon films about the production, consumption, and disposal of electronics, bottled water, cosmetics, and other "stuff," as well as the rhetoric that perpetuates these consumer patterns. The project was "created by Annie Leonard to . . . amplify public discourse on a series of environmental, social and economic concerns and . . . to build a more sustainable and just world" (Leonard, 2010).
- Artist Lucy Raven's (2009) 50-minute film *China Town* "traces copper mining and production from an open pit mine in Nevada to a smelter in China, where the semi-processed ore is sent to be smelted and refined. Considering what it actually means to 'be wired' and in turn, to be connected, in today's global economic system, the video follows the detailed production process that transforms raw ore into copper wire—in this case, the literal digging of a hole to China—and the generation of waste and of power that grows in both countries as byproduct."
- Ann Watters's first-year composition reader *Global Exchange: Reading and Writing in a World Context* (2005) offers many potentially useful readings, with an entire chapter on health and the environment.

2. One model of rhetorical analysis that we looked at was Wendell Berry's essay "Living in the Future," from his 1977 *The Unsettling of America: Culture and Agriculture*. Here Berry responds to a 1970 article in *National Geographic*, critiquing its bald, unmeasured praise for industrial agriculture.

3. A great example for the alternative genre is Cesar Chavez's 1986 "Wrath of Grapes Boycott Speech." In this well-researched and rousing public document, Chavez effectively illustrates the inseparability of public health, workers' rights, and environmental justice issues, balancing rational, emotional, and personal appeals.

References

Appiah, K. A. (2006). *Cosmopolitanism: Ethics in a world of strangers.* New York: Norton.

Ballenger, B. (2009). *The curious researcher.* New York: Longman.

Barry, J. (2006). Resistance is fertile. In A. Dobson & D. Bell (Eds.), *Environmental citizenship* (pp. 21–48). Cambridge: MIT Press.

Berry, W. (1977). *The unsettling of America: Culture and agriculture* (pp. 56–79). San Francisco: Sierra Club Books.

Chavez, C. (2008). Wrath of grapes boycott speech. In B. McKibben (Ed.), *American Earth: Environmental writing since Thoreau* (pp. 690–695). New York: Library of America.

Dobrin, S. I., & Weisser C. R. (2002). Breaking ground in ecocomposition: Exploring relationships between discourse and environment. *College English*, 64(5), 566–589.

Funari, V., & De La Torre, S. (2006). *Maquilapolis: City of factories* [Motion Picture]. U.S.A.: CineMamás.

García Márquez, G. (2008). *One hundred years of solitude*. Gregory Rabasa (Trans.), (pp. 293–313). New York: Harper Perennial.

Hallowell, C., & Levy W. (2004). *Listening to earth: A reader*. New York: Longman.

Heise, U. (2008). *Sense of place and sense of planet*. New York: Oxford University Press.

Hitt, J. (Producer). (2003, December 5). *No island is an island* [Audio Podcast]. Retrieved from http://www.thisamericanlife.org/radio-archives/episode/253/the-middle-of-nowhere

Hollett, D., & Mathew, W. (2008). *More precious than gold: The story of the Peruvian guano trade* (pp. 9–19, 76–83, 118–142). Cranbury, NJ: Associated University Journals.

Jensen, D. (2009, July). Forget shorter showers: Why personal change does not equal political change. *Orion*, 18–19.

Koeppel, D. (2008). *Banana: The fate of the fruit that changed the world* (pp. 34–76, 84–98). New York: Penguin.

Leonard, A. (2010). *The story of stuff*. [Website]. Retrieved from http://www.storyofstuff.com/

Mann, C. C. (2011, May). The dawn of the homogenocene: Tracing globalization back to its roots. *Orion*, 16–25.

Monterroso, A. (1995). *Complete works and other stories*. E. Grossman, (Trans.), (pp. 3–9). Austin: University of Texas Press.

Neruda, P. (1994). *Five decades: Poems 1925–1970*. B. Belitt, (Ed. & Trans.), (pp. 78–79). New York: Grove.

The new American dream. [Website]. (2010). Retrieved from http://www.newdream.org/

Owens, D. (2001). *Composition and sustainability: Teaching for a threatened generation*. Urbana, IL: National Council of Teachers of English.

Raven, L. (2009). *China town*. Retrieved from http://www.lucyraven.com/index.php?/project/chinatown/

Redmon, D. (2006). *Mardi Gras: Made in China*. [Motion Picture]. U.S.A.: Carnivalesque Films.

Rushdie S. (2008). *The jaguar smile* (pp. 3–21). New York: Random House.

Skaggs, J. M. (1995). *The great guano rush: Entrepreneurs and American overseas expansion* (pp. ix–16, 159–170). New York: St. Martin's Press.

Snyder, R. L. (Producer). (2005, December 2). *Dreams of distant factories* [Audio Podcast]. Retrieved from http://www.thisamericanlife.org/radio-archives/episode/303/david-and-goliath

Soluri, J. (2005). *Banana cultures: Agriculture, consumption, and environmental change in Honduras and the United States* (pp. ix–x, 1–17, 75–103, 128–160). Austin: University of Texas Press.

Taylor, J. G., & Scharlin, P. J. (2004). *Smart alliance: How global corporations and environmental activists transformed a tarnished brand* (pp. x–xxi, 1–16). New Haven, CT: Yale University Press.

Watters, A. (2005). *Global exchange: Reading and writing in a world culture.* Upper Saddle River, NJ: Pearson Prentice Hall.

8

SUSTAINABLY GROWING FARMERS OF THE FUTURE

Undergraduate Curriculum in Sustainable Agriculture at the University of Kentucky

Keiko Tanaka, Mark Williams, Krista Jacobsen, and Michael D. Mullen

In 2007, the University of Kentucky's (UK's) College of Agriculture (COA) established an undergraduate curriculum of sustainable agriculture as an individualized Bachelor of Science degree program. The curriculum aims to meet current and future needs for individuals with sustainable agriculture expertise, including trained farmers, technical consultants, and others. Three conceptual pillars of sustainability—*environmental stewardship*, *economic profitability*, and *social responsibility*—are integrated into the curriculum by requiring students to take courses from a range of disciplines: from plant and animal sciences to sociology, economics, and ethics. Faculty members from multiple departments serve as instructors and advisers to students. Through this multidisciplinary curriculum, students are expected to develop in-depth foundational knowledge, analytical tools, and critical evaluation skills grounded in a holistic understanding of agriculture systems.

The curriculum combines practical field knowledge with a scientific understanding of soil management and conservation, crop physiology, livestock production, integrated pest management, agro-forestry, human nutrition, and community food systems. Both majors and minors are required to complete 3 credit hours of Apprenticeship in Sustainable Agriculture (SAG

397), which involves working on a community-supported agriculture (CSA) enterprise located at the organic farm on the UK's Organic Farming Research and Education Unit. In addition, students are encouraged to undertake internships at other farms, perform research, and engage in other experiential and service learning activities.

This chapter discusses the successes and challenges of the curriculum. First, we briefly summarize the recent history of changes to Kentucky agriculture, which sets the stage for an account of how the sustainable agriculture curriculum was developed. Second, we review key components of the curriculum and discuss philosophical and pedagogical justifications for its organization. In the third section, we discuss key successes and challenges for the future and sketch our plan for modifications. In particular, we emphasize the importance of creating a safe, productive learning space that facilitates the dialogue between traditional and newer agriculture audiences in the classroom.

Context: Kentucky as a Burley Tobacco State

Our undergraduate curriculum in sustainable agriculture emerged as Kentucky agriculture and farming were undergoing structural transformations. With rapid urban migration of farmers, loss of farmland to suburbanization, and industrialization of food production in the last century, farming has increasingly become a less viable occupation, while agriculture has become a major global industry (Imhoff, 2007; Lyson, 2004). By the early 1980s, major agribusiness corporations (e.g., ConAgra, Archer Daniels Midland [ADM]) controlled every step of food production and distribution, from input production (e.g., seed, fertilizer) to food consumption at the dinner table (Hendrickson, Heffernan, Howard, & Heffernan, 2001).

Kentucky has experienced pressures for transforming the structure of its agricultural system similar to those in the rest of the nation. Unlike many other states, Kentucky has maintained a relatively high number of small family farms because of their dependence on burley tobacco as a major cash crop. Tobacco is produced on relatively small acreages because of the significant labor requirement, but it is a relatively high value crop. In 2007, there were 85,260 farms in Kentucky. In the last three decades, the national average farm size has been around 450 acres, while the average farm size in Kentucky was 167 in 2007 (USDA National Agricultural Statistics Service, 2009).

In 2004, the price support program for tobacco, created in the 1930s, was discontinued with the tobacco quota buyout legislation. This created both opportunities and challenges for tobacco-dependent farmers and communities for reenvisioning agriculture in Kentucky. The deregulation in the tobacco market resulted in the consolidation of tobacco farms and a decline in domestic tobacco prices. Between 2002 and 2007, the average size of a farm growing tobacco increased from less than 4 acres to 10.8 acres (Snell, 2009). During the same period, the number of tobacco farms declined by 72 percent, from approximately 30,000 to 8,113, and total acreage in tobacco fell by 21 percent (Snell, 2009). The loss of tobacco as a major cash crop meant that Kentucky farmers were in immediate need of alternative crops and production systems. Many rural communities with a high number of tobacco farms began a search for new economic opportunities.

Across Kentucky, there is a growing interest among farmers in agricultural diversification, sustainable and/or organic farming practices, and alternative marketing such as CSA and farmer's markets, which increased from 5 in 1976 to 126 in 2009 (Futamura, 2007; Kentucky Department of Agriculture, 2009). More consumers are concerned with the impact of their food purchases on their family's health (Brislen & Tanaka, 2010). A core group of faculty members in the COA felt that it was imperative that UK, as the main land grant institution in the state, meet this growing demand for training students and citizens in agriculture and related industries with sustainable agriculture expertise.

Building the SAG Program

The SAG curriculum initiative is an outgrowth of a lengthy and well-considered process by faculty members. For years, interest in sustainable agriculture education, research, and outreach was growing among faculty and staff within the COA. On June 6, 2003, this interest led to an ad hoc meeting of 22 faculty and staff members from eight different units. A core group then wrote and submitted a proposal to the USDA-Cooperative State Research, Education, and Extension Service (CSREES) Higher Education Challenge Grant program aimed at developing an undergraduate curriculum in sustainable agriculture. In September 2005, a few months after receiving funding, Mullen, the COA Associate Dean of Instruction, established the Sustainable Agriculture Curriculum Committee (SACC), with Williams as the chair and Tanaka as a member. The basic charge of the SACC was to develop an integrative undergraduate curriculum and associated minor in sustainable agriculture with the following four goals:

- To provide students with fundamental knowledge, practical field experience, integrative skills, and an understanding of agriculture in the broader society;
- To prepare students for careers in production agriculture, allied industries, and other public and private sector employment opportunities, including land management and natural resource conservation;
- To engage nonagricultural students through a new minor in sustainable agriculture so that agriculture enjoys a broader societal support base; and
- To create within the Commonwealth an academically rigorous program that has the potential to enhance farm profitability, reduce the environmental effects of agriculture, and strengthen the social connections between farmers and consumers.

Throughout the latter portion of the fall of 2005 and the spring of 2006, the SACC met regularly and discussed the philosophical goals of a sustainable agriculture program and the practical logistics of creating a rigorous, comprehensive, and viable curriculum. Part of this process included evaluating similar existing curricula, and collecting Web-based feedback from stakeholders in response to a solicitation for comments. In May 2006, the final draft of the curriculum proposal was approved by a unanimous committee vote and submitted to the COA (see table 8.1).

Philosophical Basis

The SACC started a debate over the philosophical basis of the curriculum with two commonly used definitions of sustainability. The first was from the United Nations Brundtland Commission's definition of sustainability: "sustainable development is development that meets the needs of the present without compromising the ability of future generations to meet their own needs" (World Commission on Environment and Development, 1984). The second definition was from the 1990 Farm Bill (Gold, 1999):

[T]he term sustainable agriculture means an integrated system of plant and animal production practices having a site-specific application that will, over the long term:

TABLE 8.1
Sustainable Agriculture Undergraduate Curriculum

DEPT.	COURSE	DESCRIPTION		CREDITS
UNIVERSITY STUDIES REQUIREMENTS				
I. MATH: MA 123 (satisfies premajor requirement)				3
II. FOREIGN LANGUAGE: Two (2) years of high school or six (6) hours of college level				-
III. INFERENCE-LOGIC: MA 123 (satisfies premajor requirement; also see USP I)				-
IV. UNIVERSITY WRITING: ENG 104; and graduation writing requirement (met by SAG 201 and SAG 490)				4
V. ORAL COMMUNICATION: Requirement is currently suspended				-
VI. NATURAL SCIENCES: CHE 105 and CHE 107 (satisfies premajor requirement)				6
VII. SOCIAL SCIENCES: CLD 102 or SOC 101; and ECO 201(satisfies premajor requirement)				6
VIII. HUMANITIES: Six hours from approved list				6
IX. CROSS-CULTURAL: Three hours from approved list				3
X. ELECTIVES: BIO 150 and BIO 152 (satisfies premajor requirement)				6
			SUBTOTAL	**34**
COLLEGE OF AGRICULTURE REQUIREMENT				
GEN	100	Issues in Agriculture		3
			SUBTOTAL	**3**
PREMAJOR REQUIREMENTS				
These are MA 123; and CHE 105 and CHE 107; and BIO 150 and BIO 152; and ECO 201; and CLD 102 or SOC 101; and the following courses:				
CHE	111	General Chemistry Laboratory I		1
CHE	113	General Chemistry Laboratory II		2
NFS	212	Introductory Nutrition		3
			SUBTOTAL	**6**
MAJOR REQUIREMENTS				
Environmental Stewardship Cluster				
ASC	382	Principles of Livestock Production		3
ENT	300	General Entomology		3
PLS	366	Fundamentals of Soil Science		4
PLS	404	Integrated Weed Management		4
PPA	400G	Principles of Plant Pathology		3
Economic Profitability Cluster				
AEC	302	Agricultural Management Principles		4
AEC	305	Food and Agricultural Marketing Principles		3
AEC	445G	Introduction to Resource and Environmental Economics		3
Social Responsibility Cluster				
GEN	501	Agricultural and Environmental Ethics		3
SOC	360	Environmental Sociology		3
SOC *or*	420	Community Analysis		3
SOC	517	Rural Sociology		
			SUBTOTAL	**36**
SUSTAINABLE AGRICULTURE CORE				
SAG	101	Introduction to Sustainable Agriculture		3
SAG	201	Cultural Perspectives on Sustainability		3
SAG	386	Plant Production Systems		4
SAG	397	Apprenticeship in Sustainable Agriculture		3
SAG	490	Integration of Sustainable Agriculture Principles		3
			SUBTOTAL	**16**
SPECIALTY SUPPORT				
BIO	325	Introduction to Ecology		4
Courses chosen in consultation with academic advisor				14
			SUBTOTAL	**18**
FREE ELECTIVES				
			SUBTOTAL	**9**
			TOTAL CREDITS FOR B.S. DEGREE	**122**

- Satisfy human food and fiber needs;
- Enhance environmental quality and the natural resource base upon which the agricultural economy depends;
- Make the most efficient use of nonrenewable resources and on-farm resources and integrate, where appropriate, natural biological cycles and controls;
- Sustain the economic viability of farm operations; and
- Enhance the quality of life for farmers and society as a whole.

The SACC also adopted the idea of three pillars of sustainable agriculture, which includes *environmental stewardship*, *economic profitability*, and *social responsibility*. However, at multiple meetings and over e-mail, SACC members discussed at length how to interpret and operationalize the definition of *sustainable agriculture* and what these three dimensions of sustainability mean both philosophically and pedagogically. Although we accepted environment/ecology, economy, and society as three constituent parts of sustainability, disagreements arose over the name of each pillar, for example, economic *profitability* versus *viability*, and social *responsibility* versus *equity* or *justice*. We were highly aware of the fact that our understanding of the three constituent parts of sustainability is grounded in our respective disciplinary background. Indeed, we appreciated intellectually engaging debates over the definition of sustainability, which helped SACC members develop a better understanding of the perspectives of disciplines other than our own.

More important, through these debates, we realized that we were in agreement on the criticism of a reductionist philosophy of "conventional" agriculture, with its emphasis on external inputs and specialization of production strategies, and on our support for the more holistic philosophical perspective of sustainable agriculture. Thus, we operationalized sustainable agriculture to emphasize the following features:

- Alternative farming approaches are employed to provide plant nutrients and control pests;
- Diversified cropping systems are emphasized;
- Animal and plant production systems are integrated; and
- There is often a conscious linkage of the consumer to the producer.

By diversifying production, reducing off-farm inputs, and creating more direct human relationships, farm operations are sustained, and the environment benefits and the agricultural economy is strengthened.

Mission and Learning Outcomes

The mission of our SAG program is to provide students with a fundamental knowledge in sustainable agriculture that is grounded in a framework integrating three conceptual pillars: environmental stewardship, economic profitability, and social responsibility. Through a combination of coursework and experiential learning, the curriculum prepares students for careers in production agriculture, allied industries, agricultural entrepreneurship, and public and private sector employment (see table 8.2). By the end of the program, students are expected to meet the following learning outcomes:

- Describe and apply the environmental stewardship component of sustainable agriculture;
- Describe and apply the social well-being component of sustainable agriculture;
- Describe and apply the economic viability/responsibility component of sustainable agriculture;
- Assess food systems using an integrated understanding of sustainable agriculture; and
- Evaluate the sustainability of a site-specific situation by applying a fundamental understanding of sustainable agriculture principles.

By using existing and new courses, the SAG curriculum is designed to provide students with training in each of the conceptual areas, with an emphasis on integrated, holistic, and systems-based approaches to knowledge production and dissemination. A key facet of the curriculum is experiential and service learning opportunities. This is an especially important issue because many students come from a nonfarming background or are learning about alternative agricultural practices with which they may not be familiar. In addition to the required Apprenticeship in Sustainable Agriculture (SAG 397), described in further detail in the next sections, students are encouraged to take external internships at other farms and sustainable agriculture institutions, participate in the development of community gardens, perform research, and other similar ventures.

UK Sustainable Agriculture Program CSA

Since the establishment of the CSA program in 2007, the number of shareholders has grown at a rapid pace (as shown in figure 8.1) and is expected to grow to approximately 200 shareholders this year. Through engaging in the

TABLE 8.2
Suggested Schedule in the Sustainable Agriculture Curriculum

Fall Semester			Spring Semester		
Year 1			*Year 1*		
Course	**Description**	**Credits**	**Course**	**Description**	**Credits**
SAG 101	Principles of Sustainable Agriculture	3	CHE 105	General College Chemistry I	3
ENG 104	Writing	4	CHE 111	General Chemistry I Laboratory	1
MA 123	Elementary Calculus	3	GEN 100	Issues in Agriculture	3
CLD 102	Dynamics of Rural Social Life	3		USP VIII: Humanities	3
	University Studies Program (USP) VIII: Humanities	3		Free Elective	3
	Subtotal	**16**		**Subtotal**	**13**
Year 2			*Year 2*		
CHE 107	General College Chemistry II	3	SAG 201	Cultural Perspectives on Sustainability	3
CHE 113	General Chemistry II Laboratory	2	BIO 150	Principles of Biology I	3
BIO 152	Principles of Biology II	3	ECO 201	Principles of Economics I	3
NFS 212	Introductory Nutrition	3	PLS 366	Fundamentals of Soil Science	4
	USP IX: Cross Cultural	3		Free Elective	3
	Subtotal	**14**		**Subtotal**	**16**
Year 3			*Year 3*		
SAG 386	Plant Production Systems	4	AEC 445G	Introduction to Resource and Environmental Economics	3
AEC 302	Agricultural Management Principles	4	SOC 360	Environmental Sociology	3
ENT 300	General Entomology	3	PLS 404	Integrated Weed Management	3
ASC 382	Principles of Livestock Production	3		Specialty Support Elective	3
	Subtotal	**14**		Specialty Support Elective	2
				Subtotal	**15**
			Summer		
			SAG 397	Apprenticeship in Sustainable Agriculture	
				Subtotal	**3**
Year 4			*Year 4*		
AEC 305	Food and Agricultural Marketing Principles	3	SAG 490	Integration of Sustainable Agriculture Principles	3
SOC 420	Community Analysis	3	GEN 501	Agricultural and Environmental Ethics	3
PPA 400G	Principles of Plant Pathology	3	GEN 300	Agroecology	4
	Specialty Elective	3		Specialty Support Elective	3
	Specialty Elective	3		Free Elective	3
	Subtotal	**15**		**Subtotal**	**16**

FIGURE 8.1
Numbers of SAG majors and minors, 2007–2011

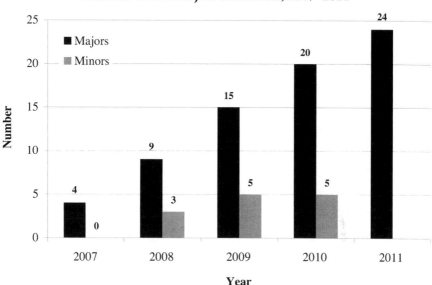

Note: The number of minors is not available for 2011.

entire production process, from transplant production to distributing the harvest to CSA subscribers, students apply foundational knowledge acquired in the SAG coursework to address concrete, everyday problems and challenges associated with farming.

CSA subscriptions are available to all the members of the UK community, including faculty members, staff members, and students. Share prices are similar to local CSA prices, and shareholders must be affiliated with UK to minimize direct competition with local farmers. The CSA lasts approximately 26 weeks, from mid-May to mid-November, with share distribution on the COA campus. Share distributions are staffed by students, with produce arranged in a farmer's market style, thus allowing for shareholders to select the content of the shares and assemble the shares themselves.

Curriculum

As described in table 8.1, students are required to complete University Studies Program (USP) requirement credits, which will be replaced with General

Education Requirement (GenEd) credits in the fall of 2011; COA requirements; and premajor requirements. Students must complete five core SAG
courses and specified courses in Environmental Stewardship, Economic
Profitability, and Social Responsibility clusters to satisfy major requirements.
Students are also required to complete 17 hours of specialty support classes
in the student's area of interest, with approval of the academic adviser,
including a newly developed Agroecology course (GEN 300, 3 credit hours).
Students must take a minimum of 9 credit hours of elective courses to
graduate.

To provide students with foundation knowledge about sustainable agriculture, four new courses were created and one existing course was modified
to become the SAG Core. Next, we briefly summarize each.

SAG 101 (Introduction to Sustainable Agriculture)

This course is the foundational course and a prerequisite for both majors
and minors in the curriculum. The course provides a broad introduction to
the "three pillars" of sustainable food production and marketing. Topics
include the definition, emergence, and growth of sustainable agriculture as
well as core principles and practices in sustainable crop and livestock production. The course includes activities designed to help students explore the
greater Lexington, Kentucky, community food system and to participate in
service learning activities, and it includes a variety of guest speakers from the
university and agricultural communities.

SAG 201 (Cultural Perspectives on Sustainability)

This course examines cultural dimensions of sustainability by helping students to survey agriculture and food systems outside the United States. Students are asked to complete a social science research project to compare
the notion of sustainable agriculture expressed through farming practices in
Kentucky with those in another country. The course is required of students,
both majors and minors, in the curriculum, and it fulfills the UK Graduate
Writing Requirement.

SAG 386/PLS 386 (Plant Production Systems)

This class provides a detailed analysis of the underlying principles of agricultural plant production systems. One of the main goals is to provide an overview of a variety of major crop production systems of the world and the

production practices of, economic importance of, and challenges to sustainable production. This course is taught from a systems perspective, integrating biophysical factors such as soil quality, crop nutrition, and water dynamics with socioeconomic factors influencing management.

SAG 397 (Apprenticeship in Sustainable Agriculture)

This course provides an experiential learning opportunity on the 20-acre Organic Farming Research and Education Unit that is a component of the 70-acre Horticultural Research Farm in Lexington, Kentucky. Under the supervision of the course coordinator and UK CSA program manager, students receive training in organic production practices including transplant production and field production, maintenance of soil fertility, and pest management. Student responsibilities also include the harvest and preparation of produce for distribution to CSA members.

SAG 490 (Integration of Sustainable Agriculture Principles)

This course is the capstone for the curriculum. The entire curriculum is designed to encourage students to consider agricultural systems as wholes in which a change to one part of the system has significant effects on all other parts of the system. In this capstone class, students are expected to bring knowledge and experience from their previous coursework and experience to bear on the issues raised. Consequently, the instructor works with the students to tailor the content of this course each year. Through experiential learning, students use different kinds of data to evaluate world agricultural systems as dynamic and interacting environmental, economic, and social entities. The course is required of students in the major.

Successes and Challenges

As an undergraduate curriculum within the COA, the SAG program has been praised by both college and university administrations for its innovative curriculum and important contribution to the university's commitment to *sustainability*. The UK Organic Farming Research and Education Unit, in which the CSA is located, has become the face of the SAG program. It brings visitors from different on- and off-campus organizations and supports various events, such as on-farm local food dinners that bring diverse stakeholders of UK COA to celebrate the college's strides toward addressing challenges in agricultural sustainability.

As already mentioned, the UK Sustainable Agriculture Program CSA has been very successful in attracting interest from students across the campus and in training students in the concrete skills necessary to operate a farm. Nevertheless, the numbers of SAG majors and minors (see figure 8.2) as well as the numbers of students enrolled in SAG courses (see table 8.3) have not increased as dramatically as one would have expected. Consequently, the SAG program continues to operate as an individualized curriculum rather than a stand-alone major program in the COA. However, with only two faculty members (Williams and Jacobsen) fully devoted to the administration of the SAG program, including teaching SAG core courses, the current rate of growth seems appropriate.

Before we discuss our plans for future growth, let us summarize our successes and challenges with the SAG core courses.

SAG 397 Apprenticeship

The apprenticeship has been extremely successful in this program. Students have consistently maintained that it is a highlight of their college experience and that they have learned how to apply the foundation knowledge acquired in the classroom in a real farming situation. At the weekly CSA delivery, the students meet with the shareholders and hear from them how the food these students grow is affecting their lives and understanding about agriculture

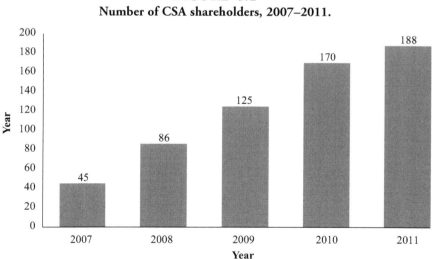

FIGURE 8.2
Number of CSA shareholders, 2007–2011.

TABLE 8.3
Student Enrollment in SAG Courses, 2006–2010

SAG		Fall 2006	Spring 2007	Fall 2007	Spring 2008	Fall 2008	Spring 2009	Fall 2009	Spring 2010	Fall 2010	Spring 2011
101	Introduction to Sustainable Agriculture	6	9	13	15	12	17	14	18	15	—[a]
201[b]	Cultural Perspectives on Sustainability				12		14		21		24
386[c]	Plant Production System					28		24		33	
395[d]	Independent Work		1						3	1	
397	Apprenticeship in Sustainable Agriculture			3	4	8	12	1	14	4	—[e]
490[b]	Integration of Sustainable Agriculture Principles						5		3		6

[a] SAG 101 was not offered in the spring of 2011.

[b] SAG 201 and 490 are offered only in the spring semester.

[c] SAG 386 is cross-listed with PLS (Plant Soil Sciences). Not all students enrolled in SAG/PLS 386 are SAG majors or minors.

[d] SAG 395 is offered only as requested by students.

[e] SAG 397 is offered only in the fall since the 2011–2012 academic year.

and food economy. Because this apprenticeship program accepts students from outside the program, SAG students have opportunities to work with students from diverse disciplinary backgrounds. Each summer, international students from countries such as Thailand, France, and Ghana have also worked on the CSA farm. This dynamic work environment has greatly enhanced learning.

At the same time, it has been difficult to maximize the consistency and quality of the student learning experience. This challenge stems from a combination of three factors.

The first is the content of the course. In the past, both instructors and students tended to spend much of the time working in the field, without time for reflections or learning. To address this, in the spring of 2010, Williams started offering weekly 3-hour seminars. In each of 15 sessions, Williams picked a specific topic (e.g., weed management, tillage, and transplant production) to examine its theoretical and scientific basis and apply the knowledge in the field. These weekly sessions allow the course to deconstruct an organic farm into individual components and then ultimately find ways to integrate them holistically into a sustainable system.

The second factor relates to the fact that many students have to balance their summer employment with this apprenticeship coursework. Ultimately, we would like to have a few paid positions for which students could apply to work more hours than unpaid students.

Third, because the apprentice program runs from the middle of the spring semester to the middle of the fall semester, the logistics of giving students credits and grades for SAG 397 through the university's system have created a problem of inconsistency among students in completing the required work hours. Since the 2011–2012 academic year, SAG 397 is offered only in the fall semester. Students enroll in the course during the spring advising period (mid-March to April) and begin the coursework in March and April, followed by summer/fall farm work to receive the grade at the end of the fall semester.

SAG 490 Capstone

This course allows students to pursue topics and projects in which they have a personal interest through collaborative experiential learning. Students generate both written and oral artifacts to be evaluated by the instructor(s). Each year, SAG 490 students take a one-week-long trip during spring break. This trip provides students with opportunities to observe various types of farming systems, support organizations, and programs for farmers; to reflect on their experience in the curriculum with both the instructors and fellow students; and to think about how to use their undergraduate training in their profession of choice. The major challenge is to continue finding adequate funding for the trip.

SAG 101 Principles of Sustainable Agriculture

This course has undergone a significant transformation: from an early emphasis on the emergence of the sustainable agriculture movement and key practices in sustainable agriculture to a format situating these concepts in the context of the greater Lexington Community Food System. This introductory course has become an important recruiting platform for the SAG major. The course is quite participatory and requires a significant amount of discussion and reflection. The major challenge in this course is to create and maintain a collegial environment in which students feel safe to examine controversial issues from diverse perspectives.

SAG 201 Cultural Perspectives of Sustainability

The course has been modified to reexamine several course concepts from SAG 101 through a social science lens and thus provide a context for students without SAG 101, and to provide an opportunity to revisit this information in more depth for students with the SAG 101 experience through social research and intensive writing. Since its inception, SAG 201 was structured to meet UK's Graduate Writing Requirement. At the beginning of the course, students tend to feel overwhelmed by the writing and research workload. This challenge has been overcome through a series of social science research methods workshops, supplementary readings, and guest speakers presenting case studies of their research.

Thus far, we have allowed students to waive the SAG 101 prerequisite in order to expose more students to the SAG curriculum. However, the depth at which this course is taught does require some background in agricultural issues, and students without the prerequisite struggled to comprehend the material and participate in class. This challenge needs to be addressed in the near future.

The Curriculum

Since we began the program in 2006, SAG has been successful in attracting high-caliber undergraduate students. However, the enrollment in the curriculum has remained low, partly due to little formal recruitment effort and partly because the sustainable agriculture movement is nascent in Kentucky compared to other states. Working with other undergraduate curricula and units within the COA and across the university will certainly help us address our challenges with student recruitment and misunderstanding about sustainable agriculture. A more difficult hurdle is articulating what our graduates can do with a degree in SAG. The SAG program has graduated only three classes at the time of this writing, and the career prospects represented are diverse but limited in number. To date, SAG program graduates have gone into farming, graduate school in business and food and agricultural policy, and management of farmer's markets. Some found jobs in agricultural extension. We envision that graduates will also find work in the non-profit sector and local and state agencies.

Conclusion

In the last three decades, sustainable agriculture has gradually become recognized as a critical area of intellectual inquiry and skill development in agricultural education. Many land grant institutions now have a program—whether research, instructional, or outreach—related to sustainable agriculture.

As we already pointed out, our program faces challenges similar to those elsewhere, including (1) the enrollment in the program remains relatively small and (2) the existing administrative structure of the university often makes it difficult, if not impossible, for faculty members with diverse disciplinary backgrounds, located in various departments and colleges, to participate in the program.

To overcome these challenges, we plan to explore opportunities for collaboration with other existing undergraduate curricula on an environment-and/or sustainability-related theme within and outside UK. Cross-listing of courses across departments and programs is one solution for the second challenge. We have just recently begun talking about the possibility of developing a national consortium among sustainable agriculture programs in various higher education institutions. We envision that students will share distance-learning, apprenticeship, and study abroad courses. This strategy will allow us to address the first and second issues simultaneously.

Advancing the dialogue in sustainable agriculture education requires addressing traditional misconceptions about the movement (e.g., that it is a "hippies' movement" or a "tree-huggers' movement") on the student and faculty levels. At the student level, tensions most frequently arise between students new to agriculture with those from traditional agricultural backgrounds because the latter fear their family heritage is being attacked. Tensions at the faculty level are more complex and nuanced and therefore require a more careful discussion that we believe is beyond the scope of this chapter.

Diffusing this tension into a productive, critically reflective dialogue frequently requires faculty members to create an environment that is inclusive, where opposing viewpoints are honored and students are encouraged to understand historic and institutional drivers that influence their notions about the definition of *sustainable* or even *farming*. This is accomplished through a balanced, neutral classroom facilitation style as well as through activities and speakers from the local community so students from all backgrounds can reflect critically on the environmental, economic, and social components of sustainable agriculture systems in the local community. By presenting course concepts in real-world, place-based contexts, students come together in shared experiences and develop more nuanced ideas about sustainable agriculture.

This nuanced definition frequently adds subtleties to their existing opinions and biases, but instructors must articulate clearly that students will not be judged for their opinions but will be evaluated according to their ability to articulate these opinions. Such an open dialogue between traditional and new agricultural audiences is critical to the retention of traditional students in SAG classes, and it helps SAG students develop a more robust understanding of more conservative agricultural perspectives, whether the students come from farming backgrounds or are new to agriculture.

References

Brislen, L., & Tanaka, K. (2010). Shopping for values: Food concerns and insights from Lexington, Kentucky. Lexington Food Assessment 2008: Consumer Survey Result. Research Report. Lexington: Department of Community & Leadership Development, University of Kentucky.

Futamura, T. (2007). *Toward the construction of "Kentucky food" in the twenty-first century: Food localism and commodification of place identity under post-tobacco agricultural restructuring, 1990–2006.* Lexington: University of Kentucky.

Gold, M. V. (1999). Sustainable agriculture: Definitions and terms. *Special Reference Briefs.* Retrieved November 23, 2010, from http://www.nal.usda.gov/afsic/pubs/terms/srb9902.shtml

Hendrickson, M., Heffernan, W. D., Howard, P. H., & Heffernan, J. B. (2001, January). Consolidation in food retailing and dairy: Implications for farmers and consumers in a global food system. Report to the National Farmers Union. Retrieved October 15, 2010, from http://libertyparkusafd.org/lp/NatureFirst%20 USA/reports%5CConsolidation%20in%20Food%20Retailing%20and%20Dairy %20-%20Implications%20for%20Farmers%20and%20Consumers%20in%20a %20Global%20Food%20System.pdf

Imhoff, D. (2007). *Food fight: The citizen's guide to a food and farm bill.* Healdsburg, CA: Watershed Media.

Kentucky Department of Agriculture. (2009). Farmer's market program. Retrieved December 15, 2010, from http://www.kyagr.com/marketing/farmmarket/directory.htm

Lyson, T. A. (2004). *Civic agriculture: Reconnecting farm, food, and community.* Medford, MA: Tufts University Press.

Snell, W. (2009). *Census data reveal significant and a few surprising changes in Kentucky's tobacco industry.* Lexington: Department of Agricultural Economics, the University of Kentucky.

USDA National Agricultural Statistics Service. (2009). *2007 census of agriculture: Kentucky state and county data.* Washington DC: USDA National Agricultural Statistics Service.

World Commission on Environment and Development. (1984). *Our common future.* Oxford, UK: Oxford University Press.

9

USING A MULTILEVEL
APPROACH TO TEACH
SUSTAINABILITY TO
UNDERGRADUATES

Stacey A. Hawkey, Valdeen Nelsen, and Bruce I. Dvorak

T he goal of this chapter is to explain how a multilevel approach has been used to provide students with training and experience in applying pollution prevention and sustainability techniques in a business setting, thus yielding short- and long-term behavior change on the job as they begin their careers. These behaviors include championing measurable waste reductions and resource conservation efficiencies, effectively advocating for business decisions about sustainability, and being skilled practitioners at making sustainability work in the business environment. An effective teaching approach for undergraduates to learn about sustainability has been built around three distinct levels, based on the experiences of the University of Nebraska–Lincoln (UNL) Partners in Pollution Prevention (P3) program. These levels are learning the technical essentials, understanding business operations, and hands-on practice.

The P3 program, which began in 1997, has offered an intensive, results-oriented, 3-credit-hour summer course in pollution prevention and sustainability for upper-level undergraduate engineers and environmental scientists. Three factors form the philosophical and practical basis for the P3 program: First, the P3 program was conceived as a partnership between the University of Nebraska College of Engineering and the University Extension as a way to reach out and extend the university's resources to help solve public needs through technical assistance. Second, the program of engineering education is influenced by the profession's longstanding commitment to sustainable development and by accreditation criteria that emphasize teamwork and interdisciplinary studies, including understanding the societal, ecological, cultural, economic, national, and global effects of engineering (Ciocci, 2004; Coyle, Jamieson, & Oakes, 2005). Last, the P3 program utilizes service learning as an educational strategy for students' projects that focus on real-world application of theories and methods to teach the application of sustainability (Bishop, Keener, Kukreti, & Kowel, 2004; Mallick, Mathisen, & FitzPatrick 2002). The course has evolved based on data from numerous qualitative and quantitative program assessments, including the collection of a variety of data to substantiate program impact and to provide an objective basis for continual program and course improvement. These program assessments include:

- Exit interviews at the end of the course and formal survey data from students to evaluate class modules and elements, including the service learning component;
- Survey data from past students and a control group of similar students who did not participate in the class (Dvorak, Stewart, Hosni, Hawkey, & Nelsen, 2011); and
- Focus group input from stakeholders related to delivery of technical assistance to businesses and delivery of education to students, as well as future approaches to sustainability education.

Selected results from these surveys, evaluations, and assessments have influenced the current approach to teaching sustainability. These continual program improvement efforts form the philosophical basis for the three levels of instruction and practice that have been incorporated into the design and implementation of the multilevel P3 course. The following section describes this multilevel approach to teaching sustainability.

The result is a multilevel approach design with its effectiveness verified. It incorporates traditional lecture, interactive class exercises, projects in the first two levels, and a service learning field experience for the third level. It employs part-time faculty, staff, and graduate students to provide the educational component for undergraduates selected as program interns. The interns are intentionally recruited as junior and senior students from a variety of engineering and science majors. They complete 2 weeks of intense training by enrolling in Pollution Prevention: Principles and Practice, a 3-credit-hour undergraduate/graduate summer course jointly offered by the Biological Systems Engineering and Civil Engineering departments at UNL and considered part 1 of the course. The typical classroom presentation in the first level immerses students in the concepts, theories, and methodologies of traditional pollution prevention and sustainability. This technical, environmentally focused foundation is supplemented in the second level with important competency development in business culture and communication, documenting and reporting impact, and advocating change. These components provide the foundation for the second level of training, which is key to achieving results in the field. After completing the class, interns spend 10 weeks in the field providing technical assistance to Nebraska businesses, performing waste assessments and waste reduction projects, and providing each client with a written report detailing waste minimization suggestions. Students are supervised and supported in their work assignments by P3 faculty, staff, and graduate students, as well as by supervisors within their assigned businesses and other program partners, such as staff in the Nebraska Department of Environmental Quality (NDEQ). Upon completion of these two levels of coursework, students apply their knowledge and skills through service learning projects to identify, research, advocate for, and help implement changes toward more sustainable business practices. The third level builds on the previous two and encompasses real-world sustainability practices that anchor the first two levels of training in experiential learning for the students.

Interns receive a $5,700 stipend as well as tuition paid for the course, which serves as a senior-level engineering technical elective. Because such an intensive, multilevel course requires more resources than traditional lecture courses, the P3 program receives supplemental funding from the U.S. Environmental Protection Agency (EPA) and the NDEQ. In addition, businesses with major projects requiring dedicated assistance from a full-time summer intern pay a portion of the cost of the service learning project.

Since the program began, more than 200 interns have assisted more than 500 businesses in 72 different Nebraska communities. These businesses range from small sole proprietorships to large multinational corporations and governmental agencies, and they operate in nearly every segment of the economy, from agriculture to manufacturing, to the health, services, and hospitality industries. P3 program staff members are largely responsible for recruiting businesses and assisting with project identification and development in order to ensure a good match between students' interests and skills set and businesses' projects and locations. Students may be assigned to assist one business for the entire 10 weeks or provide brief, less in-depth assistance to a variety of businesses.

Pedagogical Approach: Theory Plus Pragmatics Plus Practice

Educational Framework

The class work that forms the basis of the first two levels of the multilevel P3 course is designed to prepare students to work on-site with businesses as experts in sustainability, to recognize when it is necessary to bring in additional experts, and to advocate effectively for change while educating business clients about the importance of environmental stewardship and sustainable operations. The class entails approximately 80 hours of classroom contact and homework time over the span of 2 weeks; followed by the third practice level of service learning field work, which can last as long as 10 weeks; and concludes with time devoted to final report development and presentations. To accomplish this multilevel approach requires a strategic blend of technical theory and methodology, the development of pragmatic skills for success in a business setting, and practice.

The class work incorporates hands-on practice in providing comprehensive pollution prevention technical assistance at a business. This practice assessment is presented in discrete stages to correspond with and complement the cognitive topics presented in the classroom. It includes actual practice in interviewing clients, conducting waste assessments, evaluating processes quantitatively, researching sustainable solutions, and communicating the results effectively with a written product. The classroom structure that integrates all components of the first two levels of the approach is reflected in the framework for the course, which is shown in figure 9.1. The structure provides students with the knowledge, skills, tools, and experiences necessary to establish a strong environmental ethic, scan and understand a situation on-site at a business, define and determine the problem(s) encountered, identify potential solutions, and communicate results and advocate for change.

Level 1: Technical Theory and Methodology

On the first level of the multilevel approach to sustainability education, students are introduced to the technical aspects of sustainability theory and

FIGURE 9.1
Orientation to the P3 learning process and product

The Concept

The Concept

| Establish ethic and position

Set tone | Scan/understand situation | Define/determine problems | Discover/identify potential solutions | Communicate results

Advocate change |

The Process: Course Modules and Internship Application

The Process

Days 1–2	Days 3–4	Days 5–7	Days 7–9
Intro to sustainability Life cycle thinking P2 definitions Regulatory structure and priorities Hazardous materials and universal waste Assessing the situation: Opening interview Company culture General recommendations Benefits and barriers Mission statements	Intro to material balance Waste assessments and calculators Practice assessment and report Complex process site visit Motors Compressed air Safety during assessments Data gathering/metrics/ documentation Report writing	Intro to P2 methods Intro to E2 Cost analysis Prescriptive P2 resources P3 partners Complex process site visit Practice assessment and report Voluntary programs Sustainability and life cycle assessments GHG calculator	Report writing: exec summary and appendices Documentation of impact and metrics forms Management of business data and confidentiality Advocating for change and reporting results Reassessments Final reports

The Product: Management Report Form

The Product

Background Section	Waste Assessment Section	P2 Opportunities Section	Management Report with
Business/project description Current practices	Process analysis	General and specific Program improvements Costs Benefits Impact forms	Executive summary Appendices Impact forms

methodology in classroom-based lectures and activities. In response to student evaluations over the years, the course has become sharply focused on teaching specific topic modules and on practicing skills and tasks needed in fieldwork application of theory. In-class discussions, laboratory exercises, and homework problems reinforce the technical theory presented during the lectures. Faculty members rely on guest speakers with practical experience and publicly available papers and articles on current and timely topics to supplement established lecture material. In addition to the more traditional engineering skills such as conducting a product material balance, preparing process mapping and flow diagrams, and completing a cost analysis, Level 1 lecture time is spent on specific topics pertinent to the fieldwork experience. Although subject to changes in the sustainability needs of the business community, technical modules are presented on topics such as the efficient operation of motors and pumps, detection of leaks and problems with compressed air systems, background in hazardous and universal waste regulations, and advanced lighting technology for energy efficiency.

Level 2: Pragmatics of Business

During the second level of classroom work, students focus on pragmatic competency development in business culture and communication, documenting and reporting impact, and advocating for change so that once they are in the field, they can become successful change agents toward more sustainable business practices. Students are explicitly taught how to understand the culture of a business and how to communicate with real-world businesspeople. Emphasis is placed on instruction in writing a technical business report with an executive summary for management audiences, e-mail and telephone etiquette, role-playing interview techniques to gather information from businesses on their environmental practices and accomplishments, and leveraging modern business culture for sustainability causes. Newer organizational models, such as environmental management systems, lean manufacturing, and sustainability tools (an example is the Global Reporting Initiative), are incorporated into the course to prepare students to function successfully in the business world.

The P3 program discovered that solely teaching the technical aspects of sustainability and expecting the resulting data to make a strong case for change did not work. Students undersold their findings and were not effective advocates. Highly motivated students can learn technical skills as introduced in the first level on their own. Teaching students to identify and communicate nonquantifiable (indirect) benefits is one step the P3 program takes in the second level of the multilevel approach to prepare students to become more effective change agents in the business. Unlike direct benefits (waste reduction, energy savings, water conservation), indirect benefits are those environmental improvements that are difficult to quantify reasonably and consistently. Examples of such indirect benefits include operating cost reductions not easily quantified, labor savings due to reductions in the regulatory burden, reductions in future liability such as health and safety, and future risks from changes in regulations related to hazardous materials and greenhouse gases. Learning modules on life cycle thinking, benefits and barriers, and documenting impact emphasize the importance of indirect benefits. Anecdotal information from reassessments of past projects emphasizes the importance of the indirect benefits in the client's decision-making process. It was also supported by a study of 20 small to medium-size businesses that showed, on average for the four indirect benefits studied, clients tended to realize indirect savings that are of a similar magnitude to direct savings (Youngblood, Dvorak, Woldt, Hawkey, & Hygnstrom, 2008). Effective sustainability education must teach students how to function as members of a diverse technical team and how to be advocates for their ideas and perspectives in the workplace. The P3 program incorporates this important topic into selected learning modules in the second level of its approach through multidisciplinary, team-based learning activities and hands-on projects. The variety of environmental and engineering majors in the cohort affords students opportunities to understand and appreciate the interrelatedness of business functions. Through the stakeholder focus groups, the P3 program learned that businesses were concerned that sustainability would be an add-on duty and cost, taking resources away from production, profits, and basic compliance, and would not be integrated across all business functions. To build a team-based focus, in addition to the practice assessment described earlier, a field experience in a complex manufacturing setting is held. It includes exercises to identify and prioritize discrete processes within the operation and develop material flow diagrams of the conditions observed. The P3 pedagogy develops students who team with other professionals in a peer-mentoring role. Significant emphasis is included to produce graduates with the expertise, experiences, and knowledge in communication, managerial, and organizational skills that enable them to be collaborators with business and organizational leaders in directing organizations toward more sustainable operations.

Considerable time is spent teaching students how to package their ideas for more sustainable practice in a usable form, write reports for management audiences, leverage the company culture to accomplish sustainability goals, and use life cycle analysis to encourage cutting-edge technologies. Through client networking, the P3 staff members learned the importance of using the right vocabulary to eliminate confusion over the term *sustainability*, and now the P3 program emphasizes this concept in student education at the second level. In a 2002 mail survey of past students, 43% reported that the internship had a positive influence on their communication skills. Several interns have reported anecdotally to P3 staff members that the technical report writing experience required of them in the course directly benefited them later on the job.

Level 3: Practice

Information from student surveys indicates that students rate the classroom course very highly in helping improve critical-thinking, problem-solving, and decision-making abilities. However, the P3 program has heard from students and businesses alike that the application of knowledge and skills is critical to getting the desired results from the educational experience. The P3 program incorporates practice into this third level of training to anchor the knowledge and skills gained from class work by having students conduct sustainability projects at actual business enterprises. The kinds of projects undertaken by interns include electricity and natural gas energy use assessments and strategies for reducing use, which also includes researching the feasibility of installing alternative energy sources (solar and geothermal); identifying source reduction strategies to eliminate and/or reduce hazardous and solid waste; and quantifying water use and losses and recommending ways to conserve resources.

The service learning work entails field experiences with varying levels of intensity. For larger, more complex, summer-long assignments, it is essential to plan the projects before the students start work. P3 program staff members assist in defining the project and preparing a preliminary work plan, and they communicate requirements for intern supervision and mentoring. For these assignments, interns spend the entire summer as active team members with one business, bringing new perspectives to issues affecting the sustainability of business operations. For small to medium-size projects requiring short-term assistance, interns assist five to eight businesses, helping each for approximately 2 weeks. Students define the projects and research the issues in real time as needed. For all projects, regardless of the size, interns generate a technical management report and present it to the business client to advocate for change toward more sustainable business practices. For each change recommended, the report includes technical information and calculations, and costs and savings related to implementation.

One of the stakeholder focus groups was concerned that sustainability is often taught in ways that do not address real-world situations. This confirmed that employers want to hire students who can demonstrate they have had hands-on experience with practical projects, that they have practice using the knowledge and skills developed in the classroom through service learning projects. This idea fits nicely with ongoing educational trends that recognize the limitations to academic content only. It was also clear from the stakeholders' comments that connections about sustainability must be drawn between and integrated throughout all of the business disciplines, and that service learning projects can provide the experiences that afford students with the opportunities to understand and appreciate the interrelatedness of sustainability across disciplines.

The survey of previous interns indicated that Level 3 of the P3 approach, with its service learning component, has enabled students to address current industry challenges successfully. In focus groups, businesses indicated that they were eager to hire students who had already developed expertise and experience in sustainability so that they could learn from, rather than be expected to teach, their new hires. The P3 program educates students to use this insight both while working with clients and in marketing themselves after graduation. Concepts and tools taught in the third level of the approach provide the framework for students to incorporate sustainability into their work after graduation through the abilities to define, measure, and report relevant environmental achievements and encourage changes within the organization toward sustainability. Results from surveys of past P3 students indicate that service learning can have a transformational impact on them, resulting in long-term changes in workplace behavior, including championing the relatively new concept of sustainability, being able to apply meaningful source reduction activities in the workplace more quickly (especially if the student has a strong environmental ethic), and being more prone to quantify the impact of their activities (Dvorak et al., 2011).

Reassessments Demonstrate the Pedagogical Approach

The P3 sustainability course began in 1997, but it was not until 2001 that faculty members began performing reassessments of previous work. Conducting reassessments of past projects has three purposes:

- To teach students how to approach and document a sustainability project effectively,
- To encourage businesses to act, and
- To collect information on what actually works and obtain impact metrics.

These three purposes align with the three levels of sustainability education in the multilevel approach taken by the P3 program.

During the initial technical assistance provided to businesses, students report the potential effects and benefits that may be realized if the recommendations made are indeed implemented. Two to three years later, students return to the client to interview them regarding the success of the previous assistance. Client-reported actual effects and benefits are collected during these reassessments of past work.

The survey of previous interns showed poor long-term effects for the first three cohorts of students, and it appears to have taken several years of program evolution to establish a strong measurable impact on students and business clients. As the technical training (Level 1) became more focused on the needs of the client and the abilities of the student, better environmental results were seen. Anecdotal comments obtained during reassessments have added technical topics to the class work, such as analyzing compressed air systems, investigating landscape and agricultural water usage, calculating the greenhouse gas effect from recommendations of students, and training the students to identify the key currencies (money, regulatory paperwork reduction, safety improvements, etc.) for decision making by the client.

Reassessment data seem to indicate that the more contact interns have with clients, the more impact the clients report; that is, clients who work full-time with an intern for an entire summer tend to report more environmental and monetary savings than do clients who receive brief assistance (Dvorak, Hygnstrom, Youngblood, Woldt, & Hawkey, 2008). With the student as an effective advocate (as taught in Level 2), in some cases reassessments provide businesses with added encouragement to implement improvements.

By collecting information about what recommendations were actually implemented and what impact they had on a business, students in the field and P3 faculty members are able to better focus on what really enhances pollution prevention and sustainability in the business community. Reassessments are geared to document fully the actual impact from the original assistance provided during Level 3 of the multilevel approach. Data collected from reassessments shows real environmental and monetary effects (as shown in figure 9.2) and confirms the viability of the approach.

Conclusion

A system for continual program improvement and timely response to the changing needs and priorities of all stakeholders, including external socioeconomic and political forces, has been critical for developing a three-level sustainability educational program and achieving long-term success. Using a continuous improvement cycle, the P3 course routinely checks with stakeholders and changes the technical theory presented in its course, strengthens and updates the business-related pragmatics, and focuses the service learning material or protocol to better meet the needs of the marketplace. This is key to keeping the course relevant and sustainable.

The P3 program uses a multilevel approach to teaching sustainability. The focus on practical, client- and results-oriented material is integral to its success. Students can gain adequate technical skills on their own. It is critical to provide them with the knowledge, skills, competencies, and experience

FIGURE 9.2
Success by the numbers: 2001–2010 savings per client (client reported data)

- Cost Savings
  – Average = $8,000/client

- Solid Waste
  – Average = $115,100 lbs/client

- Hazardous Waste
  – Average = $6,800 lbs/client

- Energy Savings
  – Average = 34,300 KwH/client

- Water Conserved
  – Average = 96,700 gallons/client

necessary to advocate successfully for change in the complexities of the modern business environment.

References

Bishop, P. L., Keener, T. C., Kukreti, A. R., & Kowel, S. T. (2004). The ACCEND program: A combined engineering that includes co-operative work experience. *Water Science and Technology, 49*(8), 73–79.

Ciocci, R. (2004). Infusion of sustainability in engineering and technology curricula. *Proceedings of the 2004 Richard Alsina Fulton Conference on Sustainability and the Environment*, Wilson College, Chambersburg, PA, 58–67.

Coyle, E. J., Jamieson, L. H., & Oakes, W. C. (2005). EPICS: Engineering Projects in Community Service. *International Journal of Engineering Education, 21*(1), 1–12.

Dvorak, B. I., Hygnstrom, J. R., Youngblood, D. J., Woldt, W. E., & Hawkey, S. A. (2008). Lessons learned concerning impact assessment: Pollution prevention technical assistance in Nebraska. *Journal of Cleaner Production, 16*(6), 751–760.

Dvorak, B. I., Stewart, B. A., Hosni, A. A., Hawkey, S. A., & Nelsen, V. (2011). Case study in intensive environmental sustainability education: Long-term impacts on workplace behavior. *Journal of Professional Issues in Engineering Education and Practice (ASCE), 137*(2), 113–120.

Mallick, R. B., Mathisen, P. P., & FitzPatrick, S. (2002). Opening the window of sustainable development to future civil engineers. *Journal of Professional Issues in Engineering Education and Practice, 128*(12), 212–216.

Youngblood, D. J., Dvorak, B. I., Woldt, W. E., Hawkey, S. A., & Hygnstrom, J. R. (2008). Quantifying and comparing a P2 program's benefits: Pollution prevention technical assistance in Nebraska. *Journal of Cleaner Production, 16*(6), 761–770.

10

GROWING SUSTAINABILITY IN HEALTH-CARE MANAGEMENT EDUCATION

Carrie R. Rich, J. Knox Singleton, and Seema Wadhwa

At its core, sustainability is a natural component of health care. Sustainability supports the basic health-care mission to provide safe, quality, compassionate, and cost-effective care. Sustainability ought to be explored as an effective form of resource stewardship, particularly as the health-care industry strives to meet societal needs and expectations during an era of intense public scrutiny and policy reform. The downstream effects of sustainability in health care are patient, employee, and community health and well-being. Armed with this knowledge, how does one integrate sustainability into health-care management training?

A New Course Is Planted

The first comprehensive health-care management sustainability course was offered at Georgetown University as the result of an expanded guest lecture presented in an undergraduate managerial ethics class (Rich, 2010). The need for an entire syllabus, Environmental Health-Care Sustainability, resulted from the mutual realization by students and educators that environmental training is fundamental to the future allocation of health-care resources (Rich & Wadhwa, 2009). Taught as a graduate-level elective, Environmental Health-Care Sustainability was the first comprehensive academic course to focus on sustainability in health-care delivery systems.

Class Purpose

Teaching Environmental Health-Care Sustainability raised awareness about environmental challenges and opportunities in health care—a topic that is atypical of health administration. The purpose of the class was to help future leaders prepare to meet industry's needs and society's burgeoning environmental expectations (*Course Evaluation*, 2010). The course explored fiscally responsible approaches for health care providers to improve environmental stewardship (Rich, 2010). Although sustainability management courses exist, such courses do not address health care–specific challenges, including human life, around-the-clock operations, hazardous waste streams, multiple regulators, infectious diseases, and privacy concerns, among others.

Course content developed for Environmental Health-Care Sustainability was specific to health-care challenges. Best practices were compiled to create a toolkit of sustainability case studies specific to the health-care industry never before shared with academic audiences. Environmental Health-Care Sustainability highlighted sustainability practices from commercial industries and academic settings to further health-care sustainability beyond the traditional paradigm.

Target Audience

Communities expect health-care leaders to be accountable for their business decisions, including the effects of their decisions on the environment (*Environment*, 2004). Health-care administrators may be held to an even higher standard of accountability than commercial industry leaders because of their commitment to the Hippocratic Oath, "First, do no harm" (*Greek Medicine*, 2010). Given these expectations, future health-care administrators are an ideal audience for Environmental Health-Care Sustainability education.

In practice, health-care sustainability programs intersect with many service lines that ultimately report to health-care administration, ranging from Environmental Services and Engineering to Marketing and Strategic Planning. Successful sustainability programs have senior leadership support, buy-in, and oversight (Wadhwa, 2010). According to a recent survey of the health-care facility industry, "70 percent of healthcare professionals indicated that hospitals need a Sustainability Manager" (*Energy Economics and Environment*, 2010). It is the responsibility of higher education to meet industry's training needs for the emerging role of health-care sustainability managers (Wadhwa, 2010).

Course Goals

The goal of the Environmental Health-Care Sustainability course was to provide comprehensive sustainability education to future health-care administrators. The course examined environmental trends and drivers of health-care delivery systems, specifically focusing on hospitals and clinics. At the completion of the course, students were held accountable for being able to understand the theoretical and operational definitions of the term *sustainability*. Beginning with the conceptual framework of health-care sustainability, known as the *triple bottom line* or *people, planet, profit*, students were asked to analyze the business case for sustainability in health care (Rich & Wadhwa, 2010). This continuing theme of the course was explored through assignments designed to identify best practices and critique established health-care sustainability initiatives used to date in delivery settings. Students were also expected to analyze the impact of the built environment on clinical, financial, and human resource indicators, and to discuss leadership strategies for improving sustainability programs (Rich, 2010).

Course Methodology

To achieve course objectives, students investigated several content areas (*Course Evaluation*, 2010). Beginning with the principle of the Hippocratic Oath, "First, do no harm," students explored how the credo applied beyond patient care to environmental stewardship. As part of the exploration process, students examined the short-term costs and benefits of implementing sustainability initiatives compared to long-term investment strategies and benefits. Three additional basic premises were adopted at the outset of class to guide exploration of specific health-care sustainability content areas. First, students were introduced to the guiding principle that patients cannot be healthy in unhealthy environments. Second, students were introduced to the concept that strategic environmental policy is strategic health policy, particularly from public health and population health services perspectives. Third, students were introduced to the concept that when society is not strategic about health-care policies, the environment and the public's health and suffers as a result. Once the class was aligned on these three basic principles, instruction took the form of deeper immersion into specific content areas such as energy management, waste management, and water management. Students investigated national information repositories—including resources from the Environmental Protection Agency—that were specifically developed for health-care sustainability providers. Students also investigated differences in costs and environmental impacts of varying waste streams. For instance, every student conducted a financial analysis and a forecast of hazardous waste management compared to solid waste management for a host health-care institution. In addition to financial calculations, students were challenged to explore the ethical dilemmas and cultural change considerations that ultimately complement potential cost savings in any health-care delivery system. Example topics that highlighted the link among environmental, ethical, and cultural concerns in waste management included device reprocessing, mercury elimination, and pharmaceutical waste management.

Students also explored practices for "greening" the operating room, reprocessing medical devices, and disposing of pharmaceutical waste safely to prevent water contamination. After examining reactive approaches to environmental health-care sustainability, students explored proactive environmental management methods. Beginning with environmentally preferable purchasing, students researched how group purchasing organizations collaborate to influence health-care product vendors to supply more environmentally friendly products, such as products without toxins and products with recycled content. Another example of preventive health-care sustainability is healthy food in health care. Students researched sustainable food in health care through case studies of local food sourcing in hospital cafeterias and hospital farmer's markets. Students also analyzed the environmental implications of health information technology and proposed their own proactive solutions. For instance, some students reflected on the idea that conversion to electronic medical records would result in less paper waste; their ideas were reinforced by case studies. Additional conversations broadened to alternative transportation, such as carpooling and public transit.

All of the aforementioned content areas were selected by the faculty instructor in collaboration with the sustainability coordinator at Inova Health System, a leader in sustainable health-care management (Inova Health System, 2011). Practice Greenhealth (PGH), the nation's leader for health-care institutions committed to sustainable, environmentally friendly practice, also provided input (Practice Greenhealth, 2008). PGH focused on the concept of teaching culture change as a key ingredient to permanently changing administrative mindsets about environmental stewardship in health care. Both the feedback of the sustainability coordinators and PGH are reflected in the Environmental Health-Care Sustainability syllabus.

How to Teach This Course

At first glance, the overview of course objectives may seem daunting, but a content breakdown by class helped make for manageable lectures. Each lecture was broken down into six parts: (1) sustainability drivers, (2) business case, (3) strategic implementation plan, (4) associated regulations, (5) tools and resources, and (6) practical application. Each class lecture covered the social, environmental, and economic drivers of the highlighted content area. For instance, during the class on food sustainability in health care, students explored how local ingredient sourcing for the health-care delivery system cafeteria can be accomplished through support of local farmers (social driver), decreased transportation (environmental driver), and decreased transportation expenses (economic driver). Next, students were challenged to explore the business case of the content area. What are the associated costs of program implementation? What is the return on investment? What is the long-term viability of the sustainability program? After answering these questions, students studied the implementation plans of host institutions. Who are the key stakeholders? What are their incentives to participate in sustainability initiatives? How is the sustainability service marketed? Part four of each lecture covered associated regulations, requiring analysis of local, regional, state, and national legalities as well as accreditation standards. This analysis helped students understand how specific sustainability initiatives complied with regulatory and accreditation standards (Course Evaluation, 2010). Recognizing that the Environmental Health-Care Sustainability students at Georgetown University were among the first in the country to learn formally about environmental health-care sustainability, every student was required to compile a list of tools and resources for future students and emerging health-care sustainability professionals. Resource compilations included assessment tools, evaluation plans, process improvement resources, suggested readings, and glossaries organized by health-care sustainability topic area. Last, for every sustainability topic discussed in Environmental Health-Care Sustainability, practical applications were integrated in classroom learning, homework, and tests.

How to Test Student Knowledge

Striking a balance between management of strategic goals and operational imperatives is the basis for socially, fiscally, and environmentally viable health-care sustainability programs. Thus, knowledge testing should reflect students' understanding of how to implement strategic and operational goals that drive sustainability programs. Testing for Environmental Health-Care Sustainability combined metrics for measuring classroom participation with practical field assignments (Rich, 2010). The grading breakdown is shown in table 10.1.

Every student was required to maintain a career journal as the basis for documenting and evaluating student engagement. The purpose of the career journal was to help students develop skills in critical, reflective thinking. By fulfilling career journal requirements, every student produced a valuable resource for future professional use tailored to their respective individual interests. Career journal assignments challenged students to embody different roles in sustainability management, from sustainability coordinators to sustainable vendors. Since completing the Environmental Health-Care Sustainability course, students have used their career journals as components of their professional portfolios to attract employer attention (*Course Evaluation*, 2010).

Through an informal survey of the Environmental Health-Care Sustainability course at Georgetown University (*Course Evaluation*, 2010), students indicated that the most compelling assignments were the midterm and final exams. The midterm and final projects provided a platform for real-time engagement with current health-care leaders attuned to environmental stewardship. This engagement facilitated extracurricular learning that buttressed

TABLE 10.1
Grading Breakdown

Evaluation	Maximum Points
Career journal	30
Field assignments	20
Midterm	20
Final	30
Total	100

classroom learning. Practical experience helped students become competitive candidates in the growing health-care market (*Occupational Outlook 2008–09*, 2010). Ultimately, students were challenged to practice the mindsets of health-care leaders about sustainable thinking, fiscally responsible behavior, and code compliant strategies.

For their research papers, students were presented with a list of topics from which to choose and were asked to research one aspect of a sustainability program at a host health-care institution. For instance, one student's passions led her to investigate health-care waste practices in a developing country. Another student examined the domestic legal implications of environmentally unsustainable health-care practices. Regardless of the research topic, students were asked to explore a set list of content areas. Beginning with topic definition and topic overview, students segued into background analysis. During this part of the assignment, students identified and assessed the relevance of regulations and community benefit in the context of environmental stewardship. Students also included their lists of tools and resources in the background analysis section. The second part of the research paper included a strategic plan, developed by each student, specific to the individually selected sustainability topic. For every strategic plan, students outlined the business case for engaging in environmental health-care sustainability as it related to the selected topic area; identified key stakeholders; presented the financial plan for start-up costs; anticipated costs during the first 3 years of operations; and wrote the marketing plan, employee training plan, and evaluation plan to measure outcomes (Rich, 2010).

Prior to submission of the final assignment, every student participated in a site visit with a local health-care system (Inova Health System) and spoke one-on-one with the sustainability coordinator. The final reports mirrored strategic planning documents that would be presented to a health-care chief executive officer (CEO). For instance, students included financial analysis to demonstrate the business cases for proposed sustainability initiatives. Several students presented their findings to peers, health-care administrators, policy researchers, clinicians, and academics at a 2010 Earth Day Conference hosted by Georgetown University, School of Nursing and Health Studies titled *First Do No Harm: Partnerships for Patient Safety Through Sustainability and Evidence Based Design* (2010). By engaging with professionals in the field, students emerged confident about convincing peers, faculty members, and future colleagues about the value of sustainability in health care.

Teaching Resources

To date, there is no comprehensive resource to teach environmental health-care sustainability to a student audience. Fragmented resources exist and are accessible through national societies for environmental stewardship, higher education, and health-care delivery. The Association for the Advancement of Sustainability in Higher Education (AASHE) is a group of colleges and universities dedicated to creating a sustainable future, but AASHE does not have resources that guide the instruction of sustainability for health care. AASHE's mission is to "empower higher education to lead the sustainability transformation by providing resources, professional development, and a network of support to enable institutions of higher education to model and advance sustainability in everything they do, from governance and operations to education and research. AASHE defines sustainability in an inclusive way, encompassing human and ecological health, social justice, secure livelihoods, and a better world for all generations" (AASHE, 2011). The AASHE mission complements the overarching mission of health-care sustainability through its support network.

As mentioned, AASHE does not provide curricular training about sustainability in health-care delivery systems, leaving a gap and opportunity for health-care sustainability curricular development. Organizations leading the field of eco-friendly health-care management do not provide training tools for academic distribution either. As a result, academic training tools are currently underdeveloped, despite emergence of nonprofit organizations, vendors, and consulting firms that offer guidance about health-care sustainability outcomes. Educators interested in health-care sustainability are requesting alternative and complementary training resources to the existing published literature (Savitz & Weber, 2006).

The Environmental Health-Care Sustainability course at Georgetown University helped raise PGH's awareness of the academic training gap. PGH demonstrated leadership by providing student access to organizational webinars. This partnership allowed students to learn from up-to-date training modules designed and led by health care practitioners. While the webinars were informative, students ultimately found the webinars to be inappropriate for academic audiences. The webinars were developed for practitioners and contained operational details not yet meaningful to students (*Course Evaluation*, 2010). Some students participated in real-time, online revisions to the Green Guide for Healthcare (GGHC), a best practices guide for sustainability in the health-care industry (Green Guide for Health Care, 2008). Students conveyed that this learning medium was again too detail-oriented and practitioner-focused to be meaningful to the student population (*Course Evaluation*, 2010). In short, academic training for environmental health-care sustainability is—to date—undersupported by higher education.

Key Collaborators

Collaboration between academic and industry stakeholders is necessary for health-care sustainability training to be purposeful and practical. The Association of University Programs in Health Administration (AUPHA) is a global network of academics and related organizations dedicated to excellence in health-care management education (Association for University Programs in Health Administration, 2011). AUPHA will play an important role in disseminating knowledge and supporting faculty development within the emerging field of health-care sustainability (Oldham & Friedman, 2010). The American College of Healthcare Executives (ACHE) is another potential platform for educating those in health-care administration about sustainability through continuing professional education. ACHE is an international professional society of health-care executives committed to networking, education, and career development (American College of Healthcare Executives, 2010). Yet another organization that could support health-care sustainability learning is the American Hospital Association (AHA), a membership-based organization that represents hospitals, health systems, and related health-care organizations (American Hospital Association, 2010). Both ACHE and AHA are key professional societies with local chapters and support networks that could assume critical roles for educating current health-care leaders about the implications of ignoring health-care sustainability (American Hospital Association, 2010).

Industry partners can add value to classroom learning and help students develop fresh perspectives that ultimately mold academic requirements to be more in concert with desired professional skill sets. The following profiles describe organizations that provided guest lectures for the Environmental Health-Care Sustainability course. These organizations are nationally recognized for their health-care sustainability commitments. They have been gracious about sharing content to support learning in higher education.

- Perkins + Will is a global leader in facility design, fusing efficient healing environments with sustainable aims. In partnership with resources shared by the United States Green Building Council (USGBC), Perkins + Will helped students discover a green building

credit system called Leadership in Energy and Environmental Design
(LEED) (Moore, 2010).

- Inova Health System is a nonprofit health-care provider in northern
  Virginia serving more than 1 million people each year. Inova helped
  students explore sustainable visioning by studying Inova's environmental mission statement that guides sustainability initiatives for
  operations and maintenance (First Do No Harm, 2010).
- Urban Ltd. is a leader in health-care sustainability consulting and
  focuses on the design and implementation of sustainability programs
  for health-care delivery organizations. Students benefited from learning about Urban Ltd.'s benchmarking practices used to evaluate core
  competences of sustainability programs (First Do No Harm, 2010;
  Urban Ltd., 2009).
- Johns Hopkins University has demonstrated commitment to environmental research in health care, helping to broaden student learning
  about how to use research to promote environmentally sustainable
  medicine (McDonough, 2010).
- Partners Health System is a leader in environmentally sustainable
  health care, especially with regard to information technology (IT).
  With relatively little information otherwise available about the topic,
  Partners Health System provided students with case studies and IT
  measurement tools (Kaiser Permanente, 2010).
- New York University faculty members shared perspectives about food
  politics and the roles of personal and social responsibility for dietary
  choices (Nestle, 2010). These perspectives complemented case studies
  of healthy food in health care shared with students by Kaiser Permanente (2010).

Educators have several options available to engage health-care sustainability
professionals. The challenges are where to start and how to prioritize
content.

Impact of Environmental Health-Care Sustainability Education

Academia has an unprecedented opportunity to train future health-care leaders to practice socially, fiscally, and environmentally responsible management (Clancy, 2010). This triple bottom line means refocusing academic
training to balance managerial ethics with cost-saving strategies (Savitz &

Weber, 2006). Currently, higher education is supporting, rather than leading, industry's need for sustainability training. If health-care sustainability were considered core to health-care administration training, environmental stewardship would become part of the industry's fiber as graduates enter the profession.

Society increasingly demands environmental stewardship. One proactive approach is for higher education to train students about corporate social responsibility awareness and the requisite workforce management skills. The alternative, a reactive approach, is for regulators, such as the Environmental Protection Agency (EPA), and accrediting agencies, such as the Joint Commission (JC), to demand environmental accountability (*Environment of Care*, 2008). The latter requires administrators to spend time and resources "putting out fires" rather than striving beyond compliance to achieve environmental sustainability.

Leading health-care delivery systems across the country are implementing the role of sustainability coordinator as part of their corporate strategic plans. Sustainability coordinators are poised to be change agents in the health-care arena. What better way to position future health-care leaders than by training them for this emerging role? Now is the time for higher education to train future health-care sustainability leaders.

References

AASHE. (2011). About the Association for the Advancement of Sustainability in Higher Education. Retrieved from http://www.aashe.org/about

American College of Healthcare Executives. (2010). About ACHE. Retrieved from http://www.ache.org/aboutache.cfm

American Hospital Association. (2010). About the American Hospital Association. Retrieved from http://www.aha.org/aha/about/index.html

Association for University Programs in Health Administration. (2011). Welcome to AUPHA. Retrieved from http://www.aupha.org/i4a/pages/index.cfm?pageid = 1

Clancy, C. (2010, April 22). *State of the science: Perspectives from AHRQ.* First do no harm: Partnerships for patient safety through sustainability and evidence based design. Georgetown University, School of Nursing and Health Studies, Department of Health Systems Administration. Washington, DC. Retrieved from http://nhs.georgetown.edu/news/2010/04evidencebased_presentations.html

Course Evaluation: Healthcare environmental sustainability: Issues and challenges. (2010, Spring). Georgetown University School of Nursing and Health Studies, Department of Health Systems Administration. Washington, DC.

Energy economics and environment: Making the three E's work together in healthcare (2010, November). International Facility Management Association, Healthcare Council and Corporate Reality, Design and Management Institute. Annual Healthcare Design Conference, Las Vegas, Nevada.

Environment of care: Hazardous materials. (2008, November 24). The Joint Commission. Retrieved from http://www.jointcommission.org/AccreditationPrograms/ HomeCare/Standards/09_FAQs/EC/Hazardous_Material.htm

Environment: Value to the investor. (2004). Global Environmental Management Initiative. Retrieved from http://www.gemi.org/resources/GEMI%20Clear%20Ad vantage.pdf

First do no harm: Partnerships for patient safety through sustainability and evidence based design. (2010, April 22). (Forum). Georgetown University, School of Nursing and Health Studies, Department of Health Systems Administration. Washington, DC. Retrieved from http://nhs.georgetown.edu/news/2010/04evidence based_events.html

Greek medicine. (2010). U.S. National Library of Medicine, National Institutes of Health, Department of Health & Human Services. Retrieved from http://www .nlm.nih.gov/hmd/greek/greek_oath.html

Green Guide for Health Care. (2008, December). Green guide for health care: Best practices for creating high performing healing environments: Version 2.2 operations section. Retrieved from http://www.gghc.org/

Inova Health System. (2011). Our environmental commitment: Inova is "going green." Retrieved from http://www.inova.org/about-inova/sustainability/index.jsp

Kaiser Permanente. (2010, October 13). Kaiser Permanente hosts "Food For Health Forum" featuring sustainable food experts and innovators. Retrieved from http:// xnet.kp.org/newscenter/aboutkp/green/stories/2010/101310sffoodforum.html

McDonough, D. (2010, Spring). *Smart growth.* Georgetown University, School of Nursing & Health Studies, Department of Health Systems Administration. Washington, DC.

Moore, D. (2010, February 24). Valley Health: Winchester medical center campus expansion. Presentation, Georgetown University, School of Nursing & Health Studies, Department of Health Systems Administration. Washington, DC.

Nestle, M. (2010, April 21). Food politics: Personal vs. social responsibility for dietary choices. Georgetown University. Washington, DC. Retrieved from https:// mediapilot.georgetown.edu/sharestream2gui/GT-Video.jsp?myname = 0d2117 cd27760d9e012821308aee0165&cid = 0d21b6201c936da3011d3e88564906e6&win dowSize = small&originalAspectRatio = false&type = video

Occupational outlook 2008–09. (2010) Bureau of Labor Statistics, U.S. Department of Labor. Handbook, environmental scientists and hydrologists. Retrieved from http://www.bls.gov/oco/ocos050.htm

Oldham, P.C., & L.H. Friedman. (2010, Spring). Preparing today's students to lead tomorrow's green healthcare organizations. *Journal of Health Administration Education, 27*(2), 127–134.

Practice Greenhealth. (2008). Practice Greenhealth, About us. Retrieved from http://www.practicegreenhealth.org/about/

Rich, C. (2010). Healthcare environmental sustainability: Issues and challenges. (Syllabus). Georgetown University School of Nursing and Health Studies, Department of Health Systems Administration. Washington, DC.

Rich, C., & Wadhwa, S. (2009, October 28). *Community partnerships & health care sustainability.* Georgetown University, School of Nursing & Health Studies, Department of Health Systems Administration. Washington, DC.

Rich, C., & Wadhwa, S. (2010, June 22). People, planet, profit. *Healthcare Development Magazine.* Retrieved from http://healthcaredevelopmentmagazine.com/article/people-planet-profit.html

Savitz, A.W., & Weber, K. (2006). *The triple bottom line: How today's best-run companies are achieving economic, social and environmental success—and how you can too.* San Francisco: John Wiley & Sons.

Urban Ltd. (2009). *Sustainable design & green consulting.* Annandale, Virginia. Retrieved from http://www.urban-ltd.com/areas/sustainable/index.asp

Wadhwa, S. (2010, November 12). Greening operations series: Implementing and growing a hospital recycling program. Practice Greenhealth, webinar series. Retrieved from http://www.practicegreenhealth.org/tools/webinars/archive/archive/529

11

TEACHING ECOTOURISM IN THE BACKYARD OF WAIKIKI, HAWAI'I

John Cusick

The failure to develop ecological literacy is a sin of omission and of commission. Not only are we failing to teach the basics about the earth and how it works, but we are in fact teaching a large amount of stuff that is simply wrong.

(Orr, 1992, p. 85)

Although classroom settings are the norm in education, field-oriented, place-based curriculum provides students with a practical understanding of natural and cultural environments. For example, University of Hawai'i at Manoa (UHM) students can go *mauka* (to the mountain) to Lyon Arboretum and participate in *in-situ* and *ex-situ* conservation biology and ecological restoration projects in a tropical rainforest, and go *makai* (to the sea) where the university maintains the Waikiki Aquarium and conducts research and education programs. In addition to other terrestrial and marine field sites, all located within a radius of a few miles from campus, and the academic expertise at UHM that support the sites, is the Waikiki tourism landscape and associated infrastructure. This setting provides equally important place-based learning and community service opportunities related to education for sustainability. The confluence of programmatic excellence at UHM and community need provides students and faculty members with opportunities to craft sustainability solutions to existing concerns that are relevant both locally and globally.

A sustainability framework for tourism suggests a reappraisal of how to nurture, not alter, environmental and sociocultural diversity so that solutions originating in the island context of Hawai'i can be scaled up to provide examples of how to live sustainably on earth. However, the financially and politically competing and cooperating stakeholders within the mass tourism sector that maintains the status quo must at some point consider a troubling fact: The geographic isolation of the Hawaiian Islands makes travel to and from primary markets in North America and Asia unsustainable, particularly in meeting the millions of annual visitors' additional demands for energy, food, and water.

Internationally, widely debated alternatives to mass tourism are informed by sustainability-related analysis and critiques. Sustainability in the context of tourism may be defined as responsible travel that protects the environment and improves the well-being of local residents. However, herein lies a typical misconception: the governor of the State of Hawai'i's tourism liaison stated that "people come here for the environment and the scenery . . . Think of ecotourism: Hawai'i could write the book in regards to ecotourism because almost every activity we have here, whether it's on the ocean or land, is an ecotourism activity" (LaFrance, 2010, p. 7).

As defined by international experts, ecotourism is low impact and usually small scale, educates the traveler, provides funds for conservation and community economic development, politically empowers local residents and fosters human rights, and averts negative effects on a destination's ecology and host culture (Honey, 1999; Primack, Bray, Galletti, & Ponciano, 1998; Whelan, 1991). Can Hawai'i write *that* book? This does not appear likely when one considers the high-impact and large-scale tourism operations of multinational corporations that dominate the industry, the contrived authenticity of cultural performances and misinformation about natural and cultural history provided by tour operators, the continuing extinction crisis for biodiversity and the devastating impacts of invasive species on native habitats, and the displacement from ancestral lands and disempowerment of local residents. In effect, the situation is described by one local expert as "a relationship with an industry that has globally demonstrated a preference towards urbanization and the systematic displacement of local and indigenous communities from their natural, cultural, and social resources, effectively reducing local self-sufficiency while exploiting human and natural resources" (Taum, 2010, p. 33).

For Hawai'i to write the book on ecotourism as suggested, there needs to be evidence of sustainability in practice, not just rhetorically. Anything less constitutes "greenwashing." Despite the rapid increase of ecotourism research conducted in well-established tourist destinations such as Costa Rica, Kenya, the Himalayas, and New Zealand, and the development of university degree programs focused exclusively on ecotourism, such research and curriculum development relative to the Hawaiian Islands contributes marginally to the discussion on alternatives to mass tourism. The pressure on the existing tourism infrastructure, and the likelihood of the impact in locations previously unvisited by tourists, suggests research and instruction related to ecotourism in the Hawaiian Islands will contribute to the goals of sustainability literacy. This chapter briefly sets the context of tourism in Hawai'i and discusses ongoing learning outcomes from teaching a course on ecotourism at UHM.

Tourism Overview

Tourism in the state of Hawai'i represents nearly one-quarter of all economic activity and employs approximately one-third of the labor force, including many UHM students. Rapid increases in the number of visitors threaten both the unique evolutionary ecology and cultural heritage of the islands. Even with an abundance of natural and cultural resources, the challenges for government, the tourism industry, and destination communities are whether they can balance environmental conservation and economic development.

The scale of tourism currently strains government resources and the tolerance of local residents who host large numbers of visitors in their communities. The visitor count in 2007 was 7.5 million in a state with a total resident population of just over 1 million, most of whom live in the urban landscapes of Honolulu on the south shore of Oahu. Tourism stakeholders have an inherent interest in biological diversity and cultural heritage because these assets have created the conditions conducive to the development of Hawai'i as a desirable travel destination. Therefore, the promotion of sustainability best practices benefits tourism and nontourism stakeholders, and minimizes negative effects that lead to erosion of public support for the tourism sector.

Increasing competition from other sun-and-surf destinations has sparked interest in niche tourism markets, such as adventure, heritage, and health and wellness, in which tourists are encouraged to depart resort enclaves and experience natural and cultural landscapes. This approach results in more visitors to places not identified in guidebooks and previously off the list of most tourist itineraries, particularly in rural communities. Not surprisingly, 62% of residents agreed with the statement that their island "is being run for tourists at the expense of local people" (Mak, 2008, p. 35).

Sustainable tourism is defined as tourism that meets the needs of present tourist and host destinations for future tourist use, and the emphasis is generally on tourism planning and management. Sustainable tourism encompasses issues of stakeholder responsibilities toward visitors and hosts, the support of development in destinations and adjacent gateway communities, and issues of environmental conservation and preservation of cultural heritage. Ecotourism is on the opposite end of the spectrum from mass tourism in terms of scale, and the *eco* label is increasingly co-opted by the tourist industry to "greenwash" activities and their impact. Nonetheless, ecotourism is capturing an increasing share of the global tourism market and, as such, is of particular interest to the state of Hawai'i.

The ecotourist profile is generally that of an experienced traveler with higher than average levels of income and education. These visitors to Hawai'i often go to neighbor islands and visit rural communities in search of encounters with nature and authentic cultural experiences. Although such profiles limit the scope and scale of "nature" and "authenticity" to neighbor islands, the fact remains that tens of thousands of visitors stay in Waikiki every day of the year, with ready access to what can be considered urban ecotourism destinations (Joppe & Dodds, 2000). That situation is what makes teaching ecotourism in the backyard of Waikiki an opportunity to situate sustainability themes in the context of a particular place that has been enormously profitable, but inherently unsustainable, for the past several decades.

Sustainability Education at UHM

Sustainability education provides new learning opportunities for an island society located in a region where tourism is a dominant economic activity. Currently, however, UHM has no courses devoted specifically to the investigation of alternative forms of tourism, particularly ecotourism, an omission that goes against trends at peer institutions of higher education. Nonetheless, the study of ecotourism has been incorporated into an upper-division course taught by the author, titled Geography of Global Tourism, which is cross-listed in the Department of Geography and the School of Travel Industry Management.

Teaching ecotourism requires an interdisciplinary approach that is informed by the social and natural sciences, as well as business and management. Lectures and guest speakers identify themes and concepts while field research associated with small-group projects encourage the independent and collaborative analysis of destinations and adjacent gateway communities. Students learn to recognize the need for input from a variety of disciplines and stakeholder groups in solving environmental problems. They become increasingly conversant across the academic continuum of sustainability studies while being trained in skills that increasingly are demanded by decision makers and environmental managers trying to balance economic health and ecological integrity. In addition, student service learning projects take advantage of the diverse environmental conditions found in the Hawaiian Islands for field research and career internship opportunities.

The learning outcomes of the course provide students with immediate understanding of the challenges societies face in the pursuit of sustainability, whether the issue is energy, water, food, solid waste management, transportation, or social equity. In textbooks, in the media, and from other voices of authority, sustainability appears to be abstract for many students. The implications of annually hosting millions of visitors and the demand this puts on resources and infrastructure is made evident to students in the form of low service industry wages, traffic congestion, crowded beaches and trails, national chain stores putting small businesses out of business, and the overall sense of placelessness associated with mass tourism destinations. Students make the connections, understanding becomes more acute, and they are motivated to suggest solutions to change direction.

Campus Collaboration and Service Learning Projects

Faculty members and students created the Sustainable Travel Education Partnership (STEP) in the Fall 2008 semester to facilitate broad stakeholder support for and promotion of sustainable best practices. STEP members helped organize four events on the islands of Oahu and Maui in 2009 that brought together public and private stakeholders to discuss conservation, respect, community, and responsibility as they relate to tourism. Equally important for students were the skills and networking acquired through planning, organizing, and hosting events that applied sustainability practices in terms of minimizing solid waste and recycling.

In all, more than 200 participants from academia, the tourism sector, federal and state resource management, conservation groups, nongovernmental organizations, and destination communities attended the events. The following questions were posed: What does sustainable tourism look like in Hawai'i? What are the challenges to reach that goal? What roles do individuals and organizations play in achieving the goal of sustainability for the Hawaiian Islands?

Key initiatives proposed by participants included:

1. Communicate host culture issues
2. Review regulatory obstacles to alternative forms of tourism
3. Promote experiential learning and internship opportunities to bridge the ecological/sustainability literacy gap of residents and visitors
4. Identify resource management concerns as they relate to and/or involve commercial tourism activities

STEP events led to the development of project sites accessible from campus for students in subsequent courses. The purpose of service learning projects is to improve student critical thinking and oral and written articulation of complex issues associated with tourism development, community economic development, environmental education, and conservation. Project sites and associated stakeholders contribute to an understanding of the current status of tourism in the Hawaiian Islands and, by extension, to global tourism issues. Project sites are in the vicinity of Waikiki and therefore are part of the larger tourism landscape of Oahu whether or not the sites actively promote themselves as tourist destinations. The next sections briefly describe a few of the project sites and student reflections on issues associated with the promotion of sustainability education.

Cultural Heritage

The Manoa Heritage Center, located in a suburban neighborhood, provides an alternative destination to those that cater to large groups. Part of the center's challenge is maintaining site integrity while simultaneously adapting and adjusting to fit the needs of residents and tourists alike.

While their first priority is to educate the children and students of Hawai'i, educating tourists and other members of the public preserves cultural heritage and instills respect for host communities. It has been a long-standing critique of tourist destinations worldwide that visitors do not see and experience a sense of place but rather occupy a concocted consumer and recreation landscape. Students agreed, however, that if visitors to Hawai'i were to have authentic experiences in the "real Hawai'i"—history, culture, and current issues and struggles, for example—they would be better informed and part of community-identified solutions to minimize Hawai'i's dependency on externalities for basics such as energy and food.

Sustainable Agriculture

The state of Hawai'i Farm Bureau recognizes the potential of farmer's markets as sites of social interaction for both residents and visitors and requested student assistance with a survey on consumer patterns and levels of satisfaction. The service learning objective was not to figure out ways to increase visitation but to utilize the weekly event as a vehicle to promote sustainability literacy.

Resident responses were generally positive. Many residents are regulars at the farmer's market at Kapi'olani Community College, which is located at the base of Diamond Head and is a major tourist destination itself. There was a noted increase in the presence of tourists, particularly from Japan, and some respondents expressed concern that the focus was becoming less about locally grown products and more about selling products to visitors.

Student recommendations included developing a website to highlight sustainability themes, including reasons for buying local products and highlighting vendors' sustainability initiatives in their business practices. Besides social networking sites, media advertisements in newspapers, radio, and television could encourage attendance to this and other farmer's markets. Brochures placed in hotels could target tourists and facilitate resident–visitor interactions.

The primary objective is to increase student awareness of food security in Hawai'i. Food vendors provide a valuable link in the supply chain to sustain local agriculture and the cultural landscapes they depend on, but farmers don't survive on good intentions. People must purchase their products so that farmers can make a living and keep open spaces for agriculture that are routinely coveted for urbanization and further development of tourism infrastructure.

Voluntourism

Voluntourism supports community activities and "cost[s] nothing more than your time and the goodness of your heart" (Whatley, 2009, p. ix). The purpose is to contribute to an organization's objectives and assist in a local community, perhaps with other visitors but ideally with residents. The experience provides valuable economic, social, and environmental benefits to communities, whether or not they are on a tourist's itinerary of destinations.

Due to rapid suburbanization and subsequent poor resource management over the past several decades, Maunalua Bay and the watersheds in East Honolulu that feed the bay suffer from environmental degradation. The abundant diversity of marine ecosystems recalled by elder community members is all but lost. As a result of community concerns, the nonprofit organization Malama Maunalua (*malama* in Hawaiian means to "care for" and "steward") partners with community organizations to coordinate restoration initiatives. Among their activities are large-scale invasive algae removals, expanded environmental science research, and partnership with schools located in the bay's watersheds. Students proposed a voluntourism campaign at a hotel located on the bay whereby visitors can donate their labor to restoration activities, beach cleanups, seasonal whale counts, and other activities.

Conclusion

Some observers, the author included, suggest that the tourism industry in the Hawaiian Islands is by definition unsustainable. Tourists arrive from distant places by airplane and routinely rent cars for local transportation rather than use public transportation or ride bicycles, let alone walk! They stay in accommodations cut off from resident communities where they consume large amounts of electricity and water, let alone food. Too often, they choose to eat in corporate-brand restaurants that serve salads with lettuce imported from California and bananas bought in bulk from Ecuador, just two sample products that are grown in the islands.

So far, significant outcomes of teaching ecotourism in Waikiki's backyard may be few and far between. But students have promoted actions by the tourist industry and government agencies to deal with some easier-to-solve problems (water and energy conservation, purchasing of local products when possible, education programs for visitors and residents, alternative forms of economic development) in the short term while working on undergraduate and graduate research projects to address more difficult and costly initiatives (green buildings, smart grid technology, transportation options, an end to dependency on fossil-fuel energy, food security, and so on).

Tourism development can create landscapes devoid of any sense of place and leave visitors wondering where they are as one destination resembles any number of others, with their associated strip malls, generic landscaping, and more commercial than green spaces. As a balance to these pressures, ecotourism can redirect visitors' activities and their money toward more environmentally and culturally sensitive relationships with resident communities and instill an ethic of effective stewardship for environmental diversity in their own home communities.

References

Honey, M. (1999). *Ecotourism and sustainable development: Who owns paradise?* Washington DC: Island Press.

Joppe, M., & Dodds, R. (2000). *Urban green tourism: Applying ecotourism principles to the city.* Conference Proceedings of the 2000 Conference in Whitehorse, Canada. Travel and Tourism Research Association–Canada Chapter. Toronto, Canada.

LaFrance, A. (2010). The big picture. *Honolulu Weekly, 20*(6), 6–7.

Mak, J. (2008). *Developing a dream destination: Tourism and tourism policy planning in Hawai'i.* Honolulu: University of Hawai'i Press.

Orr, D. (1992). *Environmental literacy: Education and the transition to a post modern world.* Albany: State University of New York Press.

Primack, R. B., Bray, D., Galletti H. A., & Ponciano, I. (Eds.) (1998). *Timber, tourists, and temples: Conservation and development in the Maya Forest of Belize, Guatemala, and Mexico.* Washington DC: Island Press.

Taum, R. (2010). Tourism. In C. Howes & J. Osorio (Eds.). *The value of Hawai'i: Knowing the past, shaping the future.* Honolulu: University of Hawai'i Press.

Whatley, K. (2009). *Preserving paradise: Opportunities in volunteering for Hawai'i's environment.* Waipahu, HI: Island Heritage Publishing.

Whelan, T. (ed.). (1991). *Nature tourism: Managing for the environment.* Washington DC: Island Press.

12

WHO WILL TEACH THE TEACHERS?

Reorienting Teacher Education
for the Values of Sustainability

Patrick Howard

The 1992 Rio Earth Summit resulted in an action plan called Agenda 21 that outlined a set of principles and practices to assist governments and agencies in implementing sustainable development[1] policies and programs. Chapter 36 of Agenda 21 affirmed education as essential for making progress toward sustainable development. The United Nations Education, Science, and Cultural Organization (UNESCO) continues to promote the role of education in pursuing the kind of development that would respect the natural environment, cultures, and the ideals of social justice and equity. One of the major thrusts of education for sustainable development (ESD) is to reorient education at all levels to address sustainability issues. This includes rethinking and revising education from nursery schools through university to include the skills, knowledge, and values related to sustainability.

In 1998, realizing that teachers were crucial to the success of any effort to use education to promote sustainability, UNESCO initiated efforts to reorient teacher training. A UNESCO Chair on Reorienting Teacher Education to Address Sustainability was established at York University in Toronto, Canada, and an international network of 30 teacher education institutions in 28 countries began planning to move the initiative forward. It is not surprising that faculties of education and teacher educators are identified as "key change agents in reorienting education to address sustainability" (Hopkins & McKeown, 2005, p. 12). When we think about it, teachers and the education and preparation they receive are critical to any effort to use education, specifically schooling, to foster more sustainable societies. But this is where things get complex. Despite all the planning and policy, the consultations, the publications, and the initiatives carried out by committees, panels, and working groups, the success of any program relies on individuals. What will it take for faculties of education to integrate the tenets of ESD across course offerings and fully participate in preparing a new generation of teachers in the knowledge, skills, and attitudes to teach for the values of sustainability? Keep in mind that this generation of teachers will, in turn, prepare children and young people to be literate, creative individuals, fully participating in the cultural, social, and environmental health of their communities.

The architects of the UNESCO plan to reorient teacher education seem to be tacitly aware of the potential of motivating individuals by connecting with the lived experience of human beings. To understand how a community might best develop sustainably, it is essential to uncover the ontological possibilities that emerge from an understanding of historical traditions, unique cultural narratives, languages, and place-based ways of knowing and acting. The UNESCO document *Guidelines and Recommendations for Reorienting Teacher Education to Address Sustainability* (Hopkins & McKeown, 2005) states that "ESD is locally relevant and culturally appropriate, . . . is based on local needs, perceptions, and conditions but recognizes fulfilling local needs often has global effects and consequences" (p. 16). The document also contains unequivocal statements that "ESD is not imported from another cultural, economic, or geographic region . . . and [ESD] it is not 'one size fits all,' but must be created to account for regional differences" (p. 16). It is my premise that these statements, while valuable, need other statements. To teach effectively for the values of sustainability, the focus must be inclusive of local needs and issues, but it also must be firmly grounded in experience and in the relational. The view of sustainability, as put forward in the UNESCO document, is informed by ecological thinking. It is associated with a focus on relationships, interdependence, and interconnectedness, but only to a degree. The lived, felt, and relational dimensions of how we, as individuals, understand the interactive and dialogical dimensions of reality contribute powerful questions to elucidate even further an individual's relationship with the values of sustainability. Despite the differences that surround the use of the terms *sustainability* and *sustainable development*, the last 20 years has seen a dramatic increase in public awareness of the issues that affect the biotic community and cultural and linguistic diversity. The past two decades have been marked by an open debate of the long-held and previously unexamined assumptions about our relationships with the earth and the challenges to sustainability. The realization and acceptance that the human journey is an undeniably relational one has yet to be explored fully in the context of its contribution to reorienting education for the values of sustainability.

Teaching for Values

In the discussion about reorienting education for the values of sustainable development, there is no mention of the longstanding educational debate around the very possibility of whether values can be taught. However, the debate about values may very well offer a great deal to what teaching for the values of sustainability may look like. Space does not permit a full treatment of the philosophical debate about whether values can be taught; however, from the Greek Sophists to Plato and Aristotle, to Wittgenstein, Dewey, Whitehead and Noddings, each has put forward a "pedagogy of values" (Semetsky, 2010) designed to elucidate the aims of education and the sense that all education is, in essence, values education. The idea that values can be taught through direct instruction has generally been found to be erroneous, yet curriculum developers continue as if this finding were not so. Moral philosopher Mary Midgley (1996) has admonished those who espouse "wild and simple claims" (p. 78) on both sides of the issue; some suggest that values can be taught and tested, transmitted through textbook and facts as any other school subject and in any classroom, and some believe it is impossible to teach values at all. And yet we sense that values cannot be taught in the traditional sense, through textbooks and instruction, divorced from the value system and the modeling of the one who is instructing, that is, the teacher. Charles Silberman (1970) writes,

> Children are taught a lot of lessons about values, ethics, morality, character, and conduct every day of the week, less by the content of the curriculum than by the way schools are organized, the way teachers and parents behave, the way they talk to children and to each other, the kinds of behavior they approve [of] or reward, and the kinds they disapprove [of] or punish. These lessons are far more powerful than the verbalizations that accompany them and that they frequently controvert. (p. 9)

Other people's influence makes a difference. Wittgenstein said, "What can be shown cannot be said" (Kenny, 2006, p. 37). In other words, values are communicated by showing, by doing and modeling and not by saying or verbalizing such values. Aristotle contends that the best way to find out what is right or wrong is to look at the behavior of a moral person. Our attitudes toward the environment are beginning to change and they continue to change; our choices about food, consumption, transportation, and cultural and linguistic pluralism require new ways of thinking. This thinking and the requisite change in behavior is difficult, often too difficult to perform on our own. We need help from outside, books and teachers who live and model the value system being fostered coming together to sustain and support the other.

Teacher education may be reoriented for the values of sustainability, but it can be undertaken only with a clear understanding of what these values are and how people best learn these values. In outlining the specific values of sustainable development, the ESD Toolkit (McKeown, 2002) refers to the Earth Charter as a reference point, recognizing that values taught in school need to reflect "the larger values of the society that surrounds the school . . . [A] full range of values influenced by local traditions, aboriginal groups, ethnic populations, immigrants, religions, media and pop culture will be revealed, inventoried and considered for relation to and inclusion in ESD" (p. 23). The Earth Charter (2001) sets out four basic values, or commitments, and 16 key principles that flow out of the basic values. The four broad commitments are respect and care for the community of life; ecological integrity; social and economic justice; democracy, nonviolence, and peace (Earth Charter, 2001, p. 2). The document *Guidelines and Recommendations for Reorienting Teacher Education to Address Sustainability* (Hopkins & McKeown, 2005) outlines practical strategies for national, regional, and community involvement in fostering these values. Recommendations on change within institutions of higher education and within faculties of education include funding, research, partnerships, and communication. These are worthwhile suggestions, but when we are designing transformational teaching practices to influence values the "[r]ecommendations on change related to engaging pre-service and in-service teachers" (Hopkins & McKeown, 2005, p. 43) are especially significant. It is recommended that teacher educators request that preservice teachers "analyze the mandated curriculum they will be teaching to identify themes related to sustainability" and "provide student teachers with opportunities to explore their own values and attitudes towards local sustainability problems while encouraging critical thinking and decision making that influence personal lifestyle and economic choices" (p. 44). These are key recommendations and allow teacher educators and preservice teachers the opportunity to access the personal and the experiential, but they do not go far enough.

If student teachers are to teach for the values of sustainability, they must be encouraged to question whether education, in its current form, may be an obstacle to realizing sustainable communities. These communities can only be fostered within an educational framework that is "visionary and transformative and must clearly go beyond the conventional educational outlooks we have cultivated over the past several centuries" (O'Sullivan, 1999, p. 4). For example, rather than simply analyzing the mandated curriculum for themes that support the values of sustainability, student teachers must also be encouraged to inquire about how curriculum guides, textbooks, classroom practices, and teacher beliefs, as the main conveyors of curriculum in the classroom, may become tools in the perpetuation of values in conflict with values of sustainability. Textbooks, including novels; current classroom practices; and teacher beliefs should be analyzed to determine embedded cultural assumptions that may or may not support education for the values of sustainability.

In Atlantic Canada, most of the recently developed curriculum documents introduce environmental science as a course of study in high school, while throughout all grades environmental education emphasizes technology, trade, and resources. Children learn about the natural world and appropriate human–environment relationships as a subset of the science curriculum. Most often, it is a biological approach with a strong focus on efficient use and wise management of resources. The underlying belief of curriculum developers is that, by understanding our reliance on the natural environment, researching endangered species, calculating ecological footprints, and memorizing the *R*s in the recycling process, our children will become ecologically literate and sensitive citizens. Can we nurture the values of sustainability by dissecting owl pellets or by diagramming the water cycle? Science reduces: Reductionism is invaluable to scientists; it is what they do. It is indispensable to all of us. But what happens most often in dissecting the owl pellet is that the owl disappears and the mouse that was her meal disappears. In the categorizing of our ocean resources, the cod disappears. In the quest for empirical certainty, in reducing an entity, a species, to its constituent parts, it disappears in abstraction. The creature is lost; the individual and the unique are lost.

Without a doubt, science has its place in environmental education. The abstraction, the impersonal, the objectifying stance of science can help us know *some things* with a degree of certainty. It has produced an invaluable body of knowledge about intricate ecological systems, the value of species, and the complexity of species diversity. The firm hope of curriculum developers is that this approach will inculcate in children a knowledge that results in a sensitive, respectful, and restrained use of nature, namely, the values of sustainability. Scientific study provides information on which we base decisions that will directly affect the health and well-being of this planet, and in turn, each of its inhabitants. However, the knowledge gained in this way forces us to ask, In what way do our children *know* the living Earth and what *value* do they give it? Wendell Berry (2000) says, "We know enough of our history by now to be aware that people *exploit* what they have merely concluded to be of value, but they *defend* what they love" (p. 39). Does the technical, resource-based bias of the sciences, with its dispassionate, objectifying language, make it incapable of bearing the burden we place on it? This is the type of question student teachers must be encouraged to confront.

These concerns motivated Marilyn Doerr (2004) to adapt William Pinar's (1975) *currere* (autobiographical reflection on educational experiences that shape self-understanding) for implementation in a high school science-based ecology course. Doerr developed a practice she called environmental autobiography to counterbalance the mechanistic objectification of the scientific approach as a means to let students "begin to emotionally connect" with the environment. Doerr explains what happened in her ecology class:

> During the times we were exploring the basic scientific principles of ecology, we were also exploring the interior lives of people interested in ecology—themselves. . . . I needed to find something that would move my students from "I know" to "I care." (2004, pp. 30, 31)

Caring and the Pedagogical Relation

Any efforts to foster in preservice teachers the requisite skills, knowledge, attitudes, and beliefs to teach for the values of sustainable development must be firmly grounded in the relational. The work of Noddings in care theory (1984, 2002) can help us better understand how the values of sustainability may best be attained by preservice teachers. Van Manen's (1991, 2002) phenomenological interpretation of pedagogy offers teacher educators a deeper sense of how to structure learning opportunities in faculties of education.

The attainment of the values of sustainability is not commensurate with the knowledge we possess. Critical pedagogy (Kahn, 2010) addresses the underlying structures responsible for the current crises; students engage in deconstructing and unpacking the assumptions largely responsible for our current crises. There is no doubt that this education in sociopolitical analysis is vital. However, the ability to critique must include not only building a knowledge base around these issues but also a deeper sensibility for the losses we have experienced from being separated from each other and from nature because of cultural ideologies predicated on competition, individualism, aggression, and consumerism. Efforts are underway to structure such learning experiences in faculties of education. (See chapter 4.) While the critique is necessary, we must, as Doerr says, be moved from *I know* to *I care*.

Noddings's work on care theory (2002) posits that values cannot be taught directly but are "defined situationally and relationally" (p. 2). We, as carers, Noddings believes, attend because we want to; "we love the ones who address us or [we] have sufficient positive regard for them, or the request is so consonant with ordinary life that no inner conflict occurs" (p. 13). Noddings describes this encounter as one of "natural caring." The *I must* is an expression of desire, not a recognition of duty. Central to Noddings's work are her components of values education: modeling, dialogue, practice, and confirmation (pp. 15–20). Modeling the values of sustainability as a way of being in the world allows teacher educators to communicate the values as they are lived in the classroom. Teacher educators who are committed to and practice interdisciplinary coursework, support participatory learning, seek ways to incorporate shared decision making, provide opportunities for teachers to reflect on their own values, and explore issues around local sustainability provide powerful opportunities to foster the values of sustainability. Van Manen (1991) calls this the living out of a relational commitment to students and "the possibility of a new pedagogy" (p. 3). This new pedagogy requires us to "stand in a relationship of thoughtfulness and openness to young people rather than being governed by traditional beliefs, discarded values, old rules and fixed impositions" (p. 3).

The second component, dialogue as open-ended, careful listening and attending, is "the most fundamental component of the care model" (Noddings, 2002, p. 16). It is also at the heart of van Manen's (1991) interpretation of the pedagogical relation (p. 83). Attending to the other, to thoughts, feelings, memories, and experiences as they come out of conversation or out of response to reading, may serve as a space to deepen a student teacher's

understanding of her or his place in the world. Dialogue called for by literature will inevitably involve questions that require knowledge, reasoning, and
even debate. But it is important that we not close off further questioning
with so-called conclusive answers. The efforts to reorient education for the
values of sustainability require an unlearning and a relearning. They call for
developing awareness that how we relate to the world and each other is
socially constructed and that education is a major purveyor of hegemonic
practices and beliefs. Preparing children based on corporate-type models of
management and efficiency (Gerstner, Semrod, & Doyle, 1995), structuring
their days in relentless pursuit of higher standardized test scores through
a competitive ethos that prefers individualism and undermines a different
consciousness, leads to preservice teacher education that simply mirrors this
wrongheaded approach. It is doubtful much can be accomplished in fostering the values of sustainability within the same consciousness that is largely
responsible for the problems in the first place. The education of the young,
and by default the education of the teachers responsible for our children's
learning, must reflect a different consciousness than one that sees the
destruction of cultures, languages, and the earth as inevitable by-products of
so-called progress. We must educate so we see ourselves as part of the web of
life, not simply isolated, self-maximizing individuals. David G. Smith (1994)
warns, "As adults we inevitably suffer the cultural diseases of our time, but
then reproduce them in our children to the degree we have not healed ourselves" (p. ii). The work of reorienting teacher education for the values of
sustainability is crucial to creating a new understanding of ourselves and our
place in communities, in the living world, and in traditions of relational
reciprocity that will sustain us all.

Note

1. Since the publication of *Our Common Future* in 1987 by the World Commission on Environment and Development, the term *sustainable development* has taken
a central place in environmental policy making. Yet the term is highly contested.
Some see the concept as highly original and as representing an innovative direction
in environmental thought, and some trace the concept back to the ancient Greeks.
On the other hand, sustainable development is viewed by some scholars to be an
ambiguous term representing anthropocentric, technical solutions to environmental
problems. Ironically, the solutions of sustainable development, say these critics, is
born of the same paradigm that caused the problems in the first place.

References

Berry, W. (2000). *Life is a miracle: An essay against modern superstition*. Washington, DC: Counterpoint.

Doerr, M. (2004). Currere *and the environmental autobiography: A phenomenological approach to teaching ecology*. New York: Peter Lang.

Earth Charter. (2001). Retrieved from http://www.earthcharterinaction.org/content/

Gerstner, L., Semrod, R., & Doyle, D. (1995). *Reinventing education: Entrepreneurship in America's public schools*. New York: Penguin.

Hopkins, C., & McKeown, R. (2005). *Guidelines and recommendations for reorienting teacher education to address sustainability*. Retrieved from www.unesco.org/education/desd

Kahn, R. (2010). *Critical pedagogy, ecoliteracy and planetary crisis: The ecopedagogy movement*. New York: Peter Lang.

Kenny, A. (2006). *Wittgenstein*. Oxford, England: Blackwell Publishing.

McKeown, R. (2002). *ESD Toolkit*. Retrieved from www.unesco.org/education/desd

Midgley, M. (1996). Can education be moral? *Res publica, (2)*1, 77–85.

Noddings, N. (1984). *Caring: A feminine approach to ethics and moral education*. Berkeley: University of California Press.

Noddings, N. (2002). *Educating moral people: A caring alternative to character education*. New York: Teachers College Press.

O'Sullivan, E. (1999). *Transformative learning: Educational vision for the 21st century*. Toronto: University of Toronto Press.

Pinar, W. (1975). *Currere:* Toward reconceptualization. In W. Pinar (Ed.), *Curriculum theorizing: The reconceptualists* (pp. 396–414). Berkeley, CA: McCutchan.

Semetsky, I. (2010). The folds of experience, or: Constructing the pedagogy of values. *Educational Philosophy and Theory, 42*(4), 476–488.

Silberman, C. (1970). *Crisis in the classroom*. New York: Random House.

Smith, D. (1994). *Pedagon: Meditations on pedagogy and culture*. Bragg Creek, Alberta, Canada: Makyo Press.

van Manen, M. (1991). *The tact of teaching: The meaning of pedagogical thoughtfulness*. London, Ontario: Althouse Press.

van Manen, M. (2002). *The tone of teaching*. London, Ontario: Althouse Press.

PART THREE

EDUCATION AS A
SUSTAINABLE PRACTICE

13

E-PORTFOLIOS IN A LIBERAL STUDIES PROGRAM

An Experiment in Sustainability

P. Sven Arvidson

I magine you are a program director at a medium-size university. What would you do if you were required to set up e-portfolios for each student in the program, starting two months from now with 30 students? There is no precedent for e-portfolios on campus, and university resources at your disposal do not include any funding. There is lots of goodwill and perhaps a graduate assistant, but you are starting from scratch. Provosts, deans, and the student development office are keenly following your progress because learning technology and assessment are priorities in their multiyear plans.

This was the position in which I found myself as the new director for the liberal studies program at Seattle University and the first teacher of the e-portfolio–imbued course. As a result of self-study and program review, the program plan was to initiate and sustain e-portfolios to focus interdisciplinary work for new majors. There were no campus examples to emulate and no monetary resources for the launch or maintenance of the project. I chose sustainability as the guiding principle, and defined it as efficient support and continuation of a good in common. According to the *Oxford English Dictionary* (OED), the word *sustain* is from the Latin *sustinere*, from *sub-* ("from below") and *tenere* ("hold"). In other words, to sustain is to support, and current ecological usage of sustainability adds the concept of efficiency. To "efficient support," I have added "continuation of a good in common." According to the OED, *to sustain* is "to cause to continue for an extended period of time" (hence, "continuation") and to "uphold, affirm, or confirm the justice or validity of" (hence, "of a good in common" because something just is assumed to be commonly worthwhile). The key to this definition of sustainability as the efficient support and continuation of a good in common is the common good. As a program initiative in learning and teaching, we see our e-portfolios sustaining a common good among students, professors, the director, the university, and ultimately the larger community in the student's life after college.

This chapter is a practitioner-based report on sustainability of the e-portfolios. After setting the context, it addresses resource conservation, intellectual development, alumni mission fulfillment, and curricular assessment. It ends with a reflection on the e-portfolio experiment, and it includes three appendices reproducing the e-portfolio introduction and assignments as students saw them.

The Context

The context for the e-portfolio is the liberal studies program, and the context for the program is Seattle University's mission. Seattle University (SU), a Jesuit Catholic school, is the largest independent university in the Pacific Northwest. As part of its mission, it is "dedicated to educating the whole person, to professional formation, and to empowering leaders for a just and humane world." The liberal studies program has 80 to 100 majors, 30% of whom desire to become elementary school teachers, and aligns itself closely with the SU mission through its definition of liberal studies and its learning objectives.

As defined at SU, liberal studies is the interdisciplinary study of the arts and sciences, and it links cognitive advancement and civic engagement in a way that cultivates humanity. There are four major learning outcomes in three areas:

Area of Jesuit Catholic mission
- Demonstrate an awareness of the Jesuit Catholic commitment to social justice

Area of interdisciplinary scholarship
- Demonstrate skills of project management, including self-directed research, critical thinking, problem solving, and written and oral communication

- Demonstrate the ability to bring two or more disciplines, intellectual approaches, or methods to bear on problems or issues of contemporary concern

Area of education
- Demonstrate a critical appreciation of the meaning of education and the role of education in developing effective civic engagement

The e-portfolio supports these outcomes by encouraging reflection and metacognition.

Liberal studies majors select from a variety of courses from other departments, within the categories of advanced writing, natural science, math, humanities, and social sciences. At the heart of the major, five sequentially arranged courses emanate from the liberal studies program. At the time of the e-portfolio launch, most of the five were new courses, never before taught, including the first in the sequence, Introduction to Liberal Studies, where the e-portfolio is introduced to students. With the program and university contexts in place, we are at the focus. I was the teacher of that first course that tried to bring the e-portfolio onto campus in the spring of 2010 with 30 new majors.

Typically, an e-portfolio is a place for students to show who they are and to display their work with reflective commentary. In this program, we wanted students to show written, critical reflection on the SU mission (and hence the Jesuit Catholic mission) and to show reflection on their own academic work. This last piece is the metacognitive thrust that underlies the whole idea of an e-portfolio in this major and that supports the goal of appreciation for the meaning and role of education. That is, we want students to think about thinking, to reflect on what it means to be a student, learner, or teacher.

I unabashedly followed the model of e-portfolios at LaGuardia Community College in New York. This model included the following content pages in each e-portfolio: Welcome, About Me, Coursework/Projects, Educational Goals, Résumé, Links, and Contact. I used Google Sites to create a basic e-portfolio site for each student and a series of milestones to scaffold the project throughout the term (see the chapter appendices).

Resource Conservation

I had to decide whether to have a paper portfolio stored in a binder or an e-portfolio stored on a website. There were certain advantages to a paper portfolio, including simplicity and enhanced privacy. But the e-portfolio has less environmental impact, which was a deciding factor. At inception, each portfolio could easily be 50 pages long, with personal reflections; introductions; dividers; and perhaps papers from other courses, poems, short stories, commentary, artwork, and more. Multiply this by two or three years until graduation for each new crop of majors, and the portfolio can be about 100 pages by end of senior year. To multiply this by 100 majors at any one time yields about 10,000 pages of student work.

Because the e-portfolio is a paperless solution, it is easily organized and stored. Self-studies and program reviews use electronic student reflection on work, anytime, anywhere, rather than in print. In addition to paper, the resource saved here is faculty and staff member time.

The main result of striving for resource conservation was the choice of Google Sites to host the e-portfolios. Google Sites is free software, which means resource savings. Second, students know Google by experience or reputation and so there was little resistance to the platform, thus saving time needed to convince students of the relevance of the project. Third, using Google Sites meant that the e-portfolios were accessible from anywhere the student might be, although other platforms probably could make the same claim. Fourth, the technology is stable, in my experience. There were very few technical problems, which meant a potential time savings for professor and students alike. Fifth, if one knows HTML language, one can tinker behind the scenes, but such tinkering is very limited. Thus, the platform is flexible enough to allow students and professors to customize the e-portfolios, but not too flexible that users get lost in options, wasting lots of time. Finally, Google Sites has many themes, colors, and fonts, which allows students to customize the look of their site without breaking the site structure set up by the professor.

Using Google Sites for e-portfolios has serious shortcomings and liabilities. The first problem is the social openness of Google Sites. My 30 student e-portfolios, created in a folder called "Liberal Studies Majors," are not insulated from other sites created in SU Google Sites. Google Sites is set up so that all university students, faculty members, staff members, alumni— anyone with a university e-mail account—can create a website or e-portfolio inside or outside "Liberal Studies Majors." This could be a potential problem. For example, a student could falsely pose as a liberal studies major, or create an "I Hate E-Portfolios" site, or worse.

A second problem is that there are essentially three sharing or privacy settings: (1) No one views your e-portfolio except you or others you personally invite through e-mail—for example, a friend, parent, or potential employer—and this other person does not have to have an SU e-mail account; (2) anyone with an SU e-mail account can view any e-portfolio, which essentially includes the rest of the university; and (3) anyone in the world can log on and view the e-portfolios. In other words, an instructor can't easily set the privacy setting so that only the 30 students (and program faculty) can view each other's e-portfolios. For sharing, my strategy was to set (as the default) each student's e-portfolio to "share with anyone at SU" and gently discourage students from changing it to "share with anyone in the world." My reasoning was that this allowed students to see each other's e-portfolios, but it shrank the possible viewers to about 10,000 (the extended university community). The fact is that no one was consistently using Google Sites at Seattle University. One year later, the liberal studies program remains the only real user of the software on campus.

A related decision I had to make regarded the ownership of the e-portfolio. At site creation and anytime thereafter, Google lets one name the owners. At origination of a particular student's e-portfolio, I named myself, the graduate assistant, and that student as co-owners. As I create student e-portfolios one year later for the new majors and new professor, I named myself (as director), the new professor, the new graduate assistant, and the student as co-owners—four persons in all. This means that any of us can change anything on the e-portfolio itself or delete the entire e-portfolio. Any owner can delete the other owners! Like most pedagogical risk-taking, a lot of trust is required between student and professor. This is one reason why the context and student buy-in to the e-portfolios is so important. (See Appendix A to learn how the e-portfolio project was introduced to students.) The fact that a rebellious student can delete the professor and graduate assistant from his or her e-portfolio is unsettling. But there is no choice if the student is to have full creative options, such as changing themes. Such freedom of self-expression seems appropriate at the college level (for example, students can choose from more than 50 unique themes, e.g., Sand, Parchment, Mint Chip). In Google Sites, if the student is not a co-owner, the student can still be allowed to edit text. However, he or she is locked out of choosing themes, which means the professor or graduate assistant must serve as mediator for self-expression. Because the ability to change the look of the site to distinguish it and to express personality seems important to student satisfaction, I will continue to set the student as co-owner.

A third major problem is that there is a gray area about who owns the site and is responsible for its content, and the small print makes it appear that Google has rights to content. This means that one of the great advantages of e-portfolios—posting actual work, not just reflections on it—is possible but not recommended. When the same assignment is used for assessment at different times in a student's career (see the mission reflection assignment in Alumni Mission Fulfillment later in this chapter) current students would get to see previous students' work. Because of the "share with anyone at SU" setting discussed earlier in this chapter, all university students have access to existing e-portfolios. And new majors are directed to see previous students' e-portfolios as inspiration for creating their own. Making the original papers available discourages originality and encourages plagiarism. Also, faculty members from all over campus would have papers from their courses posted in the student's e-portfolio. It is impractical to obtain permission for each of these. One could also imagine that excellent papers could easily be downloaded off the e-portfolio site and sold to students around the globe. Originally, in the first course that involved e-portfolios, I instructed students to post their actual papers on their e-portfolio. By the second course in the series that used the e-portfolio, I realized my mistake after talking to other administrators. In this second course, I instructed these same students to delete their actual papers from the site. For those students who failed to meet the deadline for this deletion, I did it for them. I explained to the students in the class that I was concerned about how their work might be used by others, and they agreed.

Intellectual Development

In interdisciplinary work, the student or scholar succeeds better with a kind of self-awareness about styles of inquiry, methodological approaches, and intellectual biases. Our liberal studies program attempts to support the self-awareness needed for good interdisciplinary work through the e-portfolio. In support of learning outcomes, the primary goal of the e-portfolio is developing the capacity for intellectual growth, and the means for achieving this goal is metacognition. By getting students to think about thinking, they are encouraged not just to be a student but to understand and express what it is to be a student. The e-portfolio project supports and continues this intellectual growth efficiently through requiring reflective commentary on coursework and projects throughout the student's career in the major.

It would be a moderate disaster to start an e-portfolio project in a major, with the hope that it should develop over the student's career, and then have it die after the first course. This is where sustainability enters the area of intellectual development for students. Sustainability, defined as efficient support and continuation of a good in common, applies to the continuation of the e-portfolio throughout the required sequence of courses that a student takes. This is difficult because courses vary in type, from intense service learning to intense research, and the full-time and part-time contract faculty members teaching the courses are also diverse in their willingness or ability to blend the e-portfolio into their syllabus.

My solution, described in this chapter, involves baby steps in unrolling the e-portfolio for this group of students. The class in which the e-portfolio is introduced—Introduction to Liberal Studies—is a prerequisite for the next-term class called Methods of Interdisciplinary Research. This creates a kind of inside-the-major cohort: students who move together from one course to the next. If the same professor who started them on e-portfolios in the first course can also teach this follow-up course, then the continuation of the e-portfolio is natural, assumed, and immediately reinforced for students. I have been able to do this for the first cohort by assigning an e-portfolio update task in the second course. This year, another professor is teaching these two courses, again as a kind of cohort, to sustain the e-portfolio learning project. In the second course, students were asked to do two things to update their e-portfolio. First, they updated information on any page of the e-portfolio. The desired outcome was to simply reconnect them to the e-portfolio after the term break. Second, in light of the major (research) project required in the new term, each student was required to reflect on and then write in the e-portfolio about her or his progress and challenges. These reflections were 300 words or so written at midterm and again at the end of the course. The desired outcome was to have students step back and assess in reflective writing their learning and development in the course. Also, this reflection allowed me to assess any individual student's reactions and progress.

Although students reflect on work in other liberal studies courses and courses in other departments in their e-portfolio, the professors of those other courses do not know students are doing this reflection. So the real challenge in sustainability lies beyond this two-course cohort. Ideally, each required course in the major would assign students some work having to do with the e-portfolio. Realistically, the e-portfolio work will likely be confined to these two courses, Introduction and Methods, and then the final capstone course, Senior Synthesis. At least this brackets the e-portfolio experience with Introduction and Senior Synthesis, with *Method* in between.

Alumni Mission Fulfillment

Every university wants their alumni to represent the university well, which essentially means exemplifying the success of its mission. This e-portfolio experiment is trying to support this in two ways. First, majors are required to write a reflective paper based on the university mission and post a 300-word reflection on the paper once it is graded and returned. Second, program faculty members and students work with career services staff members to transition the e-portfolio from academic to vocational. I discuss each of these two in turn. The goal is to sustain the moral and intellectual character of the student through his or her transition to a career.

The first way to try to ensure university mission fulfillment is to have students assess, formally and critically, the role of the mission in their lives. This mission assignment is nearly identical in the first required course (Introduction) and in the capstone course (Senior Synthesis). After the student's five-page paper is returned, he or she posts a 300-word reflection on the paper to the e-portfolio. This e-portfolio reflection on the five-page paper is therefore a metacognitive activity.

The assignment itself asks students to reflect on the university mission and various related readings. The students are told to "find and express the nexus between these readings and who you are as a student and a person." They are also directed to include a full, personal mission statement at the end of the paper. Students in the Senior Synthesis course are encouraged to consult their previous product from this assignment in the lower-level course in order to encourage an awareness of subsequent development. So the first piece in the puzzle to support university mission fulfillment is to make sure that students know the mission, can critically reflect on it, and have attempted to relate it to who they are and who they want to be.

The second piece is for faculty members, students, and staff members to join in transitioning the e-portfolio from academic to vocational. Again, with the definition of sustainability as efficient support and continuation of a good in common, the goal is to sustain the relevance of the mission *after* graduation. Frankly, we have not yet reached this goal, in part because the e-portfolio is still less than a year old. The university has invested in and hosts an impressive alumni network, however, where former students can connect with employers and companies. Alumni can also post their résumés on the online alumni network. The theory is that the upper-class students will transition the student e-portfolio into an alumni e-portfolio.

The reality is that the most we can do right now is use the student e-portfolio to encourage vocational discernment. The reflective aspect of the e-portfolio encourages this vocational discernment, as does the requirement to post a résumé and educational goals. The use of the e-portfolio in the Senior Synthesis course should also boost reflection on career choices after undergraduate education because it is the course in which students most acutely face life after college. In Google Sites, students can invite prospective employers to view their e-portfolio (none of this first group has done so at this point). So the second way to support university mission fulfillment is to make sure that students explore vocational possibilities by including a résumé and vocational reflections while it is still a student e-portfolio. It is hoped that this connection between vocation and education (and institutional mission) is maintained at some level as the student develops a career.

Curricular Assessment

Efficiency is a large part of sustainability. No one wants to do work twice or try to re-create data after it has been unnecessarily lost. Our liberal studies program will be using the e-portfolios to aid longitudinal and cross-sectional assessments of learning, making program reviews and self-studies more about reflection than reconstructing lost data.

I have already mentioned a major piece of the longitudinal assessment of learning: the identical mission assignment in the introduction and capstone courses in the major. This assignment directly addresses one of the four major learning outcomes: the one about the Jesuit Catholic mission of social justice. As director, I receive all these assignments electronically and store them. It becomes empirical evidence, a strong, readily available before-and-after statement of learning for deans, university-wide committees, self-study, accreditation preparation, or program review.

The e-portfolio contains student reflections on their own learning over time, at least loosely chronicling their learning in the major or in general. So the e-portfolio offers additional longitudinal evidence of the other learning outcomes in the major having to do with managing and executing interdisciplinary work and with educational metacognition. All of this is readily available in the e-portfolio.

As a teacher, I can immediately see the impact of a particular assignment in the course once it is handed back with grading and comments, and the students must now post a reflection on the assignment. I can sample a number of reflective entries by students to get a cross-sectional view of how the assignment was approached by students, and how they feel about it after the fact. As a director, I can do the same at a higher level. For example, in the second offering of the introductory course, another professor will be leading a new group of majors through the e-portfolio process. I can check at various points in the term, view e-portfolios, and make some general assessments about how the course is going. In fact, as we prepare to launch that course, I find myself in the position of being the information technology person for the course to ensure the standardization of the e-portfolio format and content in the major.

Finally, students assessed the e-portfolio project and generally found it valuable. In my view, the key to the success of this e-portfolio experiment is trust. Successfully instituting e-portfolios in the curriculum in a major takes an incredible amount of trust between students and the instructor so that the project is seen as worthwhile from the beginning.

Reflections on the E-Portfolio Experiment

Interdisciplinary programs, such as liberal studies, are often poorly understood by other chairs, directors, or even deans. This can result in problems of perception concerning program status in a college division, academic rigor, and goals of the degree. Therefore, such programs must find ways to be leaders in innovation on their campuses. An e-portfolio that supports learning outcomes in the major is one way to lead in innovation if conditions allow. Our experiment has received positive university-level recognition for the liberal studies program on our campus.

Professors and directors should know the benefits and liabilities before proceeding with this experiment. The following list captures what I discovered.

Professor benefits: the e-portfolio
- Adds significant extracurricular dimension to courses
- Encourages student reflection on current coursework
- Reveals students as individuals
- Makes courses appear more relevant and current

Professor liabilities: the e-portfolio
- Must be incorporated as a legitimate part of courses
- Technology learning curve can be steep, even for a tech-savvy professor

- Preparation, planning of sites, and organization of information in sites for students consumes valuable time
- Raises questions of privacy and ownership of content
- Continuation through the student's career is not guaranteed, and the e-portfolio could be a one-time event

Director benefits: the e-portfolio
- Makes possible various simple, easily accessible, longitudinal and cross-sectional assessments
- Makes advising more personalized and efficient
- Makes the major appear relevant and current
- Functions as a unique recruiting tool for the major because it can be a market differentiator

Director liabilities: the e-portfolio
- Adds responsibilities around curriculum, technology, and legal and moral issues
- Requires training and advising of department faculty members for use in courses
- Requires specific, problem-solving capacities in Web technologies
- Taxes existing faculty and staff resources without additional compensation

The future of e-portfolios at Seattle University and in the Liberal Studies program is not guaranteed. Administrators are working on an e-portfolio for all university students tied to a new core curriculum (and I have received valuable advice from them along the way). This could take years to implement. In the meantime, Google could change its policies or Seattle University could change its unstated policy of allowing me to use Google for e-portfolios. In that case, I could just go to another vendor. But moving the active e-portfolios, which could number in the hundreds in the next several years, would be prohibitive. It may require a complete overhaul of the HTML coding—for each e-portfolio. I will continue with the experiment, however, because it serves my student learning outcomes and my program very well, for now.

E-PORTFOLIO: INTRODUCTION

Overview

Liberal Studies (LBST) 201 introduces you to the two main aspects of liberal studies as a discipline; the philosophy, history, and social context of the interdisciplinary pursuit of scholarly projects; and the reflection on what it means to be a responsible intellectual. Supporting the reflective aspect, the e-portfolio is a process that involves you in thinking about thinking—a metacognitive reflection on being a student. An essential part of this reflection is a required portion of your e-portfolio dedicated to reflection on the SU mission in light of its Jesuit Catholic tradition. The portfolio project introduced in this foundational course, and the metacognitive element native to liberal studies as a discipline and embedded in each required course, help you discern the arc of your career in the major.

For students interested in a career in education, the portfolio project can become a teaching portfolio, which has long been recognized as a valuable tool in teacher education. Through the portfolio project, you can reflect on your accomplishments as you head toward academic, personal, and vocational discernment.

E-portfolio and the Curriculum

- Each LBST class is project-centered, and projects are well known as the best learning model for interdisciplinary work. No other majors at SU are explicitly project-centered, and this distinguishes the major. The liberal studies program is a campus leader, and so are you.
- In this course, the e-portfolio is the main project. It is the only project in the major designed to sustain your academic life through to the Senior Synthesis.
- You may invite potential employers or references to view your e-portfolio. They will be able to see you in your best light, as a student

and as a person. There can be a purposeful progression from an academic to a vocational e-portfolio.

Expectations and Criteria

- Creativity is encouraged, but the page titles—Welcome, About Me, Coursework and Projects, Educational Goals, Résumé, Links, Contact—must remain.
- Criteria will develop as we go.
  - The most important part of your e-portfolio project is the Coursework and Projects page. You can already start posting reflections there if you like.
  - The work you post is accompanied by a brief description of the assignment and reflective commentary on it.
  - Your first *required* posting of your reflection on your work will have to do with your mission assignment.

FIRST MILESTONE

Due: **Wednesday, April 28 by 4:00.** Late completion of the First Milestone will affect final grade.

There is nothing to submit; professor will simply view your e-portfolio.

Instructions

1. Post three reflections for three assignments for Coursework and Projects page, including Mission Paper. At least one of the three assignments must be from a non-LBST course. For each assignment, describe the assignment instructions and reflect on your work on the assignment.
2. Complete the Sidebar (see later in this appendix)
3. Complete the Welcome page (see later in this appendix)
4. Complete the About Me page (see later in this appendix)
5. Complete the Contact page (see later in this appendix)

General Criteria and Guidelines for E-Portfolio

These criteria may be changed by the professor as the e-portfolio project develops; for example, additional criteria may be added.

Timeliness—Deliver Milestones on time.

Style—Be consistent between and within pages; for example, don't use 14-point Verdana on one page and 10-point Times New Roman on another. You can still be creative.

Navigation/Organization—Finding information and getting from page to page must be simple. Links you have added, for example, on your Coursework and Projects page, must work and be uniform.

Page Text—Text must be grammatically correct, informative, reflective, and inviting and can be playful.

Page Completion

Coursework and Projects—Build to at least six assignments, including Mission Paper and three non-LBST courses. Each must recount assignment instructions and a reflection about your work on the assignment.

Sidebar—This page should include your photo (if not, talk to professor about it), name, e-mail address, and navigation links to all main pages.

Welcome—This page should be inviting. The text should welcome viewers to the site.

About Me—This page should be informative and personalized, and should tell your story.

Educational Goals—Your goals should be informative and somewhat specific.

Résumé—Your résumé should be as developed as possible. Beware of posting your address and phone number.

Links—You should have between four to seven links to other sites. Each link should be annotated briefly to explain what the site is and why you have featured it.

Contact—Include your e-mail or other forms of contact. The professor strongly discourages posting phone numbers and addresses.

FINAL MILESTONE

Due: **Wednesday, June 2, by 4:00 (our last class day).** Late completion will affect final grade.

There is nothing to submit; professor will simply view your e-portfolio.

General Criteria

Seven Pages—You must have the following pages in this order: Welcome, About Me, Coursework and Projects, Educational Goals, Résumé, Links, and Contact.

Timeliness—Deliver Milestones on time.

Style—Be consistent between and within pages; for example, don't use 14-point Verdana on one page and 10-point Times New Roman on another. You can still be creative.

Navigation/Organization—Finding information and getting from page to page must be simple. The links you have added, for example, on your Coursework and Projects page, must work and be uniform.

Page Text—Text must be grammatically correct, informative, reflective, and inviting and can be playful.

Complete Online Assessment—By June 2, 4:00 p.m., go to the e-portfolio site, click on the Assessment link, and complete it.

Page Completion Criteria

Coursework and Projects—Your Coursework and Projects page will eventually include reflections on at least six assignments. One of these must be the Liberal Studies, SU mission paper. For the rest, include three assignments from non-LBST courses. Each must have an assignment description and reflection. The assignment description reports in your own words what the task was and what you were asked to do by the professor. The assignment reflection is a metacognitive report concerning the assignment.

Sidebar—Your Sidebar page should have your photo, name, e-mail address, and navigation links to all main pages.

Welcome—Your Welcome page should be inviting. Text should welcome viewers to the site. The Welcome page will be less detailed than the About Me page.

About Me—The About Me page should tell your story. It should be informative and personalized. It is more specific than the Welcome page. Remember the general criterion of good grammar. No one wants the impression "about me" to be "I can't write well"!

Educational Goals—Your Educational Goals page should be informative and somewhat specific. Think about near-term goals, such as courses you are looking forward to or skills you are hoping to enhance. Long-term goals can include books, travel, and the transition from academic to vocational discernment.

Résumé—Your Résumé page should have your résumé as an attachment (preferably in .pdf format but Word is okay) and it should have a brief summary (50 word or less) of what one will find on your résumé. The résumé could include your vocational goals or skills, or a listing of work experience. Staff members at the SU Career Center can help you construct or enhance your résumé. Make an appointment to work with a professional at the Career Center. Beware of posting your address or phone number on the Web. The professor is not recommending that you post these types of personal contact information.

Links—Your Links page should have from four to seven links to other sites. Each link should be annotated briefly to indicate what the site is and why you have chosen to feature it.

Contact—Your Contact page should have your e-mail address or other form of contact information. The professor is not recommending that you put your address or your phone number on this site.

14

THE PAPERLESS CLASSROOM

Justin Pettibone and Kirsten Allen Bartels

Engagement with one's larger community is a common theme in the classes offered by Grand Valley State University (GVSU) and the liberal studies department where we teach. Spending our semesters teaching the importance of taking society's problems seriously and the importance of acting on behalf of these problems got us to look internally, and we found an area for us to practice what we preach. We decided that we could experiment with more responsible ways of teaching by confronting the large amounts of paper we had to produce (copying and printing) during the course of the semester.

This initial observation was the spur to several conversations between the two of us. At first, these conversations were often fatalistic laments at how much paper we were using, followed by (perhaps a bit defensively) a half-hearted justification for it because neither of us knew whether or how we could change our paper use. Our excuses were perhaps familiar: "I don't want to risk becoming less effective in my teaching" or "I'm just not that tech savvy to rely on computers for everything!" But after two semesters of these conversations, we realized that there was a disconnect between the message our classes send to our students (do the right thing, even when it's hard!) and our own unwillingness to make some hard calls with regard to our pedagogical habits. Paper use became an ethical issue for us, an imperative that would back up what we were teaching in our classrooms in some form, regardless of the specific class.

We both liked the way we did things, using paper to distribute readings, assignment sheets, grading rubrics, quizzes and tests, and other teaching necessities. Both of us regarded the idea of migrating our work to electronic format with a fair amount of skepticism. (After all, there's no ethical obligation to act when something *can't* be done, right? Using the status quo as a protective shield or convenient excuse for inaction, or hiding behind policies to remain in a comfort zone, makes it easier to look for reasons and justifications not to do something than to do something.) Despite this initial ambivalence, we came up with an idea to start a pilot paperless teaching program to determine whether and how one *could* go paperless. In the process, we faced quite a few unexpected challenges, but we were able to persevere. In the end, we found the process valuable not just from an ethical and experimental viewpoint, but also because it caused us to rethink our pedagogical approaches, showing us new ways to communicate and connect with students.

Perhaps at this point, we should pause to introduce ourselves, not to make ourselves stand out in any way, but rather to do the opposite. We want to show that when it came to our teaching styles, different as they were and are, and when it came to paper use, we were average. We both teach a wide range of courses for an interdisciplinary department at GVSU. Justin is a student of philosophy currently pursuing his doctorate in American studies at Michigan State University. Kirsten has a multidisciplinary background, having studied geology, environmental studies, classics, and literature. We both fondly remember being undergraduate students in our twenties. We both remember life before texting, and even before e-mail, and both of us are resistant to inconvenient change.

Starting was hard. First we had to ask ourselves just how much printing and copying we actually do over the course of a semester. How much toner, paper, and electricity are used to reproduce our syllabi, quizzes, handouts, and supplemental readings? And how much is simply too much? Many instructors have raised these questions before, no doubt—and many have acted on these questions. How could we follow suit? We printed and copied and passed out tons of paper (literally, *tons*, over the years) to our students. What if we stopped? What if we didn't print or copy a single sheet of paper for any of our classes for an entire year? Without knowing how to stop, we just decided to jump in and commit to not wasting paper.

When we calculated our estimated paper cost for one academic year, we were shocked. Following the manufacturer's information on our office printers and the copier down the hall, we found that each one of us spent between $4,000 and $8,000 per year on the paper we distribute to our classes. *Each!* These figures were was based on a 4/4 teaching load, with approximately 30 to 35 students per class, and our teaching habits. After recovering from the shock of determining these dollar amounts, our commitment to this project was solidified, but our apprehension didn't go away. One of our biggest concerns was that if we made a transition in our teaching styles, the students absolutely must still receive the same quality of instruction from us.

To succeed, we realized that we needed to communicate with each other about our objectives in the classroom and about how our experiments with alternative paperless strategies affected those objectives. We needed to be completely open, honest, and transparent about the good and bad of how we taught because we needed to lean on each other and learn from each other. And because our lives were about to change, and old habits, as they say, die hard. Suddenly printed rubrics to grade in-class presentations, giving tests and quizzes in the standard manner, distributing assignment guidelines, and even copying syllabi were no longer options for us. For two people who had used typewriters in college, this was intimidating.

We realized that we needed to rely on good software and appropriate hardware to make the transition. From this grew the idea to make our little experiment an incentive program, to help us reinvent our approach to technology in our teaching. We needed to find technology that we could use in the classroom. Our office computers were standard-issue desktops that were useful but they wouldn't be much help in our project. Because we are very different people, we identified different needs. To meet those needs, and with the full support of our department head and dean, we applied for minigrant funding from GVSU's Sustainability Initiative, and we were given $500 each for the technology of our choosing. Justin purchased a laptop computer, while Kirsten opted for a smaller netbook. The individual selection of technology was to facilitate ease in the transition, and it is the center of this sustainable initiative. We needed to be allowed to teach according to our strengths and to find the technology that would enhance our teaching, not detract from it. With our grand idea and our shiny new toys, we set out to change the mindset of faculty members throughout our university.

And so the semester started, with all of our handouts and readings and syllabi converted to .pdf files and loaded on BlackBoard (our university's online learning platform), where students could access them anytime. In our first week of classes, at midterms, and at the end of the semester, we surveyed our students to get their impressions of the project; to solicit any suggestions from them for making it work (because they're all more tech-literate that we are); and, most important, to find out if their learning experience was changed by the project. We were also concerned that, while we saved thousands of dollars in printing for our department, we had merely pushed that cost onto the students, which would have defeated the purpose of the project. Our surveys showed that approximately 37% of the students in our classes said that they would refrain from printing as well, and 24% responded that they'd do *some* printing. In fact, the vast majority of students (over 70%) were excited about the idea, although 52% did have concerns.

As the semester went on, we found that some of the concerns held by us and our students were well-founded. The project posed challenges that we never envisioned. It required shifting our mindset and adjusting our pedagogy to reflect our sustainable practices. It also involved learning to use technology in ways that neither of us had ever imagined. Shortly after we made our commitment to paperless teaching, GVSU piloted a new version of BlackBoard. The new version was not as user-friendly as the previous version, in our opinions. This change led to a variety of issues that tried the patience of both faculty members and students. Students had no problem with the fact that everything, including the syllabus, was on BlackBoard, but all too often, the system was unavailable for periods throughout the semester. Students laughed with (and probably at) Kirsten when she magically made the course website communicate in Italian. Having no idea how this happened and no skills at reading Italian, the class was forced to adapt. In Justin's class, students generally liked submitting their assignments online, but compatibility issues often made those assignments impossible to access on Justin's computer. Through it all, the students remained understanding about the myriad issues inherent in the launching of new software because they were as committed to the idea as we were. Without their support, we wouldn't have made it through the year.

In the end, only about 7% of students surveyed said that they felt they were learning less effectively because of the paperless instruction, while 92% said that they were learning with the same or higher levels of effectiveness. Generally, students had positive feedback about the goals and execution of the project after completing our paperless instruction classes, too. The most pointed criticisms from students were regarding accessibility to our online content. Some students didn't have Internet access at home, some students felt some anxiety about not being able to check BlackBoard for changes with enough regularity, and some feared that they wouldn't get important information on time. Some students also felt that the program didn't go far enough. The project was for us, the instructors, not to distribute any paper. After a few technological frustrations, we reviewed our grant application and noted that we didn't say anything about students not turning in paper to us.

We saw this as a way of skirting some issues with compatibility that electronic submission of assignments had caused. A few students did take us to task for this and thought that we should find a solution that they thought was more in the spirit of the project.

We learned a great deal over the course of the two semesters of which the pilot program commitment was a part. We learned that one of us has far less patience for the technology required for the paperless classroom to work. We altered teaching approaches to make use of online readings and quizzes. We both escaped the H1N1 flu epidemic because we were not handling students' papers and therefore we were not trading germs, and in fact both have remained healthier since eliminating the paper exchange. We found that while Justin detested assessing student papers online, Kirsten provided better and far more readable feedback in the paperless mode.

Regardless of the differences in how we each fulfilled our commitments not to use paper, we can offer a few pieces of advice to those considering making the paperless leap. First, let your students know what you're doing. By and large, the millennial generation that makes up the vast majority of our students understands the importance of going green, and they feel good being a part of it. They're even willing to put up with some hassles to do so. So if you can't access your files or get your grades back as quickly as you would have otherwise done, most likely they'll understand. Second, use whatever tools are at your disposal to their fullest potential. We're quite lucky at GVSU: Each classroom that we teach in has a projector and screen (often more than one) connected to a standardized computer station and document camera. These machines are great for reviewing assignments, referring to texts, giving quizzes, and so on. Make sure to become comfortable using such equipment and know what it can do. Incorporating paperless technology into your teaching repertoire likely has a lot of potential. Third, learn some new programs. There are a lot of great options for making lectures more multimedia, which makes it much easier to move away from paper handouts. Prezi, iTunesU, Wimba, and even Facebook and Twitter can be helpful in and out of the classroom. Set up groups for online discussions, and bring these into your class instruction. The more ways you can communicate with your students, the better. Don't feel intimidated by these new forms of technology, and be sure to set parameters that are comfortable for you. For example, Justin often uses online discussion boards to start discussion in his classes. The goal of these online activities is always clearly defined: A certain number of posts per week is required (not so much that it gets to be an impossible task to read through, however). These online discussions have been quite successful. Students generally show up to class more prepared and more willing to join in when they have already done the online discussion. Fourth, trust yourself, but don't fool yourself: The transition to paperless instruction will be a challenge, but not one that you can't meet!

We're both happy we undertook this project and allowed it to change our methods. Initially we both regretted our shift away from paper. We missed simplicity and ease of using paper. At times, we wondered if going back to paper would free us. But we managed to survive the issues and bond more closely with our students. Although we know we saved paper and toner, we reflect back on our project and wonder about the true costs and benefits. Trees will grow, if allowed. They are a renewable resource. And yes, we saved the energy that would have been used for copying and printing. But what about the inherent eye strain with reading on a flat screen? (Kirsten would much rather blame her newly acquired need for reading glasses on anything other than her "advancing years"!) Finally, what about the non-renewable resources required to manufacture the laptop computer and netbook? The carbon footprint of manufacturing one Dell laptop is approximately 770 pounds of carbon. By contrast, the carbon footprint of printing one ream of paper is 18.5 pounds. But given the sheer number of pages printed and copied, our estimated carbon savings for our first year is estimated to be 3,000 pounds. Although this estimate is rough at best (it does not calculate the energy required to run either the computers or the printers), it is something to think about. The benefits of sustainability are not always as simple and straightforward to calculate as we would like. But we feel that we took a step in the right direction, and we will always pause before printing.

15

COMMUNICATING
SUSTAINABILITY

Teaching Sustainable Media Practice

Alex Lockwood, Caroline Mitchell, and Evi Karathanasopoulou

A s Sacha Kagan (2008) states, "The word 'sustainability' has become very fashionable in the first decade of the 21st century, and its widespread use has led to all kinds of definitions and interpretations, some of which are missing most of the substance of the concept" (p. 15). Our aim in this chapter, and the ongoing project it draws from, is to explore a richer concept of sustainability as a "cultural change process [that] requires the advancement of learners' skills and competencies" (Kagan, 2008, p. 15). Such an advancement of skills and learning through education is not only a means for achieving a far-off goal of sustainable development; it is also an inherently sustainable practice in itself.

Sustainability and Transformative Learning

We are not suggesting that our teaching of sustainable practice is aimed solely at sustaining current structures of capitalist ownership and control within our particular fields (the global mass media) or to produce employable graduates. Rather, we approach teaching as a process of transformative learning that offers students and teachers together a "shift of consciousness that dramatically and permanently alters our way of being in the world" (Morrell & O'Connor, 2002, p. xvii). Such learning aids students in the development of the skills and knowledge required for *transformative criticism*, an approach put forward by Edmund O'Sullivan (2002) that "questions the dominant culture's . . . visions of continuity." For O'Sullivan, this is the first step in a three-step process: after (1) locating such structures that neglect or obstruct sustainable practices or maintain destructive patterns, practitioners of transformative criticism then can (2) offer a vision of what an alternative to those dominant forms of culture could look like, and then (3) point to a process of change in creating new cultural forms that are functionally appropriate for sustainable practice, *and then begin practicing them*. In light of humanity's catastrophic transgressions across planetary boundaries (Rockström et al., 2009), of which climate change is perhaps only the most mediated example, such transformative criticism is, we argue, central to the future not only of higher education, but of our planet itself.

We agree with O'Sullivan that what this means for ourselves and our students will be explored in practice. But rather than focusing on the production of content (curricula, programming) *about* sustainability, students and educators would instead "foreground" (Haraway, 1989) this three-stage operation of transformative criticism to locate sustainability as the instigating question in each educational moment, thus initiating Kagan's "cultural change process" to develop sustainable capacity and creativity. The first practice transformed, therefore, will always be the process of learning as it is enacted; the competencies and skills that develop from this learning, directed toward specific cultural forms and their required means of production, will then be shaped in ways sensitive to the aims of transformative criticism. Each encounter (whether in the classroom, the community, or the media studio) will begin by asking: Is what we are doing sustainable? Or, in O'Sullivan's (2002) words, do our teaching, media, and lifestyle practices contribute to a "surviving, critiquing and creating" of our current political-economic system, to replace it with one that does not "lead to human suffering and environmental disaster" (p. 4).

To give one example, following the recent announcement that the United Kingdom's (UK's) new coalition government planned to raise tuition fees and cut 100% of the UK's teaching budget for arts and humanities subjects from the 2012–2013 academic year,[1] students at our university organized a live television debate, which was broadcast as voting on the proposal took place in Parliament. The students who conceptualized and organized this event had just been through an initial pilot for our sustainability project (discussed later in this chapter). They will not be affected by the rise in tuition fees or the teaching budget cuts, yet by engaging with transformative criticism and the foregrounding of sustainable learning practice, they (1) identified the location of what they considered a formally inappropriate and socially unjust dominant cultural formation, and (2) through their media practice, offered space for an alternative vision of this cultural formation while (3) already practicing the competencies of compassion, self-motivation, and motivating others, plus a range of behaviors seeking to ask questions of broader cultural sustainable survival. We hope that the replication of our pilot project will lead to additional such student-led practices, and that such practices during students' formal education will lead to a dynamic awareness of their own power in "the advancement of . . . skills and competencies" (Kagan, 2008, p. 15) relevant to today's local and global challenges.

We are also exploring how these practices are formed through community media, in particular community radio, rather than mainstream media as a location for developing sustainable content and working practices in personal, local, and universal contexts. We distinguish community radio from mainstream public service and commercial radio where radio is not made *for* people but *by* them. As Lewis (2006) states: "[T]he community or communities for whom the station exists manage the policy, make the program, and deliberately choose to broadcast content suited to their needs and not obtainable from mainstream outputs" (p. 25).

Preparation for the Global Media Industries

The media are fully integrated into the rituals and practices of everyday life (Moores, 2000) to the extent that, according to Byron Reeves and Clifford Nass (1996) *"media equates real life"*: We perceive story and narrative presented in the media as real places and real people. Yet as integral as television, radio, the print press, and new media technologies are to people's lives, the rapid and unique changes affecting the global broadcast, print, and digital media industries have asked questions of the sector's own sustainability (e.g., see Deuze, 2008). The related question for media educators is, How relevant can the teaching in media departments and journalism schools be in light of such changes?[2] Few expect the media (local, national, and international) to continue with its present structures and outputs. But what new media forms the industry will adopt to safeguard its democratic and oversight roles are still to be realized. While social, economic, and cultural practices have been central to the conversation, the salient concept of sustainability remains on the periphery of communications debates.

This relative exclusion of sustainability from the conversation over the future of communications comes despite the importance of the media in contributing to widespread understanding and commitment to sustainable development processes. We are halfway into the UN's Decade for Education for Sustainable Development (ESD) 2005–2014, which recognizes that "[j]ournalists and media organizations have an important role to play in reporting on issues and in helping raise public awareness of the various dimensions and requirements of sustainable development" (UNESCO, 2005, p. 25). Yet the critical tendency, as Blewitt (2006) suggests, is to view the media industries "as a major cause of many social and political ills, ranging from child obesity to international terrorism" (p. 160) rather than a starting point for the transformation of culture.

For us and our students, this offers an opportunity, from within the potential disintegration of current global media business structures, to re-evaluate a sense of sustainable practice for those industries. As O'Sullivan (2002) notes, "[B]reakdown, or crisis, motivates the system to self-organize in more inclusive ways of knowing" (p. 2) where current crises states can be transformed for "the reconciliation of social justice, ecological integrity, and the well being of all living systems on the planet" (Kagan, 2008, p. 15). Students may also have the opportunity to participate actively in alternative community-led media, which, combined with media studies, can offer them a critique of, and an alternative to, the mainstream media. In community radio, with appropriate training and community development processes, participants can represent their own versions of this reality, which may be very different from that portrayed by the mass media (see Mitchell & Baxter, 2006). The inclusion of teaching about community media in practice enables students to explore and experience how community media projects themselves need to achieve long-term sustainability (see Jallov, 2005, and Girard, 2007, for case studies). What better way to do so than by teaching sustainable communications practice to media students and by using sustainable methods of media production and development that might even, at the same time, prepare them for the job market?[3]

Our Communicating Sustainability Project: Sparking Sustainability

Situated in northeastern England, Sunderland is a new UK university that gained university status in 1992 and provides teaching and research facilities for around 17,000 students. The city of Sunderland itself has a history of heavy industry and was once renowned as the largest shipbuilding city in the world.[4] The university's media center was built on the site of the old ship-yards on the banks of the river Wear, after the last yard closed in 1988. Regeneration and sustainable practice is central to the future of the department, particularly in light of a fundamental shift in the government's economic support for the teaching of arts, humanities, and social sciences in the UK.[5] Some initial funding from the UK's Arts, Design and Media Higher Education Academy (http://www.adm-heacademy.ac.uk) has allowed academic staff members to develop curriculum interventions around sustainable media practice under the concept of "sparking sustainability" within community media, integrating experiences of sustainability in student life and the lives of people of northeastern England.

The Sparking Sustainability project aims to secure the long-term sustainability of the media department's community radio station Spark FM. The student-led and volunteer-run media station (http://www.sparksunderland.com) has a 5-year license to broadcast to the students, the local community, and (via the Internet) beyond its geographical borders. The running of the radio station is integrated into the Broadcast Journalism and Media Production programs, and it is forging links to other journalism courses in the department.

The project is based on classroom interventions that prepare students in creating and producing sustainable audio broadcast, video, print, or online articles. While ostensibly about producing broadcast, print, or online story content covering sustainability issues, the integrated goal of the project is, in fact, the development of sustainable media practice among our students and staff members. We shaped the delivery of our project around the belief that sustainability is a "process or strategy of moving toward a sustainable future" (Kagan, 2008, p. 15) that requires the development of skills and knowledge, or competencies. As Barth, Godemann, Rieckmann, and Stoltenberg (2007) suggest, such competencies have a broad and encompassing flexibility and are "expected to enable active, reflective and cooperative participation toward sustainable development" (p. 418). It is worth listing the eight competencies that Barth et al. identify as central to higher education's contribution to the process of moving toward a sustainable future:

1. competency in foresighted thinking;
2. competency in interdisciplinary work;
3. competency in cosmopolitan perception, transcultural understanding, and cooperation;
4. participatory skills;

5. competency in planning and implementation;
6. capacity for empathy, compassion, and solidarity;
7. competency in self-motivation and in motivating others; and
8. competency in distanced reflection on individual and cultural models.

These competencies are neither media-specific, nor do they fit with any mainstream understanding of sustainability, if such understanding is viewed as simply aligned with a sustainable development agenda. Each classroom intervention draws on the idea of developing these competencies within a higher education setting to offer students the opportunity for that "shift of consciousness that dramatically and permanently alters our way of being in the world . . . and our sense of possibilities for social justice and peace and personal joy" (Morrell & O'Connor, 2002, p. xvii) that is at the heart of a transformative learning experience. In particular, the teaching team was interested in competencies in participatory skills (4 in the list); capacity for empathy, compassion, and solidarity (6); and self-motivation and in motivating others (7). We focused on the advancement of these skills by both modelling the competencies (working in a participatory manner as educators) and focusing elements of the interventions on those areas (e.g., having students support each other in group sessions).

Interventions in the Classroom

As already suggested in this chapter, sustainability for our project is not just about environmental stewardship and recycling. For example, the UNESCO Decade of Education for Sustainable Development lists eight areas of activity, including cultural diversity and gender equality (UNESCO, 2005). This was important for the project because we were drawing on problem-based pedagogies to "spark" student engagement and self-determined understandings of sustainability in personal, local, and universal contexts. This followed the belief that self-led learning focused on what is important to the individual is a central part of a transformative learning experience. Much of the thinking behind how we then structured the classroom interventions was drawn from the "Positive Education" work of Martin Seligman, at the University of Pennsylvania. Seligman's (2009) work posits that the teaching of well-being leads to better learning. That is, "increases in wellbeing likely produce increases in learning, the traditional goal of education" (p. 5).

The workshops then begin from the basis of discovering what sustainability means to the students in their lives and student media practice. A *before survey* is conducted. From our pilot conducted in May 2010, we discovered that, while many students do understand sustainability to be about traditional environmental activities (64%), they also have a spark of awareness about the other possible and potential meanings of the word. For example, we found that 65% associated sustainability with managing resources, and at least 12% connected it with personal well-being.[6] When asked to write a sentence on what sustainability meant to them, answers included:

- A procedure that is useful, effective, and reliable yet provides all these in the healthiest of manners
- Living/working in a way that can be continued into the future
- Defeating entropy, preventing heat death; long-term you can only delay it, never stop it

When asked if they were to "act more sustainably tomorrow than today," 26% said they would use less energy, and 19% said they would recycle more, but 14% also said they would "talk to people more" and 13% said "rest."

This exploration of the concept of sustainability is then used to stimulate media content creation via the mechanism of a student competition to produce broadcast, video, or print content on the themes of sustainability *as it is understood by the students*, and not according to some predefined script. Content sessions are facilitated so that students work together to develop ideas, pitches, and briefs for work, thus developing their competencies in participatory skills (4 from the list already mentioned), and competencies in self-motivation and in motivating others (7 from the same list). Although competitive incentives are used, prepared materials on example content are specifically chosen to develop the students' capacities for empathy, compassion, and solidarity (6 from the list). For example, broadcast clips of previous radio programs are used with a specific human interest story; beyond this, the methods of the team in producing the content are drawn out by identifying and analyzing the sustainable practices used in the making of the material. Students are encouraged to approach and develop links with their local community and youth audiences, with the understanding that community media properties will be sustainable in the long term only if and when they are integrated into the local community beyond the learning institution. When asked in the *before survey*, 89% of respondents said that they had initiated contact with student groups, yet this resulted in only 26% of contacts leading to programming or partnership development. These figures fell to 56% and 21%, respectively, for initiating contact with youth groups in the local city community. This information is presented to emphasize that community links were not so much more difficult to establish (than student links) once initial contact had been made. This was intended to direct programming ideas toward content about sustainability, and it would also be, in effect, sustaining media practices focused on integrating the radio station with the community.

The project ended in May 2011. Additional interventions occurred in November and December 2010 and January 2011. The competition for content materials closed in February 2011, and all participants were asked to complete an *after survey* to gauge the impact of the interventions on student skills and knowledge, both about sustainability and sustainable practice. An awards ceremony took place in March 2011. The data to be analyzed will point the way to a national program that can further integrate the core competencies of teaching sustainability into the curriculum of media students across the United Kingdom.

Conclusion

As Sacha Kagan (2008) argues, a focus on developing core personal and interpersonal competencies, and a fundamental belief in both transformative and positive educational practices, are the best means to achieve long-term sustainability within and beyond higher education for our students and ourselves as media practitioners. Our Sparking Sustainability project focuses on such broad and encompassing competencies as outlined in this chapter because such "processes involve all-out reflexivity about 'ourselves' in a wide sense (from individual routines to social institutions to power networks). They develop reflexivity skills of different types, appealing to a diversity of human qualities, beyond the limited types of rationality tapped by most scientific discourses and beyond the limitation of imagination embedded in established rules and routines" (Kagan, 2008, p. 18). It is only by moving beyond these "limited types of rationality" in teaching communications and media practices that tomorrow's journalists and today's students will be equipped not just for jobs in the industry, but for reconfiguring those industries to meet the nexus of economic, social, cultural, and environmental challenges we now face. Any emphasis on *teaching sustainability*—such as asking students to report on local environmental planning issues, for exam-ple—must be accompanied by the processes of *acting sustainably*, which means addressing our own educational practices. The underlying goals of the educational intervention itself are to help students "learn how to learn" and—we add—learn critically and hopefully. As Paulo Freire says in *Peda-gogy of Freedom*, teaching is "an intervention in the world" (Freire, 2001) and we ourselves are both critical and hopeful that these interventions are in some way a contribution to the urgent debate about whether our current cultural institutions and processes are any longer " 'formatively appropriate' " (O'Sullivan, 2002) for a sustainable future.

Notes

1. See Prince (2010).
2. See McAdams (2010).
3. The UK prime minister, David Cameron, made special note of the impor-tance of environmentally sustainable industries when he visited northeastern England, where Sunderland is based; see Watt, Wintour and Edemariam (2010).
4. For example, see Tighe (2010).
5. On October 20, 2010, the UK coalition government formally proposed to Parliament to cut the entire teaching budget for arts, humanities, and social sciences, which is, as Stefan Collini (2010) writes, "a redefinition of higher education and the retreat of the state from financial responsibility for it."
6. The pilot workshop intervention was conducted with 33 participants, from the Spark FM radio station staff members, other journalism students, and members of the teaching staff.

References

Barth, M., Godemann, J., Rieckmann, M., & Stoltenberg, U. (2007). Developing key competencies for sustainable development in higher education. *International Journal of Sustainability in Higher Education. 4,4,* 416–430. doi:10.1108/14676 370710823582

Blewitt, J. (2006). *The ecology of learning.* London: Earthscan.

Collini, S. (2010, November 4). Browne's gamble. *The London Review of Books.* Retrieved from http://www.lrb.co.uk/v32/n21/stefan-collini/brownes-gamble

Deuze, M. (2008). Understanding journalism as newswork: How it changes, and how it remains the same. *Westminster Papers in Communication and Culture, 5*(2), 4–23.

Freire, P. (2001). *Pedagogy of freedom.* Lanham, MD: Rowman & Littlefield.

Girard, B. (2007). Empowering radio: Good practices in development & operation of community radio: Issues important to its effectiveness. Research conducted for the Program on Civic Engagement, Empowerment & Respect for Diversity, World Bank Institute, Washington. Retrieved from http://comunica.org/radio 2.0/archives/69

Haraway, D. (1989). *Primate visions*. New York: Routledge.

Jallov, B. (2005). Assessing community change: Development of a "bare foot" impact assessment methodology. *The Radio Journal*, 3(1), 21–34.

Kagan, S. (2008). Sustainability as a new frontier for the arts and cultures. In S. Kagan & V. Kirchberg (Eds.), *Sustainability as a new frontier for the arts and cultures* (pp. 14–25). Frankfurt, Germany: Verlag für Akademische Schriften.

Lewis, P. M. (2006). Community media: Giving "a voice to the voiceless." In P. Lewis & S. Jones (Eds.), *From the margins to the cutting edge, community media and empowerment* (pp. 13–41). Cresskill, NJ: Hampton Press.

McAdams, M. (2010, October 14). Journalism education: Irrelevant, or lacking context? *Teaching Online Journalism*. Retrieved from http://mindymcadams.com/tojou/2010/journalism-education-irrelevant-or-lacking-context/

Mitchell, C., & Baxter, A. (2006). Organic radio: The role of social partnerships in creating community voices. In P. M. Lewis & S. Jones (Eds.), *From the margins to the cutting edge, community media and empowerment* (pp. 69–100). Cresskill, NJ: Hampton Press.

Moores, S. (2000). *Media and everyday life in modern society*. Edinburgh: University of Edinburgh Press.

Morrell, A., & O'Connor, M-A. (2002). Introduction. In E. O'Sullivan, A. Morrell, & M-A O'Connor, (Eds.), *Expanding the boundaries of transformative learning* (pp. xv–xx). New York: Palgrave.

O'Sullivan, E. (2002). The project and vision of transformative education: Integral transformative learning. In E. O'Sullivan, A. Morrell, & M-A O'Connor (Eds.), *Expanding the boundaries of transformative learning* (pp. 1–12). New York: Palgrave.

O'Sullivan, E., Morrell, A., & O'Connor, M-A. (2002). *Expanding the boundaries of transformative learning*. New York: Palgrave.

Prince, R. (2010, October 20). CSR: Student fees to double from 2012 as university budgets slashed. *The Telegraph*. Retrieved from http://www.telegraph.co.uk/news/ newstopics/spending-review/8076246/CSR-student-fees-to-double-from-2012-as-university-budgets-slashed.html

Reeves, B., & Nass, C. (1996). *The media equation: How people treat computers, television and new media like real people and places*. Stanford, CA: CSLI Publications and Cambridge University Press.

Rockström, J., Steffen, W., Noone, K., Persson, Å. Chapin, F. S., . . . & Foley, J. (2009). Planetary boundaries: Exploring the safe operating space for humanity. *Ecology and Society*, 14(2), 32–65.

Seligman, M. (2009). Positive education white paper. Retrieved from www.flourish ingschools.org/Positive_Education_FSWhitePaper.pdf

Tighe, C. (2010, October 18). A long drive to prosperity. *Financial Times*. Retrieved from http://www.ft.com/cms/s/0/1f515596-da47-11df-bdd7-00144feabdco.html# axzz1EcGFwBej

Watt, N., Wintour, P., & Edemariam, A. (2010, April 23). David Cameron targets north-east and Northern Ireland for spending cuts. *The Guardian*. Retrieved from http://www.guardian.co.uk/politics/2010/apr/23/david-cameron-paxman-squeeze

UNESCO. (2005). United Nations decade of education for sustainable development (2005–2014). Retrieved from http://www.unesco.org/en/education-for-sustainable-development/decade-of-esd/

16

ROADBLOCKS TO APPLIED SUSTAINABILITY

Bart A. Bartels

I n 2008, individuals in downtown Grand Rapids, Michigan, were asked about sustainability. Of the 50 polled, none knew the definition of sustainability, yet most considered it "too expensive."[1] Presently, *sustainability* is a product to be marketed by everyone, from car companies to coffee shops. Universities are no exception. A *Princeton Review* survey found that 64% of prospective students would consider information about how green an institution is either "strongly," "very much," or "somewhat" in making a college choice ("2010 College Hopes and Worries"). Grand Valley State University (GVSU) is one option for those students. It is known as a leader in sustainability, with colleges and universities looking to my department, the Sustainable Community Development Initiative, for collaborative guidance on their journey. This chapter explores the integration of sustainability initiatives at colleges and universities, including the roadblocks incurred and the possible routes to success, using GVSU, not as the ultimate authority, but as an example of one institution that is traveling the path.

Defining Sustainability Versus Implementing Sustainability

Prior to starting on a journey, it is wise to have an idea of the destination. The quest for a perfect definition, though, can become one of the roadblocks on the journey toward sustainability. According to the Global Development Research Center, there are more than 100 definitions of sustainability and sustainable development (Global Development Research Center, 2011). The most commonly used is that found in the Brundtland Commission's 1987 report, *Our Common Future,* more commonly known as the Brundtland Report. This United Nations document introduced the concept of sustainable development, describing it as "development that meets the needs of the present without compromising the needs of future generations" (World Commission on Environment and Development, 1987). This broad conceptualization accommodated initiatives of all disciplines. In the more than two decades since the Brundtland Report was published, many refinements have been made to the term: broadening it, narrowing it, making it more and less exclusive. Authors have coined sustainable phrases to differentiate their books from the others, thereby further segmenting the meaning. Although sound, overuse, misuse, and multiple meanings can render a word meaningless, often causing energy that could propel the ideas forward to stagnate instead in debates, discussions, and even diatribes on the definition.

At a recent sustainability conference (that shall go nameless to avoid any possible embarrassment), a 45-minute discussion to define the conference theme welcomed attendees. While academia benefits from philosophical debate, and higher education is a natural venue for such discussion, this forum as an introduction to the topic seemed to undermine the purpose of the conference. Surely those hosting a conference on sustainability would have agreed on at least a working definition of what their conference is about. The session left attendees with the perception that the presenters did not agree on its meaning and with little hope of finding the answers they came to the conference to find. Action was again stalled, and this kind of inaction is often disheartening to those wishing to make an immediate difference.

To move past this roadblock, it has been effective in meetings that I have attended to move away from a definition and back to a concept. While some see this as deevolution, the forward progress of implementing Brundtland's primary concepts refute that position. Brundtland's key concepts are need and limitation:

- the concept of *needs*, and in particular the essential needs of the world's poor, to which overriding priority should be given; and
- the idea of *limitations* imposed by the state of technology and social organization on the environment's ability to meet present and future needs (World Commission on Environment and Development, 1987).

Getting back to the basics seems to empower those looking for a way to move forward. Harvey Brooks states, "Ideally it [sustainability] should be defined so that one could specify a set of measurable criteria such that individuals and groups with widely differing values, political preferences, or assumptions about human nature could agree whether the criteria are being met in a concrete development program" (Beckerman, 1996, p. 144). This more inclusive conceptualization of sustainability helps overcome the multidisciplinary versus interdisciplinary paradigm that people are largely reluctant to acknowledge. For instance, projects may invite members from several disciplines to participate, but thoughts are not readily exchanged across disciplinary boundaries; thus, participants are unable to capture interdisciplinary benefits. One important example of such differences between disciplinary views of sustainability is highlighted by Michael Toman (1992): "[E]cologists and economists view sustainability in very different ways." Toman points out that economists tend to view natural capital as a product that can be replaced by human capital, while ecologists tend to view natural capital as having no practical substitutes. To integrate multiple perspectives, respect, understanding, and common ground seem to be more beneficial than the quest for an all-encompassing terminology. Finding the commonalities and common goals, while often more challenging than might at first be assumed, has moved many a plan from the meeting phase to successful implementation.

The triple bottom line, which takes into account social, environmental, and economic factors to make better decisions as global citizens, reinforces the need to consider the cultural implications of any sustainable initiative or effort. The triple bottom line also puts the economic aspect on an equal footing with the environmental and social factors in an attempt to remove the perception that sustainability is "too expensive." While individual disciplines may place more emphasis on any one of the three legs, David Ewoldt's definition can help us move past disciplinary boundaries. Ewoldt (2007) combines past, present, and future generations with economic, environmental, and sociocultural constraints:

> Sustainability means to integrate our social and economic lives into the environment in ways that tend to enhance or maintain rather than degrade or destroy the environment; it is a moral imperative to pass on our natural inheritance, not necessarily unchanged, but undiminished in its ability to meet the needs of future generations; and it entails finding, and staying within, the balance point amongst population, consumption, and waste

assimilation so that watersheds and bioregions can maintain their ability to recharge and regenerate. (May 13)

Ewoldt and Toman have lent support to the Brundtland concept, added a missing perspective or providing clarity to the commonly used definition, and have allowed meetings that I have attended not merely to cross disciplinary boundaries, but also to help erase those divides to focus on the common goal or action.

Measuring Student Involvement

The common goal, the common good, and *the best interests of all involved* are indeed promising touchstones that can focus people on action rather than on mere semantic disputes. Like sustainability, however, these terms are used in ways that both motivate and paralyze. The common good might not be so common. What is good for the west side of town may be viewed as a detriment to the east. Goals set in the near term may have adverse effects on the distant future. Bryan Norton's convergence hypothesis would advocate resolving differences in preconceptions with action rather than theoretical agreement. "We hope that, under favorable conditions in which inhabitants of a place have committed to cooperative action through partnership or adaptive management process, they can focus attention on possible objectives that can unite people behind action in pursuit of shared goals" (Norton, 2005, p. 507). To garner widespread support, it is important to keep a wide range of stakeholders informed and include their input to determine the best path forward, a unifying objective. Raising awareness is a critical component to any campus sustainability initiative. For many students, the university setting provides the first exposure to sustainability and the opportunities for involvement that it provides. Indeed, in their first year students seek to participate in groups and initiatives with similar interests. Student involvement and engagement allows students to learn that what seem like impassable roadblocks in fact often turn out to be mere bumps in the road as they strive to find their voice, make a difference, and get involved. At GVSU, students have a wide variety of ways to get involved with sustainability efforts. Examples include joining a student organization such as the Student Environmental Coalition, the Community Garden's Farm Club, or the Student Sustainability Partnership. Other options are to take part in the energy competitions held in campus housing units or to take part in a national campus residence competition called Recyclemania. These organizations and programs provide outlets for activity and venues to share information that all contribute to the common good.

As with many aspects of university actions, documentation is an important factor in gauging success. Documenting student involvement in sustainability efforts and initiatives can be quite useful, but it is also subjective to some degree. Graduate assistants and interns working on sustainability are easy to account for, but what about the rest of the stakeholders? The Sustainable Endowments Institute evaluates student involvement at colleges and universities in its College Sustainability Report Card (Sustainable Endowments Institute, 2010). The Report Card uses five indicators to evaluate student involvement, including the following:

Residential Communities
- Offering residential housing options around sustainability themes

New Student Orientation
- Integrating sustainability into new student orientation

Internships/Outreach Opportunities
- Offering sustainability internship opportunities for students on campus
- Providing student positions through supported eco-rep programs or similar initiatives

Student Organizations
- Having active student organizations that prioritize campus sustainability efforts and that achieve significant results in their efforts to advance sustainability on campus

Sustainability Challenges and Competitions
- Overseeing sustainability challenges and/or competitions on campus or with other colleges at least once a year

While these sustainability indicators create a competitive atmosphere among institutions and give impetus for each college and university to act on the scored criteria, it leaves the majority of students unaccounted for. What about all the projects done on campus and in the community to benefit the economy, the environment, and fellow citizens? What about the service learning hours that do not occur under the auspices of student organizations?

In an effort to account for involvement in sustainable projects, one ends up back at the beginning of this chapter, looking for the perfect definition of sustainability. But how do you count participation in sustainable activities when there is no agreement on what activities should be counted? Questions about documentation can include, for example: To qualify as a sustainable project, does the project have to benefit all three factors of the triple bottom line? What if a group of students cleans up a beach but at a cost that is prohibitive? What about students mentoring elementary classes that have little to offer the environment? What if students do such a fine job keeping a neighborhood clean that a city worker is laid off? When it comes to defining whether a project should be classified as sustainable, the process can be subjective, and at times it depends on the individual goals of those making the determination. Questions have also been raised about whether enough emphasis is being placed on results, considering that the metrics focus on participation. Shouldn't we be more concerned about what is being done than about how many participants are involved?

In an effort to keep track of all sustainable efforts at GVSU, we have tried to simplify the complex and go back to the basics of sustainability and sustainable development. Yes, documenting student involvement can be cumbersome and ambiguous, but that doesn't mean it should be a roadblock. And no definition of sustainability says anything about it being easy. To promote sustainability involvement effectively, a multifaceted plan must be enacted by administrators, faculty members, and the students. Education for sustainable development is being embedded throughout the curriculum, with more than 200 courses currently offering sustainability content (Grand Valley State University, 2008). Grand Valley students are now taking over 14% of their credit hours in sustainability courses. In addition, more than 10% of our students are involved in sustainability projects outside the classroom. Efforts are being made to document results, including those not measured in monetary terms. Goals are being modified to place as much emphasis on results as participation.

Institutional Openness and Support

GVSU is ever mindful that enacting change is always subject to resistance. The university is fortunate enough to have not only a student-driven—or bottom-up—initiative, but also a presidential—or top-down—directive. At Grand Valley, that message was reinforced when sustainability was added to the strategic plan as the seventh value of the university. In that declaration, the institution stated, "Grand Valley State University values the guiding principles of sustainability in helping to meet the current needs of our faculty, staff, and students without compromising the needs and resources of future generations" (Grand Valley State University, 2009). This statement takes the broad and inclusive definition from the Brundtland Report and applies it to a university setting. Having sustainability as a value gives reason to actions taken. When an institution's leaders are committed to sustainable best practices, value is added to the work performed. It is then up to the faculty members to embed the new value into the curriculum.

The pace at which sustainability has been instilled into the campus classrooms and culture has indeed been swift. By many measures GVSU is a leader is sustainability on a national scale, but national recognition is of little concern to a student who asks, "Why aren't we doing more?" Even though the university leadership is encouraging and is embedding sustainable practices, the real driving force comes from the students. One initiative after another can be pointed to as shining examples of an impassioned student who didn't take no for an answer.

Start-up capital is often a constraint to sustainable projects. How does an institution of higher learning support sustainable projects run by students? Grand Valley supplied support through minigrants, seed money of up to $500, to help get projects started. The university has recently rolled funding of the minigrants into the Sustainable Community Reinvestment Fund. The reinvestment fund was set up to create efficiencies and value for the GVSU community that would then funnel the savings back into the fund. Cost savings would then fund future sustainable projects, making the whole process sustainable. The benefit of combining conservation projects with those without monetary gain is that efficiencies can finance value creation. The higher the return on conservation projects, the more money that is available for environmental stewardship and social equity projects.

In 2007, an ambitious student was adamant about removing lunchroom trays from the campus cafeterias. It took much lobbying, but eventually she was granted a trial run in one of the lunchrooms. Protests were immediate. Complaints about the new-found difficulties were rampant. A few football players were furious about having to make more than one trip to the food counters, but the rage was overcome by a petite female student who took the time to explain. By standing at the end of the lunch line, she was able to meet each complaint with a factual response. Water conservation figures, soap reduction, and financial savings figures were given as reasons for the inconvenience of carrying a plate and a glass at the same time. Once students understood the reasons for the change, the policy was embraced and spread to the other dining areas. This initiative started by one student now saves over 1.75 million gallons of water a year and 50 pounds of soap a week, and has reduced food waste by an astonishing 30%, a result that was not originally anticipated.

The following year, a class project created the community garden. The philosophy class wanted to address health issues by raising awareness about the benefits of locally grown produce using organic practices. The group was allowed to use a plot of land at the edge of campus without a long-term commitment from administration. Three years later, the small class project has transformed into a community outreach program involving local elementary schools, the campus day care center, and Upward Bound students.[2] It is also the source of many interdisciplinary sustainability projects, including business students writing a business plan, communications majors providing a marketing strategy to generate revenue at the on-campus farmer's market, a public administration class helping with grant writing, biology students assisting with soil amendments, and a geography class providing mapping research. The collaborative effort is expected, after only 3 years, to expand what was a small class project into a community-supported agriculture program.

A third example started in 2008 and is gaining momentum. Plastic water bottles are a favorite target of student angst. Many campuses have groups looking to ban the sales of plastic bottles in vending machines. Grand Valley's Student Environmental Coalition, a student organization, started such a movement. This passionate group, with legitimate concerns about the needless transportation of water and issues caused by manufacturing plastic bottles, now ran head on into the economic factor of sustainability. The sale of bottled water is the biggest revenue source for the campus vendor, and a long-term contract was in place with the bottling company. The students had to adapt, and adapt they did. The following year, the Student Environmental Coalition changed the focus to education. Awareness-raising events were held to highlight the advantages of tap water, and taste tests were organized comparing tap water to the much more expensive bottled variety. The Students On Tap project is now taking the next step and looking to partner with the facilities office to retrofit several drinking fountains to provide refillable water bottle dispensers, with light-emitting diode (LED) readouts that measure the number of plastic water bottles diverted from the landfills.

Avoiding Green Fatigue

In the last few years, the passion for action on campuses has become more emboldened. A term now known as *green fatigue* is being used to describe the malaise brought on by inactivity and meetings that only lead to more meetings. Stakeholders are increasingly frustrated by roadblocks to activity. They have grown weary of hearing bureaucratic reasons for inaction rather than solutions to problems. The last thing they want is to sit in a series of meetings to discuss definitions or strategic policy. Student involvement today is about action, and if mistakes are made, corrections to the action can be made later. In the opinion of many, it is far better to take action and learn than to take no action. This kind of drive is changing the culture of educational institutions. Finding a reason to avoid action is no longer acceptable. Students are engaged and push for progress on their stated initiatives, whether the initiatives follow policy guidelines or not. The voice of today's students comes from a passion that deserves and demands to be heard. It is the place of the educational institution to advise and provide direction for students who are energized and motivated to the point of engagement. Enabling leads to innovation, and innovation reduces or even eliminates green fatigue.

As we move forward in finding ways to promote sustainable involvement, there are indeed numerous obstacles to overcome. Whether it is confusion over the definition of sustainability, inadequate metrics for involvement, resistance to change, or the apathy of green fatigue, it is the responsibility of educational institutions to inspire the creativity and innovation to succeed, to support the efforts of risk takers, and to lead. While administrators, faculty members, and students are all on the same path of sustainability, whoever is leading might want to pick up the pace.

Notes

1. Grand Valley State University CAP 400: Advertising/Public Relations Campaign class project. The course was taught by Peggy Howard.
2. Upward Bound is a federally funded TRIO program that supports high school students for college entrance. The community garden hosted about 20 Upward Bound students for participation in the sustainable agriculture program.

References

Beckerman, W. (1996). *Through green-colored glasses: Environmentalism reconsidered.* Washington, DC: The Cato Institute.

Ewoldt, D. (2007, May 13). What does sustainability really mean? Relocalize.net: The Relocalization Network. Retrieved from http://old.relocalize.net/what_does_sustainability_really_emean

Global Development Research Center. (2011). Sustainable development definitions. Retrieved from http://www.gdrc.org/sustdev/definitions.html

Grand Valley State University. (2008). 2008 sustainability indicator report. Retrieved from http://www.gvsu.edu/cms3/assets/1ACDDEF0-A15A-67B1-F268 BE06B2416593/documents/2008/2008-sustainability-indicator-report.pdf

Grand Valley State University. (2009). Strategic positioning 2010–2015: Values. Retrieved from http://www.gvsu.edu/strategicplanning/values-17.htm

Norton, B. (2005). *Sustainability: A philosophy of adaptive ecosystem management.* Chicago: University of Chicago Press.

Sustainable Endowments Institute. (2010). College sustainability report card 2011: Indicators. Retrieved from http://www.greenreportcard.org/report-card-2011/indicators

Toman, M. A. (1992). The difficulty in defining sustainability. *Resources, 106,* 3–6. http://www.wsu.edu:8080/~susdev/Toman92.html

2010 college hopes and worries survey report. (2010). *Princeton Review.* Retrieved from http://www.princetonreview.com/uploadedFiles/Test_Preparation/Hopes_and_Worries/HopeAndWorries_Full%20Report.pdf

World Commission on Environment and Development. (1987). Chapter 2: Towards sustainable development. *Our Common Future.* UN Documents. Retrieved from http://www.un-documents.net/ocf-02.htm

PART FOUR

LEADERSHIP AND REFORM STRATEGIES FOR LONG-TERM INSTITUTIONAL CHANGE

17

TEACHING SUSTAINABILITY LEADERSHIP

Courtney Quinn and Gina Matkin

E ffective leadership is the process of creating and sustaining positive change. The dearth of strong cohesive leadership in the environmental community is frequently cited as one reason for failure to make more significant progress toward sustainable systems. Consequently, in popular and academic literature, new integrative leaders are being sought to shape a sustainable future. Teaching upcoming leaders from various disciplines about the interaction of sustainability and leadership skills may be one of the most important tasks for education. In this chapter, we discuss the need to teach sustainability leadership and our approach to educating a new generation of leaders to address today's most pressing issues.

To begin the discussion on the education of sustainability leaders, we provide an overview of leadership studies and its relationship to sustainability. We examine how this crossing of fields encourages a new type of leader. Particularly, we focus on our approach and philosophy to teaching leadership for sustainability. We describe how we use leadership theory to inform curricula and pedagogies for undergraduate and graduate students from a variety of social and physical disciplines. We give details on how we help students explore both the larger philosophical questions regarding leadership for sustainable organizations and communities, as well as practical applications of leadership skills. Specific examples from a course entitled Environmental Leadership are utilized to explore the teaching of sustainability leadership, but we believe the concepts and strategies we use here could be applied to other leadership courses, too. The study of leadership is a unique field that provides an opportunity to support student success and give students the tools to envision and create a sustainable future.

Leadership Studies

Humans have been concerned with leaders and leadership for centuries. The study of history has primarily been a study of leaders (Bass, 1990). As a formal practice, leadership studies is a research-based, multidisciplinary field that focuses on influence exerted by a person (or persons) in order to guide, structure, and/or facilitate activities and relationships in pursuit of a common task or goal. In the past, leadership for economic, social, or environmental gain was considered a distinct research area.

Economic Leadership

Beginning with the Industrial Revolution and continuing into the 20th century, theories of effective leadership focused on effective business management. Taking their cue from ancient writers concerned with gaining and retaining power, such as Machiavelli (1513), researchers studied how to create an organizational culture that translated into economic profit (McGregor, 1960; Taylor, 1911).

Social Leadership

The study of leadership has always been about relationships between people, as well as between groups, organizations, cultures, and even eras. Well-known leadership theories such as charismatic (Conger & Kanungo, 1994), transformational (Burns, 1978), authentic (Avolio & Gardner, 2005), and leader member exchange (Graen & Uhl-Bien, 1995) all focus on various aspects of relationships. These relationships form the basis of our culture and thus help shape everything, from a dyad to a social movement, to a society and beyond.

Environmental Leadership

Only a few models of environmental leadership have been offered (Gardner, 1995; Manolis et al., 2009; Portugal & Yukl, 1994). Some research has focused on the characteristics of environmental leaders (Egri & Herman, 2000). The majority of scholarly activity revolves around variables that predict or influence pro-environmental behavior, including an individual's values and beliefs (Schultz et al., 2005), environmental knowledge (DeChano,

2006), and motivations toward the environment (Pelletier, Tuson, Green-Demers, Noels, & Beaton, 1998). Gordon and Berry (2006) note that environmental leaders are trying to solve problems that have long-term solutions, complex interactions of issues and people, scattered scientific information, a need for interdisciplinary cooperation, and an emotionally charged and often contentious surrounding atmosphere. This makes for a rather difficult task.

A Move to Sustainability Leadership

Given the inherent complexities of moving toward a sustainable system, a new consciousness is emerging, one that increasingly recognizes that leadership for economic prosperity, social well-being, and environmental sustainability are not separate goals. For too long, leaders have focused on a single aim without seeing the interconnections among economic, social, and environmental health. Just as leaders need to consider all areas of their organization simultaneously, sustainability leaders must focus on the interwoven whole of healthy, natural, and human communities. We are being called on to reexamine our definitions of, and assumptions about, leadership (Ferdig, 2007), which in turn forces educators to reconsider why and how we teach leadership. Our students will face complex problems that will require leadership from people in formal positions of power as well as active community members. Educators must help our future leaders understand the interconnectedness of local and global issues and to practice working together to find and implement creative solutions.

Teaching Sustainability Leadership

The need for sustainability leaders has never been greater. The interactions among population, consumption, and technologies compound the challenge. Institutions of higher education must engage the development of sustainability leaders. This work requires interdisciplinary action. Because most teaching and research in universities remains within highly specialized disciplines, it is difficult to offer students an education that bridges these divides. However, the discipline of leadership studies can be one such bridge. Students from every major are interested in, and can benefit from, classes on leadership. Classes on leadership expose students to economic, social, and environmental issues and provide the opportunity for students in different majors to work together to solve problems that cross disciplines.

A Course on Environmental Leadership

The course Environmental Leadership has been available through the department of Agricultural Leadership, Education, and Communication at the University of Nebraska–Lincoln for more than a decade. The course, designed for upper-level undergraduates and graduate students, provides an opportunity to examine historical, current, and future leadership and leaders in the environmental movement. We explore western social narratives (such as individualism, industrialization, and consumerism), global environmental narratives, stories told by individual leaders, and theories of behavior change relating to the environmental movement. This overview provides students with necessary contexts to explore environmental issues and how they relate to social and economic concepts. We highlight leadership theories needed to evaluate and address the complexities of sustainability.

Many extant leadership theories can inform our understanding and teaching of sustainability leadership. Visioning and stories, significant life experiences, and theories of behavior change guide our sustainability leadership curriculum. In this chapter, we discuss each leadership theory and how it applies to sustainability leadership, and we provide an example of use in the classroom. Students' required readings for each topic are found in table 17.1.

Visioning and Stories

A core tenet of seminal leadership theories is visioning (Bass, 1990; Conger & Kanungo, 1987; Farling, Stone, & Winston, 1999; Greenleaf, 1977). Most leadership theories consider communicating a vision to motivate people to action to be a hallmark behavior of a leader. To articulate this vision, leaders use stories (Gardner, 1995). Leaders tell stories about themselves and those they lead; where they are coming from and where they are going; and what should be feared, struggled against, and dreamed about (Gardner, 1995).

The theory of charismatic leadership proposes that leaders offer a story decidedly different from the status quo (Conger & Kanungo, 1987). Kaak (2010) thus proposes that sustainability leaders have a vision and set of values that run counter to their industrial forebears. What makes the vision process a challenge for sustainability leaders is that, except in times of crisis, members of society are not looking for an unfamiliar or new story (Gardner, 1995). Many questions arise that we must help students address when teaching visioning and sustainability leadership, including: (1) Does the general population feel we are in a time of crisis? (2) If not, what impact does lack of

TABLE 17.1
Examples of Required Readings for Sustainability Leadership Topics in the Course Entitled Environmental Leadership

Topic	Example Readings	Chapter or Article
Visioning and stories	Gardner, H. 1995. *Leading Minds*	"A Cognitive Approach to Leadership"
	Hopkins, R. 2008. *The Transition Handbook*	"Harnessing the Power of a Positive Vision"
	Shellenberger, M., & Nordhaus, T. 2007. *Break Through: From the Death of Environmentalism to the Politics of Possibility*	"Death of Environmentalism"
Significant life experiences	Chawla, L., 1998. "Significant Life Experiences Revisited: A Review of Research."	
	Kooser, T. 2002. *Local Wonders: Seasons in the Bohemian Alps*	
	Louv, R. 2005. *Last Child in the Woods*	
Behavior change	Bamberg, S., & Moser, G. 2007. "Twenty Years after Hines, Hungerford, and Tomera: A New Meta-Analysis of Psycho-Social Determinants of Pro-environmental Behavior."	
	Hopkins, R. 2008. *The Transition Handbook*	"How Peak Oil and Climate Change Affect Us: 'Post-Petroleum Stress Disorder'" "Understanding the Psychology of Change"
	Yes! Magazine, Issue 52	"Why We Find It So Hard to Act against Climate Change"

concern have on the vision that sustainability leaders are trying to convey through their stories?

For a discussion of sustainability leadership and visioning, we include the negative visions and images so often portrayed in the media. Students relate to doom-and-gloom scenarios because popular media frequently use such images. Students quickly relate to the Shellenberger and Nordhaus (2007) piece. In our experience of classroom discussions, this is where many students become stuck. They ask, "What can I do? I'm just one person." In response, students read a selection that offers a positive vision. "It is one thing to campaign against climate change and quite another to paint a compelling and engaging vision of a post-carbon world in such a way as to enthuse others to embark on a journey towards it" (Hopkins, 2008, p. 94).

To engage students actively in the classroom, teams of students choose an issue and draw a poster, write a news article, or role-play a story of a positive future that considers the environment, people, and economics as an integrated whole. In our quest for sustainability, we need leaders who create a positive vision through the ability to tell a story about where we have been and where we need to go.

Significant Life Experiences

Avolio (1994) notes that individual leadership tendencies may be directly or indirectly linked to key life experiences. The question, "Which life experiences shape leaders' development?" has been asked by environmental leadership researchers. Through interviews, researchers have found that spending time outdoors as a child, time with influential adults, reading books, negative experiences of environmental destruction, and a deep connection to a place can influence environmental leaders (Chawla, 1999; Palmer, 1993; Tanner, 1980). Arnold, Cohen, and Warner (2009) found similar responses among young environmental leaders.

For class discussion, we focus on the importance of outdoor experiences and a sense of place. During this unit, we like to hold at least one class period outside or take a field trip to a local natural area. To discuss significant life experiences and a sense of place, we encourage instructors of sustainability leadership to use reading selections written about the place where most students are from or where the class is located. A field trip to the location gives students a novel way to experience and discuss the role that our sense of place has in sustainability leadership. Next, students discuss possible implications of the predominantly indoor and structured life of many children today. After sharing their own childhood outdoor experiences, students discuss our rapidly changing society and childhood experiences, and consider possible long-term effects on sustainability leadership.

Behavior Change

The ultimate goal of sustainability leaders is to change behavior. Whether this occurs through a new worldview that values sustainable behavior, policies that promote actions to benefit people's prosperity and that of the planet, or individual commitment to change, sustainability leaders seek to motivate us to change our current way of life. Of course, this is more easily said than done. Therefore, leadership theories on behavior change have much to offer students of sustainability leadership.

Lewin's (1951) change theory considered behavior change to consist of unfreezing, moving, and then refreezing group standards. Bartunek and Moch (1987) provide a theory of first-, second-, and third-order behavior change. This change theory applies to both individuals and organizations. First-order change is merely the tacit reinforcement of current understandings. Second-order change involves conscious modification of present ways of thinking. This is similar to what the environmental movement has been trying to accomplish. Third-order change occurs when people are aware of their present mental schema and therefore are able to change it as they see fit. Sustainability leaders seek third-order change in both themselves and others. Hardman (2009) found that sustainability leaders deliberately focus on their personal awareness and are willing to "surface and change one's mental models." Ferdig (2007) notes that sustainability leaders embrace changing dynamics and recognize that the process of change fuels creativity and innovation.

For a preclass assignment, students reflect on a time when they wanted or needed to change a personal behavior. This gives them a personal connection to the material. In class, we use Bamberg and Moser's (2007) model of pro-environmental behavior as a framework to discuss other readings and a visual way to debate causes of our action or inaction. The model combines Schwartz's norm-activation model (1977), which supposes pro-environmental behavior is based on prosocial motivation, with Ajzen's theory of planned behavior (1991), which assumes behavior is primarily motivated by self-interest. We evaluate the role of guilt and fear in rendering people incapable of acting on environmental issues. Students discuss the role of social norms in guiding which issues are discussed in the political arena as well as around the dinner table.

Learning From Experience

To give students a personal connection to the course material and make learning more concrete, students are required to complete a project during the semester. The goal of the project is to develop a plan that can create change in awareness or behavior. The project can be individual or team-based. This three-part project requires students to use the leadership theories they have learned and to integrate concerns for people, prosperity, and the planet.

Part one requires students to collect information and data on a topic of interest to them. Students also research current local, national, and international leadership on the issue. Student topics can begin from their interest in social justice, economics, or pro-environmental behavior. For example, an environmental studies student may research the waste stream in her or his community by gathering data on the garbage and recycling services in her or his town. A business major may research companies that are both profitable and do not use sweatshop labor. Students report their findings to the class. The class then helps their peers consider aspects of sustainability not originally researched. If the student researching a community waste stream neglected to collect data on the cost to taxpayers or individual citizens for garbage and recycling pickup, other students and the instructor can guide the student to collect additional information. Students then share their completed research with the instructor and one additional classmate for a peer review before proceeding to part two.

In part two, students are required to become immersed in their issue. They conduct interviews and collect stories of and about leaders and the people, organizations, or policies they are seeking to influence. Students are encouraged to become *participant observers* and assist an organization, business, policy maker, or individual while the student observes and experiences the organization's or person's leadership. Students can go to an organizational meeting, attend an event, or participate with an individual testifying at a policy meeting. Students then create a written report that analyzes whether the leadership they witnessed included concern for people, prosperity, and the planet.

Part three requires students to create a sustainability leadership plan for their chosen topic. This plan can be for an event, a campaign, or even a business. The requirement is that students explicitly consider people, prosperity, and the planet as an integrated whole. For example, the environmental studies student must not neglect economic concerns about tax increases to fund recycling programs. The business student should consider the environmental consequences of natural resource extraction and disposal in the making of their proposed product or service. Students use collected data and experiences to create, explain, and justify their goal(s), objectives, and strategies. In addition, students envision and create a written or visual story of their results as if they have already been achieved. This story can be in the form of a newspaper article, poster, play, online video, or other type of report. The final plan and future vision is presented to the class.

At our university, this course is taken by students from many different disciplines. It is not uncommon for students to remark in their journals, assignments, or course evaluations that the opportunity to explore the connections among the environment, people, and economics was eye-opening. In addition, students value the opportunity to work on a project of personal value to them while practicing their leadership skills. One student noted, "In the future I am going to use what I learned to encourage my employees to have the same attitude I had when it comes to creating change. We can all be innovators and try to create a better place for business and the environment."

Conclusion

Currently, there is limited scholarly work focused on sustainability leadership. Economic and social leadership have received considerable attention by scholars and practitioners, and environmental leadership is just now emerging. At this time, an integration of leadership is needed that includes all aspects of a sustainable future. In this chapter, we reviewed existing leadership theories we use to teach environmental leadership and the continued development of a holistic curriculum. Creating a positive vision through stories, fostering significant life experiences, and understanding the process and impediments to behavior change are critical topics that any leader, but specifically sustainability leaders, needs to consider. Our hope is that the practical in-class ideas described here can spur more classes toward a focus on sustainability leadership.

Leadership is the process of creating change. The complexities of simultaneously considering economic, environmental, and social needs create a need for leaders with a broad array of understanding and skills. Therefore, we expect a lot from our leaders. We seek leaders who have "clarity of mind, spiritual depth, courage, and vision" and who are modest and understand patterns and connections between people and nature (Orr, 2003). We want leaders who are intelligent, articulate, charismatic, and media-savvy (Joly, 2004); who are strong, dedicated, and focused (Lindenmayer & Likens, 2010); and who have the willingness to examine and change their mental models while facilitating multiple stakeholder engagement in the same process (Hardman, 2009). It is the responsibility of educators to help students develop and practice the skills and explore the ideas that will allow them to lead society to a sustainable future. While we recognize that a single course cannot foster all such characteristics and skills required of our future leaders, we regard our course as a small start that may spur larger changes in individuals, departments, institutions, and ultimately the rest of society.

References

Ajzen, I. (1991). The theory of planned behavior. *Organizational Behavior and Human Decision Processes, 50,* 179–211.

Arnold, H., Cohen, F., & Warner, A. (2009). Youth and environmental action: Perspectives of young environmental leaders on their formative influences. *Journal of Environmental Education, 40*(3), 27–36.

Avolio, B. J. (1994). The "natural": Some antecedents to transformational leadership. *International Journal of Public Administration, 17*(9), 1559–1581.

Avolio, B. J., & Gardner, W. L. (2005). Authentic leadership development: Getting to the root of positive forms of leadership. *Leadership Quarterly, 16,* 315–338.

Bamberg, S., & Moser, G. (2007). Twenty years after Hines, Hungerford, and Tomera: A new meta-analysis of psycho-social determinants of pro-environmental behavior. *Journal of Environmental Psychology, 27*(1), 14–25.

Bartunek, J. M., & Moch, M. K. (1987). First-order, second-order, and third-order change and organization development interventions: A cognitive approach. *Journal of Applied Behavioral Science, 23*(4), 483–500.

Bass, B. M. (1990). From transactional to transformational leadership: Learning to share the vision. *Organizational Dynamics, 18*(3), 19–31.

Burns, J. M. (1978). *Leadership.* New York: Harper & Row.

Chawla, L. (1998). Significant life experiences revisited: A review of research. *Journal of Environmental Education, 29*(3), 11–21.

Chawla, L. (1999). Life paths into effective environmental action. *Journal of Environmental Education, 31*(1), 15–26.

Conger, J. A., & Kanungo, R. N. (1987). Toward a behavioral theory of charismatic leadership in organizational settings. *Academy of Management Review, 12*(4), 637–647.

Conger, J. A., & Kanungo, R. N., (1994). Charismatic leadership in organizations: Perceived behavioural attributes and their measurement. *Journal of Organizational Behaviour, 15,* 1–14.

DeChano, L. M. (2006). A multi-country examination of the relationship between environmental knowledge and attitudes. *International Research in Geographical and Environmental Education, 15,* 15–28.

Egri, C. P., & Herman, S. (2000). Leadership in the North American environmental sector: Values, leadership styles, and contexts of environmental leaders and their organizations. *Academy of Management Journal, 43*(4), 571–604.

Farling, M. L., Stone, A. G., & Winston, B. E. (1999). Servant leadership: Setting the stage for empirical research. *Journal of Leadership Studies, 6*(1), 49–72.

Ferdig, M.A. (2007). Sustainability leadership: Co-creating a sustainable future. *Journal of Change Management, 7*(1), 23–35.

Gardner, H. (1995). *Leading minds: An anatomy of leadership.* New York: Basic Books, pp. 3–21.

Gordon, J. C., & Berry, J. K. (2006). *Environmental leadership equals essential leadership: Redefining who leads and how.* New Haven, CT: Yale University Press.

Graen, G. B., & Uhl-Bien, M. (1995). The relationship-based approach to leadership: Development of LMX theory of leadership over 25 years: Applying a multi-level, multi-domain perspective. *Leadership Quarterly, 6*(2), 219–247.

Greenleaf, R. (1977). *Servant leadership: A journey into the nature of legitimate power and greatness.* Mahwah, NJ: Paulist Press.

Hardman, J. H. (2009). Regenerative leadership: Theory and practice for transforming people and organizations for sustainability in business, education, and community. *Journal of Environmental Assessment Policy and Management, 8*(3), 259–280.

Hopkins, R. (2008). *The transition handbook: From oil dependency to local resilience.* White River Junction, VT: Chelsea Green Publishing.

Joly, K. (2004). Stop the train! *Conservation Biology, 18*(1), 4.

Kaak, P. (2010). The agrarian mind and good leadership: Harvesting insights from the literary field of Wendell Berry. In Benjamin Redekop (Ed.), *Leadership for environmental sustainability* (pp. 145–157). New York: Routledge.

Kooser, T. (2002). *Local wonders: Seasons in the Bohemian Alps.* Lincoln: University of Nebraska Press.

Lewin, K. (1951). *Field theory in social science: Selected theoretical papers.* Chicago, IL: University of Chicago Press.

Lindenmayer, D., & Likens, G. (2010). The science and application of ecological monitoring. *Biological Conservation, 143,* 1317–1328.

Louv, R. (2005). *Last child in the woods: Saving our children from nature-deficit disorder.* Chapel Hill, NC: Algonquin Books.

Machiavelli, N. (1513/1992). *The prince.* Toronto: Dover Publications.

Manolis, J. C., Chan, K. M., Finkelstein, M. E., Stephens, S., Nelson, C. R., Grant, J. B., & Dombeck, M. P. (2009). Leadership: a new frontier in conservation science. *Conservation Biology, 23,* 879–886.

McGregor, D. (1960). *The human side of enterprise.* New York: McGraw-Hill Book Company.

Orr, D. (2003). Walking north on a southbound train. *Conservation Biology, 17,* 348.

Palmer, J. A. (1993). Development of concern for the environment and formative experiences of educators. *Journal of Environmental Education, 24*(3), 26–30.

Pelletier, L., Tuson, K., Green-Demers, I., Noels. K., & Beaton, A. (1998). Why are you doing things for the environment? The Motivation Toward the Environment Scale (MTES). *Journal of Applied Social Psychology, 28*(5), 437–468.

Portugal, E., & Yukl, G. (1994). Perspectives on environmental leadership. *Leadership Quarterly, 5*(3/4), 271–276.

Schultz, P. W., Gouveia, V. V., Cameron, L. D., Tankha, G., Schmuck, P., & Franek, M. (2005). Values and their relationship to environmental concern and conservation behavior. *Journal of Cross-Cultural Psychology, 36,* 457–475.

Schwartz, S. H. (1977). Normative influence on altruism. In L. Berkowitz (Ed.), *Advances in experimental social psychology,* vol. 10 (pp. 221–279). New York: Academic Press.

Shellenberger, M., & Nordhaus, T. (2007). *Break through: From the death of environmentalism to the politics of possibility.* New York: Houghton Mifflin.

Tanner, T. (1980). Significant life experiences. *Journal of Environmental Education, 11*(4), 20–24.

Taylor, F. W. (1911). *The principles of scientific management.* New York: Harper & Brothers.

18

TEACHING SUSTAINABILITY TO FUTURE MUSEUM PROFESSIONALS

Sarah S. Brophy

The Green Museum class (part of the Graduate Museum Studies program at the George Washington University [GW] and Certificate of Museum Studies at the University of Delaware [UDel]) addresses environmental sustainability in museums, historic sites, gardens, zoos, and aquariums. Museums benefit from the public trust, and they must safeguard this public trust; sustainability is an important aspect of this safeguarding. As charitable institutions, they are responsible to their communities for their environmental impact and for conserving their financial resources. As preservation organizations, they are responsible for protecting art, artifacts, historic sites, and natural resources. As educational institutions, they are responsible for engaging and teaching the public about important issues that are important historically, now and in the future.

The children's museums, science centers, and those caring for living things were early adopters of this green responsibility. Next were those involved in building projects who hired architects skilled in sustainability. The rest of the museum community has been slow to change, however. The economic recession, the complexity of green practices and options, and museums' institutional aversion to risk are all barriers to increasing the level of environmental sustainability.

Yet this resistance to change toward a more sustainable way of operating is at odds with the expectations of many recent graduates, who have finished secondary school and college in the most recent wave of environmental awareness. These individuals are actively recycling, saving water and energy, and thinking about organic foods and local sources. They are proactive in their lives and eager to learn about and implement the new technology—green bling—commonly perceived as the greenest practice.

To bridge the gap between students' expectations and current practices, the graduate-level Green Museums course focuses on understanding the process of decision making around sustainability and on the process of bringing about change among peers. The expectation is that students completing the course will be prepared to facilitate increased environmental sustainability in their future workplaces regardless of the existing museum culture and views of sustainability. Our learning goals are that students will successfully demonstrate understanding that:

1. Increasing the degree of environmental sustainability in the practices of people and organizations is a process of patience, education, and continued learning for all parties.
2. Researching, assessing, and then choosing are critical skills in green practice.
3. Modeling green practices oneself is the best way to encourage change, but that it is as challenging and complex for one to *model* as it is for an observer to *adopt.*

Challenges

Teaching this class has three particular challenges:

1. Fitting all the reading material into a single course while adapting every semester's syllabus to reflect changes in the museum field and in green practice
2. Allowing time to address trending issues during the semester
3. Recognizing that environmental sustainability, being an ecosystem topic, does not lend itself to linear study or to a steady progression through the course

Managing Reading Materials

A topic as complex as the field of sustainability seems to expand continually: Available research increases as does the quantity and diversity of materials. In the last 2 years, the amount of museum-specific articles on green practice has quadrupled. While this increase provides higher-quality reading material, it adds challenges in the selection of assignments. Each semester requires comprehensive restructuring and adaptability as the course progresses. Educational delivery programs such as BlackBoard and Sakai make it easy to provide articles, and video and website links electronically. These tools allow instructors to keep the resource materials current for each semester and to make midcourse additions for trending topics.

Incorporating Trending Issues

With the influx of new information, I often allow a news story or fresh trend to displace any prepared basic presentations. For example, zoo professionals actively debate the use of products, particularly snack foods and candy, that include palm oil. These products are available at zoo cafés and at special events; an example of a special event is opening zoos for Halloween trick-or-treating. But the monoculture harvest of palm oil destroys habitat for orangutans, Bengal tigers, and Asian elephants when the farmers clear-cut forests and impinge on habitat to plant palms. This topic is both timely and topical, and the course's goal is to develop the students' ability to collect and assess information and then use it to make effective decisions. Taking time to explore and address issues like this is critical to the course. This relatively new debate became an important topic for group work (described later). Adaptability is an important component of a course about sustainability, and we abandoned the preset class presentation and found other ways to engage with the topic of producing palm oil and other topics like it.

Recognizing the Lack of Linear Progression

Recognizing the need for adaptability and implementing the subsequent changes are very different tasks. I tend to think linearly, so I would prefer to organize a course with a similar progression. Yet a linear progression for this type of class is challenged not only by the need to interject timely and topical material but also by the topic's nature. Because an ecosystem has so many interconnections, and sustainability is about natural and re-created ecosystem services, it is very difficult to design a single, obvious content sequence. To provide a clear but interconnected structure, I have adopted the categories of Leadership in Energy and Environmental Design (LEED) to help frame class topics: sustainable sites, water efficiency, energy and atmosphere and indoor environmental quality, and materials and resources. The museum-specific topic of collections care fits squarely into energy and atmosphere and indoor air quality, and exhibit design fits nicely into materials and resources.

This is not because I do or do not endorse LEED, but because LEED is a useful assessment method that students will continue to experience in their careers.

Course Format

The classes mix readings, discussion, museum visits, guest lecturers, and group work to facilitate engagement and learning. The group work includes decision scenarios, debate, and the creation of mock museums to explore concepts in a variety of ways. On their own, students keep journals of green practices (their own and others') and organize a project that improves environmental sustainability in an organization. The journal and the project are consistently the most effective parts of the class.

Class Work: Readings

In addition to a wide variety of articles discussed in the class, I assign a minimum of four books, excerpts, or journals, depending on the class format. *The Green Museum: A Primer on Environmental Practice* (Brophy & Wylie, 2008) serves as our core text. As with other aspects of the course, the selection was not straightforward because the timing of the introduction of the book is problematic. If students read it first, it overwhelms them with new information and options, but if they read it later in the course, they may not have the foundation needed to grasp the complexity of what we see in museum visits. The solution seems to be to require it in advance for six-week courses, and midway for full-semester ones. Although the number of articles is increasing regularly, "Green and Lean," known as the "Green Issue," of *Exhibitionist: The Journal of the National Association for Museum Exhibition* (Jennings, 2009), remains the only green text from the exhibits field currently available. A handbook for green exhibitions—designed and field-tested with support from the National Science Foundation—should be available in 2014 and will become a regular part of the course.

To grasp fully the multitude of issues inherent in sustainable practices, regarding sustainability from a broader viewpoint is pivotal. To accomplish this goal, two texts are selected: *Climate Change, Past, Present & Future: A Very Short Guide*, by Warren D. Allmon, Trisha A. Smrecak, and Robert M. Roas (2010), and *The Consumer's Guide to Effective Environmental Choices: Practical Advice from the Union of Concerned Scientists*, by Michael Brower and Warren Leon (1999). *Climate Change* helps establish baseline knowledge for all students, and *The Consumer's Guide* illustrates that data and appearance often conflict, making green decision making very complex. *Cradle to Cradle: Remaking the Way We Make Things*, by William McDonough and Michael Braungart (2002), gets students thinking about life cycle analysis and is the basis for our "close the loop" principle. I often supplement these with a few chapters from *Making Sustainability Work: Best Practices in Managing and Measuring Corporate Social, Environmental and Economic Impacts* by Marc J. Epstein (2008) to help students understand risk aversion in nonprofits, and the process of managing sustainability plans and goals institutionwide.

Together, these readings prepare the students to discuss the quadruple bottom line: people, planet, profit, and program as a decision-making tool. We acknowledge the challenge of first costs, or green premiums, as a barrier for museums interested in implementing green practices and green construction, then review the concept of evaluating institutional options not just by the cost of a green activity but also by the benefits, or costs, related to the planet (environment), people (visitors, staff members, and members of the community), and program (the museum's mission and its work at collecting, preserving, and interpreting objects, history, and art, and educating the public). Again, the lack of linearity makes this a complex process but, as discussed later in the chapter, the process is important in making difficult choices on complex topics.

Class Work: Discussion

One-third of the classes are simply lectures and discussions based on Power-Point presentations with images of museums, specific construction components, sample exhibits, and representative program activities. For each of these images, we evaluate the pros and cons of each green example and discuss what factors students should consider if they were responsible for, for example, participating in a decision about allowing daylight into certain exhibit galleries, selecting lighting designs for collection spaces versus the gift shop, or identifying materials for more sustainable exhibit installations within a museum. Because decision making is often based on core principles, we use the core principles listed here to provide structure for the evaluation:

1. Think like an ecosystem: The class is about the environment and every activity creates multiple effects.
2. Close the loop: This course is all about life cycles of goods, practices, and living organisms, so we must evaluate each practice or material from its source to next use, not source to landfill.

3. Do more than one task: Activities are more efficient if each creates synergy and achieves multiple goals.
4. Educate inside and out: Teach yourself, your colleagues, and the public so that we can "green" the world more quickly.

Class Work: Museum Visits and Guest Lecturers

GW is in Washington, DC, and benefits greatly from proximity to many excellent museums. We visit four or five sites each semester. Museum staff members lead the visits, based on a loose topical outline discussed in advance. Their willingness to discuss failures and successes makes these experiences particularly valuable. Visits have included the National Museum of Natural History, where students studied sustainable practices in collections management, building rehabilitation, and the café; and the National Building Museum, where students considered how the museum has branded itself as a green resource through the design and promotion of green exhibits and programs. Students explore green historic preservation at Lincoln's Cottage and Visitor Education Center (National Trust for Historic Preservation), energy efficiency retrofits at the National Gallery of Art, and sustainable practices for living collections and outdoor sites at the National Zoo. Because so few sites are confident in green exhibit practices, we visit with an architectural firm responsible for designing and installing the interior spaces of the U.S. Green Building Council's (USGBC's) LEED Platinum headquarters.

While site visits are time-consuming and often require burning fossil fuels, guest lecturers provide content and real-world experience at a lower sustainability cost. We use Skype to "bring in" speakers from the Utah Museum of Natural History to talk about their construction project. They narrate a PowerPoint presentation and respond to student questions. This gives the class an opportunity to discuss museum operations in a state with a different climate, geographical barriers, opportunities, and community expectations. For example, choosing a site for the new museum required relocating a very popular mountain biking trail and addressing natural open space resource management, problems not encountered in our urban Washington, DC, setting.

For a trending topic, we invited Cecily Grzywacz, conservation scientist at the nearby National Gallery of Art and chair of the American Society of Heating, Refrigerating and Air-Conditioning Engineers (ASHRAE) committee on standards for museums (heating and air-conditioning), to present a review of the present debate on relaxing the standards for interior climate control. Museums that share collections for exhibits, such as paintings, furniture, and documents, are required to commit to certain standards in exhibit conditions. The narrow expectations for heating and cooling and humidity controls are very energy-intensive. Changes to these guidelines could mean significant energy (and cost) savings for many museums, and these changes would be more in line with actual practice for those unable to achieve the strict guidelines. This topic will come to a head as these students take permanent jobs, so they must be well versed in the discussion and prepared to participate. Her visit means the students now have a personal connection to a leader in the field, and she encouraged them to contact her in the future, whether as a student or once employed in the field, if they have specific collections conservation questions, or if they would like to visit the National Gallery of Art to see her work.

Class Work: Group Work

The class, divided into four teams, completes two types of decision-making activities as group work: a team approach to decision making, and team approaches to designing the ultimate green museums. Over parts of three class meetings, beginning midway through the course, student teams tackle the idea of creating their ideal green museums. The four teams are randomly assigned a museum type: art, history, historic house, cultural, science, nature, and so on. The teams select appropriate physical features (green roof, gray water, photovoltaic [PV] panels) and program ideas (recycling, café, education options), and then create institutional mission statements. They establish their geographic regions, community sizes, and any other special characteristics to define the museums' settings. Then they start drawing and annotating. A marker-on-paper activity forces them to slow down as they assess and incorporate green options so they can design a coherent, sensible museum. At the end of the semester, they present to the class as a whole with the theory behind their museums, and they describe why they chose to include or exclude certain aspects of green practice.

Sometimes a trending topic lends itself to a decision-making activity. As previously discussed, we address the use of palm oil. After an in-class presentation to provide background information and to review the connection to museum operations—from fundraising to café menus—the students are divided into two teams, one to fight *for* palm oil use and the other to fight *against* its use. The challenge can be worded as follows: Given the palm oil situation, how can zoos encourage responsible sustainable practices that protect animal habitat and local employment, while continuing their programs in support of animal life and educating the public? Each team has an Internet researcher to support them as they develop a position, and each team has 45 minutes to prepare. The process of making a solid case requires all their faculties in weighing pros and cons, and incorporates all aspects of museum management. The side benefit of this particular discussion is that, as they make their cases, using all that they know about how museum decisions must support museum missions, and how to use the quadruple-bottom-line process, they discover their own solution by maneuvering two opposing ideas—for and against—into the best museum choice. While one team realizes that it must create the case for *sustainably sourced* palm oil, the second team creates one against *un*sustainably sourced palm oil. Even when asked to do so, neither team can or will argue for unsustainably sourced palm oil through a monoculture that threatens animal habitat.

Student Work: Journals

For half of the semester, students record six journal entries for three types of environmentally sustainable or unsustainable practices: personal, observed, and professional (both observed and recommended). Students cannot use professional examples from our class visits to museums, but otherwise they can collect entries whenever and wherever they find them. The entries range from trying harder to remember to take reusable bags to the grocery store, to complete conversion to local and organic eating; from noticing which museums have smart recycling options that are used often by the public, to tracking down the right staff member to ask why the museum isn't recycling!

Without fail, the journals illustrate significant change in students' awareness of green practices and their degree of engagement. Very often the students go beyond simply reporting an observation to researching their questions online and proposing a new or better application for themselves or for museums. By the end of the journal process, every student demonstrates excitement, surprise, and pleasure in his or her increasingly green practices, and an increased commitment to sustainability. Most entries include observations of how the student or others resisted a change, or how the student found a way to facilitate change. These key learning moments help students facilitate change during their class projects and, it is hoped, in their jobs.

Because many do not realize that their classmates are making the journey in similar fashion, at least twice during the journal period I invite each student to describe a journal entry of his or her choice. This activity has a 100% response rate: no silences, no uncomfortable looks, just pure eagerness to share. Students discover that others had the same difficulty convincing, for example, roommates to take shorter showers or colleagues to recycle paper. They could share tips on which bars serve the least expensive local beer and food. The topics often resurface during later classes, and students continue to support each other with ideas for increased personal and professional sustainability. Separately, when I review students' journals for grading, I am careful to read each entry and add comments to perhaps half of them. These range from "Me, too!" and "I didn't know that" to "Check out the National Building Museum shop as a good example." This personal connection reinforces the concept that everyone is learning—including the professor—and that any one of us has something to teach the rest of us. It creates a collegial atmosphere that reinforces the importance of continuous learning.

Student Work: Projects

Originally, my goal was for the students to complete a greening project at the museum where they intern or at a related organization (not within their family because that added too many complications). Examples were starting a recycling program from scratch, developing a complete preferred materials purchasing guide, or creating green exhibit guidelines. Completing a greening project turned out to be too ambitious for the students to implement successfully in the course's time frame, so now the projects are kept very simple: changing from a paper newsletter to an electronic one, beginning paper recycling, or researching and developing a guide to existing green features, for example. All project reports include a project assessment completed before the project begins, a description of the activities attempted, and the observed and measured results. Because full implementation is often impossible in the time frame of one course, it is a welcome benefit, but not the project goal. This approach supports our mantra that institutional greening is a journey, not a destination. Students are graded on the thoroughness of their assessments and observations, and on their ability to adapt to the changing situation, not on the final result. Without exception, students discover the following:

1. The unevenness of people's knowledge and perceptions of green practice
2. The complexity of changing people and habits
3. How change is often small and incremental

4. The way that environmental sustainability practices can build momentum among individuals and groups in a way that promises continued change after the project's completion

We take two class periods for students to report on their projects in person, in addition to the electronic report they give me. The presentation gives them an opportunity to celebrate their successes and laugh about the struggles. They can use any format they like, but they must stick to a 10-minute time frame. They often use cartoons, or images from collections, such as Edvard Munch's *The Scream*, to illustrate stories that are unfailingly funny. The students quickly see a pattern of human resistance to change, and they recognize the complexity of organizational structures, both of which they will experience repeatedly as they pursue environmental sustainability in their careers.

Student Work: Final Exam

The only exam is the final. Because so much of the class focuses on decision making, only 25% of the final exam covers vocabulary and basic short-answer questions, while 75% consists of essays. Students know in advance that the exam will have four challenge questions (of which they will select three) that encourage them to demonstrate the concepts and decision processes they have learned. They have 2 hours to complete the exam. Because the topic is both large and intricate, containing the response time forces them to demonstrate not how much they know, but how well they use what they have learned.

Greening the Course Delivery

Much of the reading is available electronically instead of in print. The *Exhibitionist*, a field-generated journal, has an issue on green exhibitions that has since been made freely available electronically (Jennings, 2009). *The Green Museum: A Primer on Environmental Practice* (Brophy & Wylie, 2008) was recently released as an e-book. Assigned articles are available in the education management systems: GW uses BlackBoard; UDel uses Sakai online. I prepare the syllabus using Century Gothic font to reduce ink use by one-third if students choose to print it. Because I live at a distance from the universities, driving to class, even transferring to public transportation halfway, is an unsustainable practice. The UDel class is a mix of online and traditional classes. This hybrid format has two bookend, face-to-face (F2F) meetings of 3 hours, or double class time, and four 90-minute online sessions. As we meet each other and begin working together, this provides support for a social presence during the intervening online class work. Then a final F2F meeting allows for group work requiring students to synthesize all they have learned and to create their ideal green museum together as they model integrated designs in their projects. I am gradually changing the GW program to a hybrid, mixing half F2F and half online, as I have done at UDel.

The online format has great instructional benefits. The topic lends itself to images of everything, from recycling containers to cutting-edge heating, ventilating, and air conditioning (HVAC) equipment and green museum buildings, so it is perfectly suited to PowerPoint delivery online. Students can choose to revisit the lecture materials as a study source and spend time in class listening and discussing rather than hurriedly taking notes. Online discussions tend to encourage participation by those students least likely to speak out in a face-to-face class, and these types of discussion allow me to divert the most talkative with a quick online research assignment to answer questions raised in class. The practicing professionals who are part of this hybrid learning group report that they find the online sessions more convenient for participation but less rewarding as a learning tool. They greatly value the face-to-face classes in the course.

The online environment also offers tools that can compensate for trying to fit too much into too little time. For example, to address vocabulary, I can use an optional self-test program so interested students can study vocabulary without consuming class time better spent on site visits and discussions. Students can retake the test until they develop mastery of the vocabulary. Many feel that the vocabulary and technical specifications are critical to their work, so until they realize that research, experimentation, and learning over time are the core of their green practice, the vocabulary self-test option satisfies their need for mastery of industry-specific terms.

The online format also allows me to encourage students to send in their own images for class discussion. At the close of each online session, I request certain types of images for the next online session wrap-up discussion. Then I present their contributed images in a PowerPoint. The student contributors describe the green roof, water wall, recycling station, interesting green exhibit, and so on, that they have discovered and that reflects our class discussions.

Is the Museum Field More Green Because of This Course?

One of the original student projects has evolved into a new recycling program for the GW Museum Studies department. I know students are practicing their green studies in their careers because they return to campus to follow up with me. One student has asked for feedback regarding green plans at her museum, one is working with me on a multimuseum project and has joined a national committee in the field, another developed new learning carts at the US Botanic Garden, and one is now a sustainability consultant. Two of these students have taken and passed the US Green Building Council's first level professional certification exam to become LEED Green Associates; both have changed their career paths to a heavy emphasis on green practice in museums. They are indeed out in the field creating change, and they have become excellent professional colleagues.

References

Allmon, W. D., Smrecak, T. A., & Roas, R. M. (2010). *Climate change, past, present & future: A very short guide.* Ithaca, NY: Paleontological Research Institution.

Brophy, S. S., & Wylie, E. (2008). *The green museum: A primer on environmental practice.* Lantham, MD: AltaMira Press. (The publisher released an e-book in 2010.)

Brower, M., & Leon, W. (1999). *The consumer's guide to effective environmental choices: Practical advice from the Union of Concerned Scientists.* New York: Three Rivers Press.

Epstein, M. J. (2008). *Making sustainability work: Best practices in managing and measuring corporate social, environmental and economic impacts.* San Francisco: GreenLeaf Publishing.

Jennings, G. (2009, Spring). Exhibitionist: Green and Lean. *Journal of the National Association for Museum Exhibition.* Washington, DC: The American Association of Museums.

McDonough, W., & Braungart, M. (2002). *Cradle to cradle: Remaking the way we make things.* New York: North Point Press.

19

ESCAPING THE STRUCTURAL TRAP OF SUSTAINABILITY IN ACADEMIA THROUGH GLOBAL LEARNING ENVIRONMENTS

Tamara Savelyeva

The lack of connection among campus greening, Education for Sustainability (EfS), and sustainability science initiatives magnifies the challenge of teaching sustainability in academia by creating a structural trap. In practice, the priority is given to a going-green approach to improving infrastructure efficiency, which promotes a one-sided understanding of sustainability among faculty members and students. The greening, EfS, and sustainability science movements at universities throughout the United States are based on the assumption that once we introduce people to a sustainability concept and show practical solutions to sustainable living, they will change their ways and the whole institution will become sustainable. Such a linear approach makes synergistic implementation of sustainability in teaching, learning, research, and campus operations particularly problematic because faculty members and students undergo separate teaching and learning curves. This creates a structural trap by simultaneously introducing sustainability at all levels of academia within an educational system that is not designed for holistic transformation. How can universities escape this trap without transforming their entire educational system? How can we merge the fields of campus greening and EfS in one model that would ignite changes in the minds of students and faculty members?

In this chapter, I describe a global learning environment (GLE) as a conceptual phenomenon and pedagogical model that addresses the challenges of the structural trap and provides an effective schema of teaching sustainability at all university levels, across different disciplinary fields and cultural backgrounds. This model was created based on the results of a 5-year empirical study of a Global Seminar (GS), an initiative facilitated by faculty members and run by students from 40 universities around the world (the United States, Mexico, Costa Rica, Italy, Australia, Sweden, Honduras, South Africa, Germany, Austria, Denmark, China, and Russia). Drawing on data from the GS project, I suggest that this model integrates the sustainability strategies present in academia today by promoting a holistic way of introducing sustainability into all levels of teaching, providing a unique capacity-building schema, and defining indicators of teaching quality for sustainability in academia.

Background

The description of the GLE phenomenon sprang from the results of an experiential study conducted to examine and model learning environments within the GS project (Savelyeva, 2009; Savelyeva & McKenna, 2011). The study involved interviews, observations, and narratives of the international GS participants, and focused on (1) faculty members' perceptions of the course aspects that made it succeed and last within different educational systems, and (2) the nuances of the course's teaching and learning practices that allowed integration of sustainability principles across disciplinary and cultural boundaries. This study was supported by the Phi Delta Beta Honor Society for International Scholars (the United States), and the Curriculum Resource Center of the Central European University (Hungary), which aimed both to understand and enhance the effectiveness of the sustainability educational movements in different countries.

The Structural Trap

Complex academic systems do not transform easily, yet they can adapt relatively quickly. This occurs because of their fragmented structures: Different parts of a university fit loosely together, operate under different rules, and do not overlap. Such structural fragmentation is a natural trait of a university system despite its unified and coherent image. It allows fast adaptation of the overall system and ensures its continuous operation. Commonly characterized as multidimensional organizations (Baldridge, 1971; Bolman & Deal, 1997), academic institutions are praised for their complexity. However, the structural fragmentation of university functions, facilities, chains of command, and other aspects is a linear characteristic. This confines any university event within a separate part of the system at a given point. Thus, fragmentation and compartmentalization excludes the simultaneous implementation of a new paradigm, such as sustainability, throughout all university dimensions. This creates problems that cannot be avoided easily. Hereafter, I refer to this issue as a structural trap.

The major issue cause by the structural trap is that the holistic transformation to sustainability is an unrealistic goal due to the linear fashion of system adaptation within a complex and compartmentalized university. The fragmented structure of a university and the confined nature of current sustainability approaches in academia create a fundamental problem within teaching and learning: Both faculty members and students undergo separate learning curves about sustainability as a concept and practice. They grasp the notion of sustainability at different rates and levels simultaneously. A complete and unified understanding of sustainability becomes unachievable in the classroom and across academic units. Another issue is the demand for fast and simultaneous assimilation to the new sustainability paradigm that makes it difficult for university faculty members, students, and leaders to escape the structural trap. Perceived as an innovation factor (Lozano, 2006) or a transformative learning agent, sustainability has to be incorporated, embedded, implemented, and introduced (Peet, Mulder, & Bijma, 2004; van Weenen, 2000) at all levels of the university system. Pressured by new sustainability assessments and regulations, universities get stuck in their own well-worn paths of adapting to sustainability, and making their efforts easily measurable for ranking and making them highly visible for recruitment purposes. They create and modify the sustainability approaches to fit the fragmented structure of their university systems.

The continuity of a university relies on its separate capacities and functions of its structural elements to pursue multiple goals simultaneously. There appears to be a fair amount of agreement in the literature (Barnett, 1990) on at least three broad goals of a typical higher education institution that can be linked to the existing sustainability movements: (1) providing for the economy, (2) forming the values of its graduates, and (3) enhancing intellectual merit through research. The three isolated sustainability movements present in academia today—campus greening, EfS, and sustainability sciences—correspond to different goals of the university system operations, programming, and research. Here, I briefly connect these three different accepted goals with the three sustainability movements.

Campus greening appears to be the strongest and the most visible sustainability movement in U.S. higher education institutions. Serving as a core measure of campus sustainability assessment system (Association for the Advancement of Sustainability in Higher Education [AASHE], n.d.), greening promotes the goal to provide for the future economy through increasing the efficiency in all university operations and favoring sustainability-related businesses. The second movement, EfS, can be linked to the traditional university goal of forming intellectual abilities and establishing the ethical values of its students. The commitment to values, ethics, and sustainability complements the action goal of campus greening, and thus a university's EfS curricula are designed to enrich students' conceptual understanding of sustainability. In comparison, sustainability science fulfills the goal of enhancing the intellectual merit of a society through outstanding scientific research. Sustainability science merges multiple disciplinary perspectives related to sustainable development and, just like the EfS, remains active only within narrow circles of specific academic departments.

The overall goal of synergetic assimilation to sustainability in academia requires an instrument for bridging the inherently fragmented structure of a university system. This can be achieved through the domain of teaching, which links all of the isolated pieces of the system together. Barnett (1990) addresses the importance of teaching situations, which are developed out of the research and leadership culture of a university. Teaching serves as a link between research priorities and leadership personnel by stimulating a mutual process of intellectual and professional development for all the participants. The view of teaching as a linking agent might justify continued epistemological attempts of finding new ways to teach sustainability and expand knowledge about sustainability in all academic fields. I believe that the detailed description of the GLE as it is presented in this study provides means for escaping the structural trap and creating opportunities for faculty members to integrate campus sustainability efforts into their teaching practices in a new and innovative way.

The Case for the GLE: Global Seminar Project

The Global Seminar (GS) is an informal consortium of international universities, agriculture and technical colleges, community colleges, and professional institutions (see figure 19.1). The participating faculty members have

FIGURE 19.1
GS institutions

UNIVERSITIES			

Cluster 1.
University of
  Melbourne, Australia
  (Coordinator)
Cornell University,
  United States
EARTH University,
  Costa Rica
University of Pretoria,
  South Africa
Zamorano University,
  Honduras
Chinese Normal
  University of Beijin
Ural State University,
  Russia (Observer)
	Cluster 2.
	Royal Vet and Agricultural
	  University, Denmark
	  (Coordinator)
	University of Western
	  Sydney, Australia
	North Carolina State
	  University, United States
	Penn State University,
	  United States
	Universidad Agraria de
	  Colombia, Columbia
	University of Boku,
	  Austria
	Uppsala University,
	  Sweden
		Cluster 3.
		Florida A & M University,
		  United States
		  (Coordinator)
		Alabama A & M
		  University, United States
		INTEC, Dominican
		  Republic
		Unitersity of Guam
		Virginia State University,
		  United States
		Delaware State University,
		  United States
		Elizabeth City State Uni-
		  versity, NC, United States
		University of Free State,
		  South Africa
			Cluster 4.
			Virginia Tech, United States
			  (Coordinator)
			Hohenheim University,
			  Germany
			Lasallian Institute for the
			  Environment, Philippines
			Universidad Autonoma de
			  Guadalajara, Mexico
			Universidad Nac. Agraria
			  la Molina, Lima, Peru
			University of Florence, Italy
			Zhejiang University,
			  Hangzhou, China
			NPSUT, Taiwan (Observer)

COMMUNITY COLLEGES
Cluster 5. Community College of Rhode Island, United States (Coordinator) Hudson Valley Community College, NY, United States Kirkwood Community College, Iowa, United States Perrotis College, Greece TAFE International, Australia

designed a sustainability-related course curriculum for the GS, which has been synchronously implemented in their respective universities since 1999. Faculty members deliver this course in conjunction with other international universities connected via educational technology. Within the GS, participants are clustered in groups of four to six institutions and are coordinated by a volunteer faculty member. The course is structured around 3 week-long learning cycles (see figure 19.2). During each cycle, participants work on a sustainability-related case study, developed by the faculty members. At the end of each cycle, students discuss the case via a videoconference.

The GS's unique, nonhierarchical, bottom-up participatory structure, as well as its teaching and learning processes, ensured the longevity of this sustainability initiative and its success at all the participating international universities. The GLE described in the next section was derived from the analysis of the GS course processes and practices.

FIGURE 19.2
GS learning cycle

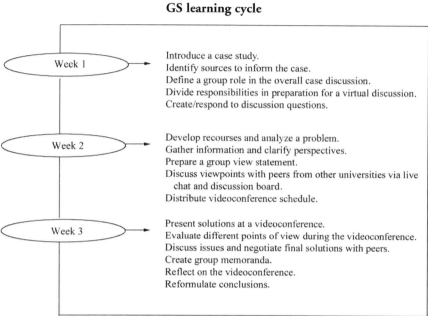

GS learning cycle figure showing:

Week 1
Introduce a case study.
Identify sources to inform the case.
Define a group role in the overall case discussion.
Divide responsibilities in preparation for a virtual discussion.
Create/respond to discussion questions.

Week 2
Develop recourses and analyze a problem.
Gather information and clarify perspectives.
Prepare a group view statement.
Discuss viewpoints with peers from other universities via live
   chat and discussion board.
Distribute videoconference schedule.

Week 3
Present solutions at a videoconference.
Evaluate different points of view during the videoconference.
Discuss issues and negotiate final solutions with peers.
Create group memoranda.
Reflect on the videoconference.
Reformulate conclusions.

GLE: Escaping the Structural Trap

As it appeared in this project, the GLE can be described as a specific property of an educational structure and not a physical space like a classroom. The GLE occurs when both faculty members and students are engaged in innovative learning exercises with the common purpose of acquiring an understanding of sustainability. The learning environment that resulted from the study of the GS project (Savelyeva 2009; Savelyeva & McKenna, 2011) included four defining characteristics: It is international, innovative, interdisciplinary, and interactive (see figure 19.3).

A culture of mutual learning, which was established by the GS participants, united the four defining characteristics of the GLE. In the context of this course, the mutual learning experience of faculty members and students implies simultaneous teaching and learning focused on sustainability, where everybody becomes a teacher and a learner. Participants build their understanding of sustainability together and learn from each other in a nonlinear

FIGURE 19.3
Characteristics of the global learning environment (GLE)

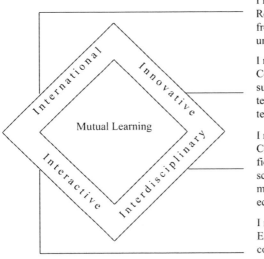

International
Reaches students and faculty members from other departments, colleges, universities, countries

Innovative
Contains new and exciting elements, such as different course formats, new teaching methods, and advanced technologies

Interdisciplinary
Connects different disciplinary fields, including sociology, soil sciences, agriculture, medicine, communications, economics, and natural resources

Interactive
Emphasizes the value of communication among the course participants

and nonhierarchical fashion. The culture of mutual learning crosses disciplinary, cultural, and administrative boundaries of each respective university and helps to overcome the inherent difficulties of learning all aspects of sustainability simultaneously. Thus, the mutual learning that occurs within the GLE makes possible the holistic assimilation of sustainability as a concept and professional practice, while forging across existing barriers and providing a means of escaping the academic structural trap. Mutual learning not only establishes a conceptual link between research and teaching (Posch & Steiner 2006); it also bridges different levels of an educational system with innovative teaching practices. It also serves as a guiding principle for the establishment of the international and interdisciplinary interactions (Nielsen, Dirckinck-Holmfeld, & Danielsen 2003; Savelyeva, 2009; Savelyeva & McKenna, 2011).

Within the GLE, the processes of teaching and mutual learning become one unifying force for the sustainability movements to interlink and create a common sustainability vision in academic systems around the world. The understanding of sustainability is often compartmentalized within natural sciences, and in general, it is perceived as the new buzzword for all universities by faculty members and students. In many cases, it is used to describe a broad range of sustainability-related issues, everything from compact, fluorescent light bulbs to climate change. The GLE ignites and frames the conversation about all the multiple meanings of sustainability among its participants and leads to a more complete personal understanding of it as a concept.

This culture of mutual learning is complemented by two important features of GLE: creation of a unique capacity-building function and promotion of self-initiated professional development schema for university faculty members. The typical capacity building present in academia today involves training faculty members with an outsider specialist during a curricular greening workshop or a sustainability seminar organized by the professional development unit of the university or department (Barlett & Rappoport, 2009). In contrast, GLE encourages faculty members to learn from one another through the mutual effort of class design and delivery rather than an external agent providing sustainability training. This capacity-building schema is truly participatory and it is best suited for the university setting for a number of reasons. First, it respects the faculty members' academic autonomy, which is revealed as a "deeply revered university norm . . . of a professor as a commander in [charge of] a classroom" (Cuban, 1999, p. 53). This is often the source of difficulties in gaining an agreement to implement a university's sustainability measures and to accept curricula greening methods. Respect for the autonomy of faculty members reduces the problematic resistance to changing teaching and learning practices. Second, GLE's capacity-building schema uses the diverse expertise of the faculty members to construct a university-specific understanding of sustainability through the interactive process of collaborative teaching. Here, GLE becomes part of a professional development exercise for the research faculty members, who have only limited training in teaching methods or pedagogical science.

Another unique characteristic of GLE made evident from this study is its ability to define new indicators of teaching quality for sustainability in academia. Current sustainability indicators, such as STARS (AASHE, n.d), do not include teaching as a component of a sustainability curricular evaluation. GLE stresses the significance of teaching situations in the overall learning experience for faculty members and students to expand their understandings of sustainability. Within GLE, teaching quality can be viewed as a projection of the intrinsic values of the faculty members across five teaching quality vectors (Savelyeva, 2009): teaching the course subject with expertise, managing the class with care, promoting course goals, providing proper and fair feedback to and from the students, and facilitating students' self-regulation and independent learning. These vectors are closely related to the students' development of generic metacompetencies and the value of relationships among the participants (see figure 19.4).

As part of their overall teaching experience, faculty members transferred their personal values and professional ethics to the students through a set of challenging situations that require a constant mutual effort to grasp the new concept. This strengthens the relationships among course participants and affects students' learning. The instructors are challenged throughout this process as much as their students are. Through overcoming these challenges together with their students, faculty members improve their teaching quality and gain a sense of professional growth. Approached in this way, GLE's teaching quality can best be described as fostering a capacity for true change and constantly improving student learning (Astin, 1980).

To truly understand GLE, it is necessary to apply a holistic approach when conceptualizing its characteristics and teaching practices by acknowledging the complexity and diversity of its unique processes and cross-boundary interactions. All GLE's elements should be perceived simultaneously to create a unified notion of sustainability teaching practices as a nonlinear entity and as a nonhierarchical, pedagogical exercise. Inspired by a culture of mutual learning, this notion is different from the contemporary sequential teaching practices. As a nonlinear model, GLE implies considerable flexibility with faculty members' teaching practices that enables the application of

FIGURE 19.4
Educational quality as a projection of intrinsic values of the instructor

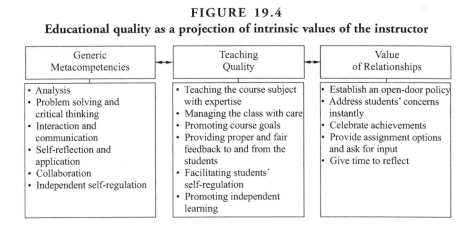

Generic Metacompetencies	Teaching Quality	Value of Relationships
• Analysis • Problem solving and critical thinking • Interaction and communication • Self-reflection and application • Collaboration • Independent self-regulation	• Teaching the course subject with expertise • Managing the class with care • Promoting course goals • Providing proper and fair feedback to and from the students • Facilitating students' self-regulation • Promoting independent learning	• Establish an open-door policy • Address students' concerns instantly • Celebrate achievements • Provide assignment options and ask for input • Give time to reflect

GLE within different disciplinary and cultural contexts. It also adapts GLE for use in different educational systems around the world.

Conclusions

Establishing a culture of mutual learning, generating a unique capacity-building schema, and defining indicators of teaching quality for sustainability in academia via the GLE highlights a path away from the existing structural trap. GLE experiences at participating universities around the world advance both current curricular and pedagogical ways of dealing with fragmentation and compartmentalization of a university system. However, GLE fulfills more than just an epistemological task of describing a new way to teach sustainability, create knowledge of sustainability in students and faculty members, and implement sustainable practices in their lives. GLE allows for viewing sustainability teaching as an ontological matter of enabling the involved individuals and universities to recognize, embrace, and promote sustainability amid an unsustainable world. By dealing with the three typical goals (providing for the economy, forming the values of its graduates, and enhancing intellectual merit through research) of a fragmented university system, GLE brings the corresponding sustainability movements (greening, EfS, and sustainability science) into agreement. GLE provides a framework for infusing sustainability within a university system in a natural, adaptive manner that fits the fragmented and multidimensional university structure. Finally, GLE can be created and simultaneously implemented on different campuses, within different disciplines, and by diverse cultures.

References

Association for the Advancement of Sustainability in Higher Education. (n.d.). Sustainability Tracking Assessment and Rating System (STARS). Retrieved December 10, 2010, from https://stars.aashe.org/pages/about/

Astin, A. (1980). When does college deserve to be called "high quality?" *Current Issues in Higher Education: Proceedings of the American Association of Higher Education, 1,* 1–4.

Baldridge, V. (1971). *Power and conflict in the university: Research in the sociology of complex organizations.* New York: Wiley.

Barlett, P., & Rappaport, A. (2009). Long-term impact of faculty development programs: The experience of Tell and Piedmont. *College Teaching, 57*(2), 73–82.

Barnett, R. (1990). *The idea of higher education.* Bristol, PA, USA: SRHE.

Bolman, L., & Deal, T. (1997). *Reframing organizations: Artistry, choice, and leadership* (2nd ed.). San Francisco: Jossey-Bass.

Cuban, L. (1999). *How scholars trumped teachers: Change without reform in university curriculum, teaching, and research, 1890–1990.* New York: Teachers College.

Lozano, R. (2006). Incorporation and institutionalization of SD into universities: Breaking through barriers to change. *Journal of Cleaner Production,14*(9–11), 787–796.

Nielsen, J., Dirckinck-Holmfeld, L., & Danielsen, O. (2003). Dialogue design with mutual learning as guiding principle. *International Journal of Human-Computer Interaction, 15*(1), 21–40.

Peet, D., Mulder, K., & Bijma, A. (2004). Integrating SD into engineering courses at the Delft University of Technology: The individual interaction method. *International Journal of Sustainability in Higher Education, 5*(3), 278–288.

Posch, A., & Steiner, G. (2006). Integrating research and teaching on innovation for sustainable development. *International Journal of Sustainability in Higher Education, 7*(3), 276–292.

Savelyeva, T. (2009). *Global learning environment: Innovative concept and interactive model for changing academia and academics.* Saarbruken, Germany: VDM.

Savelyeva, T., & McKenna, J. (2011). Campus sustainability: Emerging curricula models in higher education. *International Journal for Sustainability in Higher Education, 12*(1), 55–66.

van Weenen, H. (2000).Towards a vision of a sustainable university. *International Journal of Sustainability in Higher Education, 1*(1), 20–34.

20

MAKING SUSTAINABILITY
A CORE VALUE

Christine Drewel

While environmental, social, and economic factors dominate the discussions pertaining to sustainability, an understanding of the values that support sustainability is essential in order to create visible and vibrant programs in higher education. This chapter will highlight four key constituencies that have an impact on creating leadership and lasting activities within higher education. Faculty members and administrators should consider these areas carefully if they are interested in promoting and expanding conversations about values and about how they are connected to sustainability initiatives. I also include brief examples from Grand Valley State University (GVSU) for illustration. Although this chapter cannot be comprehensive in scope or depth, it is my hope to begin articulating the importance of discussing core values in relation to sustainability and sustainable initiatives in higher education.

The word *core* has linguistic connections to the Latin *corpus*, or "body," and those values we hold deep within us we often refer to as connected to our hearts. Sustainability most certainly is linked to the environment and to economic and social factors, but another, often neglected area speaks to our hearts. Sustainability, both as idea and practice, connects to our core values. Sustainability and living in a sustainable manner are important to people; it touches many of us deeply and offers us a way to contribute to our communities in a meaningful way. Although the underlying values may vary among institutions, higher education provides a forum for discussion and a platform for actively engaging sustainability both in ideology and in praxis.

Four main constituencies that influence the theory and practice of sustainability in higher education are the administration, the faculty, the students, and the surrounding community. Each of these groups has a different set of values and reasons for supporting, remaining indifferent to, or discouraging sustainability. Their values are not necessarily conflicting or hierarchical, however; promoting dialogue and establishing relationships and understanding among the four sets of values is essential in order to create a deeper and lasting commitment to sustainability.

Development of Values: Administrative Support and Articulation

Without the support of the administration for both the practical and philosophical aspects of sustainability, any programming, curriculum development, or event planning is unlikely. While the support can vary depending on the institution, having sustainability connected to the strategic plan, mission, vision, or value statement indicates a lasting and visible commitment. Because administrators and faculty members typically participate together in the drafting process, and because revisions normally take several years, such statements can have a lasting impact on the vision and direction of the institution in relation to sustainability.

Administrators also face increasing demands for fiscal transparency; the values of the institution must also include economic sustainability. In his article, "Academic Values, Institutional Management and Public Policies" (2007) David Ward, former president of the American Council on Education, highlights many of the financial and management constraints facing the administration of higher education institutions, including increasing pressures from globalization and decreasing state funding. He argues that universities are "places of disputation, skepticism and questioning" and that "those values may well be critical" as higher education institutions confront the many changes they must make to keep up with globalization (p. 20). Issues of sustainability intersect economically with local, regional, and global problems; administrators can and should constructively and intentionally align their institutional values in a way that is fiscally sustainable and connected to the global community, too.

The administration and faculty at GVSU have built sustainability directly into the institution's value statement. Because GVSU has been recognized as a leader in sustainable practices and initiatives, the following may provide a model statement for other institutions to consider integrating into their mission, vision, or value statement, too:

> Grand Valley State University values the guiding principles of sustainability in helping to meet the current needs of our faculty, staff, and students without compromising the needs and resources of future generations. We are committed to working with our community partners to create a sustainable future for our university, our community, and our region. We will model applied sustainability best practices in our campus operations and administration, education for sustainable development, student involvement, and community engagement by promoting social responsibility, encouraging environmental stewardship, and creating efficiencies and value for the work we perform. We will provide our students with excellence in education for sustainable development by imbedding theory, systems-oriented thinking, and service learning into our curricular and extracurricular programs. (Grand Valley State University, 2010c)

The statement provides a broad perspective on the many areas that the work of the university encompasses. It also addresses the three other constituents addressed in this chapter: faculty members, students, and surrounding communities.

Development of Values: Faculty Perspectives and Integration

Ideally, the three main areas for which faculty members are responsible—teaching, scholarship, and service—would be integrated seamlessly into daily academic life. In reality, many faculty members inherit the courses they teach, are bound by the constraints of the syllabus of record and perhaps by general education or other program requirements, and do not always have the luxury of teaching in areas that are perfectly aligned with their scholarship interests. Integration and articulation of values, sustainability, and sustainable practices into these areas requires time, reflection, and intentionality: aspects of faculty life that are typically fragmented or neglected entirely. If we, as faculty members, cannot value and create integrative processes in our own academic lives, how can we expect our students to accomplish this goal?

Laura Rendon, author of *Sentipensante (Sensing/Thinking) Pedagogy: Educating for Wholeness, Social Justice and Liberation* (2009), promotes a holistic approach to the process of integrative learning. She writes that integrative learning "recognizes connections among diverse ways of knowing but also emphasizes the relationship [among] mind, body, and spirit, and the connection between the outer life of vocation and professional responsibility and the inner life of personal development, meaning and purpose" (p. 134). Faculty members can align their pedagogies with the values of sustainability and thus teach in a manner that is integrative and meaningful.

Though ideas connected to sustainability appear throughout many programs and curricula at GVSU, the Environmental Studies (ENS) Program and the Liberal Studies (LIB) Department offer students direct paths to integrating the idea into their coursework. ENS offers a minor with a strong emphasis on sustainability that engages sociocultural, physical and life sciences, and economic and political perspectives on the environment (Grand Valley State University, 2010a). The minor is compatible with a wide variety of other majors and career choices. The LIB major offers students an individualized study plan resulting in either a B.S. or a B.A. with a unique emphasis area, which can engage sustainability from interdisciplinary perspectives (Grand Valley State University, 2010b). There has been a dramatic rise in the number of students pursuing degrees that allow them to incorporate sustainability and sustainable practices into their curricular and co-curricular activities. Both ENS and LIB are part of the innovative Brooks College of Interdisciplinary Studies, which values creative and collaborative engagement in local and global communities.

Development of Values: Student Perspectives and Engagement

Student awareness and participation is essential to sustainability in higher education. Many of the essays in this book have highlighted best practices and model programs that prove that the students both care about and want to contribute to sustainable lifestyles. The millennial generation, in particular, is engaged and eager to make a difference. Neil Howe and William Strauss, authors of *Millennials Go to College* (2007), argue that the current generation of students is both optimistic and confident, traits that align with the underlying values of sustainability. "Whatever problems are facing their world, Millennials assume that they can be fixed. At the same time, they accept that these solutions will take a substantial amount of planning, work and sacrifice. They see their own generation as key to addressing these problems" (p. 111). Furthermore, they are team-oriented and "love group work, cooperative activities like volunteer service, and participating in something larger than the individual" (p. 125). Providing students with opportunities, raising their awareness through event planning and speakers, and encouraging support of student organizations all help engage students in conversations that they can connect to their values directly. And they do want to discuss their values, both in and outside the classroom.

In *When Hope and Fear Collide: A Portrait of Today's College Student,* authors Arthur Levine and Jeannette Cureton (1998) explain that students today need a curriculum that highlights and emphasizes communication, the study of human heritage, an understanding of environmental issues, and an understanding of their own individual roles in order to develop a sense of efficacy and an understanding of their own and respect for others' values. Levine and Cureton explain:

> Students must learn the meaning of values, be able to distinguish between values and facts, understand the difference between relative and absolute values, and differentiate [among] good, better, and best values. They also need to develop mechanisms for weighing and choosing among values. Finally, they need to comprehend how values function in our society and in their lives: the changing nature of values over time, how values fit into cultures, the place of values in an individual's life, and what happens to minority values in a society. (p. 165)

Although students may have difficulty articulating their values at first, they are eager to discuss how material presented in the classroom, no matter what the disciplinary perspective, applies to their lives. As many of the chapters in this book have addressed, issues connected to sustainability encompass multiple disciplines; getting students to understand the underlying values and applications simply requires a commitment to active and problem-solving pedagogies and service learning.

Students at GVSU can become involved in numerous organizations that value and engage sustainability issues. These organizations include the Soil and Water Conservation Society, the Student Environmental Coalition, and Students for Fair Trade. New organizations form each year, and they often collaborate and share resources for events and activities. GVSU also facilitates annually the highly visible Campus Sustainability Week, which is entering its seventh year. The Sustainable Community Development Initiative partners with campuswide departments to host events, speakers, panel discussions, concerts, and other activities for students, faculty members, and the surrounding community.

Developing Values: Community Perspectives and Involvement

The surrounding communities need to be integral and active partners with academic institutions; creating partnerships, internships, dialogues, and programs can raise awareness of sustainability and foster sustainable development. Understanding the values of the surrounding community is the first step in the process. Many higher education institutions already have a substantive history and key relationships with their surrounding communities, but they have little understanding of the underlying values of their community members because questions that would reveal such values are rarely asked. Initiating conversations about values should come first; action and engagement should follow.

The main campus of GVSU is located on an 876-acre campus near the town of Allendale, Michigan, approximately 12 miles west of Grand Rapids. The Grand River borders the campus on the east, and most of the campus buildings sit on plateaus among deep, wooded ravines. The institution, which also has vibrant campuses throughout the region in Holland, Muskegon, Traverse City, and Grand Rapids, has cultivated active relationships with sustainability as an integral part of and way to connect with the surrounding communities. As early as 1976, GVSU offered curriculum and community engagement through its Urban and Environmental Studies Institute, which was "established to focus the resources of Grand Valley on the quality of life in West Michigan" through research, teaching, and community service (Grand Valley State Colleges, 1976, p. 149). Students examined problems that the city faced, attended city commission meetings, and constructed internships and service learning projects connected to urban and environmental problems. While a discussion of the classes, programs, and service learning opportunities that GVSU has offered its students throughout the years is beyond the scope of this chapter, the underlying value is that, from its founding, GVSU has consistently formed relationships with the surrounding community.

GVSU has been a recognized leader in sustainability initiatives and sustainable campus programming, and it consistently strives to develop its commitment to outside communities locally, regionally, and nationally. GVSU was recently recognized by the *Princeton Review* as one of the country's most environmentally responsible colleges (Grand Valley State University, 2010d) and it received national merit in the Sustainable Endowment Institute's 2011 Campus Sustainability Report Card.[1] It actively sponsors speakers, panels, and conferences for students, faculty members, and the community to engage and discuss sustainability. GVSU also hosted "Future Cities/Green Town Grand Rapids 2010," a 2-day conference that was sponsored by the Michigan Municipal League, Michigan Department of Energy, Labor and Economic Growth, the Michigan Department of Natural Resources and Environment, the City of Grand Rapids, and others. The conference provided tours of Leadership in Energy and Environmental Design (LEED) certified buildings and dialogues about the future of energy in Michigan, climate mitigation, and many other topics connected to sustainability (Grand Valley State University, 2010e).

Conclusion: The VALUE of Values?

The discussion about the degradation of values in higher education has been ongoing and intense. Consumerism, individualism, and corporatization have gained serious influence in our institutions, and the values connected to these forces often run contrary to the values underlying sustainability. Although many higher education institutions "talk the talk" of sustainability, even administrators, faculty members, and students with the best of intentions can find it difficult to "walk the walk." To begin addressing sustainability as a principle or idea, and sustainable practices as a way of life, we must begin considering the deeper undercurrents of sustainability and its value and meaning for us as humans.

The values connected to sustainability are inherently interdisciplinary and integrative; no one area of study should be excluded from the discussion. Anthony Kronman's book *Education's End: Why Our Colleges and Universities Have Given Up on the Search for Meaning* (2007) argues that the humanities, whose primary job was to wrestle with questions like "Why are we here?" and "How ought we to live?" are essential to the development of students, faculty members, and the institutions themselves. We cannot afford to let the voices and perspectives of these areas be ignored. Parker Palmer and Arthur Zajonc, in their book *The Heart of Higher Education: A Call to Renewal* (2010), also support deeper conversations about meaning and values:

> Values such as compassion, social justice and the search for truth, which animate and give purpose to the lives of students, faculty, and staff, are honored and strengthened by an integrative education. But to be truly integrative, such an education must go beyond a "values curriculum" to

create a comprehensive learning environment that reflects a holistic vision of humanity, giving attention to every dimension of the human self. Integrative education honors communal as well as individual values and cultivates silent reflection while encouraging vigorous dialogue as well as ethical action. (p. 152)

While it is difficult to provide a one-size-fits-all approach to articulating what the underlying values are or should be for higher education institutions, to initiate reflection and dialogue, the following acronym may be useful: VALUE = Vision, Awareness, Listening, Understanding, and Empathy. Whatever the sustainability program, course, project, initiative, or idea, if the four constituencies (administrators, faculty members, students, and community members) are interested in integrating values into their dialogue, these five values may provide a starting point.

> *Vision*—Vision may include direct inclusion of sustainability in the university's mission, vision, or value statements, but it applies in a more general way. Faculty members, students, staff members, administrators, and members of the surrounding community need to express their vision for the future, and how and why sustainability and sustainable practices fits into it.
>
> *Awareness*—Often, many grassroots projects, ideas, and activities are already occurring within the institution, student organizations, classrooms, and community. Raising awareness of these endeavors could be as simple as creating a website or making an announcement in a classroom or meeting, inviting and including all groups and perspectives. The problems that sustainability attempts to solve require multiple approaches and liaisons; communicating about the issues and the impact that individuals and groups are having while engaging in sustainability is a practical value.
>
> *Listening*—Listening is an often overlooked but imperative value. Without actively listening to the concerns, needs, and ideas of each of the four constituencies (administrators, faculty members, students, and community members), productive dialogue cannot occur. While each group will undoubtedly have its own agenda and hope for whatever the project or activity may be, the first step in any engagement is to ensure that all voices are heard and to listen without judgment or bias.

Understanding—Although difficult to measure or assess, understanding of each others' perspectives is a value that is at the heart of sustainability. Knowing why we are doing what we are doing, how we have an impact on and are connected to each other and our causes and initiatives, and why each person matters and can make a difference is all part of creating understanding.

Empathy—In his book *A Whole New Mind: Why Right Brainers Will Rule the Future*, Daniel Pink (2006) stresses the importance of integrating the value of empathy in all aspects of business, education, and our daily interactions with each other. He says, "Empathy is the ability to imagine yourself in someone else's position and to intuit what that person is feeling. It is the ability to stand in others' shoes, to see with their eyes, and to feel with their hearts" (p. 159). Pink contends that empathy is an ethic for living, makes us human, brings joy, and is an essential part of living a life of meaning (p. 165). Empathy is a natural extension of the values of listening and understanding; to engage productively in sustainability and sustainable practices, we must be able to put ourselves into the minds, hearts, and places of those with whom we are working.

Administrators, faculty members, students, and members of the communities surrounding higher education institutions can all benefit from integrating values into their conversations about sustainability, sustainable practices, and sustainable development. Although the details of how and why each institution includes values into their dialogue will undoubtedly vary, each of the four constituents can enrich and engage sustainability in a deeper and more meaningful way if they do.

Note

1. See Grand Valley State University (2010f; 2010g). The Princeton Report evaluates how sustainable practices were applied in nine areas: administration, climate change and energy, food and recycling, green building, student involvement, transportation, endowment transparency, investment priorities, and shareholder engagement. Grand Valley State University received an A- ranking.

References

Grand Valley State Colleges. (1976). *Catalog: 1976–77*. Allendale, MI: Grand Valley State Colleges.

Grand Valley State University. (2010a). Environmental Studies Minor. Retrieved from http://www.gvsu.edu/ens/

Grand Valley State University. (2010b). Liberal Studies Department. Retrieved from http://www.gvsu.edu/liberalstudies/

Grand Valley State University. (2010c). Strategic positioning 2010–2015. Retrieved from http://www.gvsu.edu/strategicplanning/values-17.htm

Grand Valley State University. (2010d). Grand Valley chosen as "green college" by *Princeton Review*. *GV Now*. Retrieved from http://www.gvsu.edu/gvnow/index .htm?articleId = 21B01FC1-D53F-1AFA-BC4854809B1ACB14

Grand Valley State University. (2010e). Conference at Grand Valley focuses on green cities. *GV Now*. Retrieved from http://www.gvsu.edu/gvnow/index.htm?article Id = 721A9729-0F6D-AABC-31673862BE266D05

Grand Valley State University. (2010f). GVSU sustainability week: A grand tradition. *GV Now*. Retrieved from http://www.gvsu.edu/gvnow/index.htm?articleId = B0A4AA5A-A02F-725C-1357A4391D00CD23

Grand Valley State University. (2010g). GVSU named a sustainable leader. *GV Now*. Retrieved from http://www.gvsu.edu/gvnow/index.htm?articleId = BDA2F8BD-C0F5-B8C5-1E30303175C0407F

Howe, N., & Strauss, W. (2007). *Millennials go to college*. Great Falls, VA: Life Course Associates.

Kronman, A. (2007). *Education's end: Why our colleges and universities have given up on the meaning of life*. New Haven, CT: Yale University Press.

Levine, A., & Cureton, J. (1998). *When hope and fear collide: A portrait of today's college student*. San Francisco: Jossey-Bass.

Palmer, P., & Zajonc, A. (2010). *The heart of higher education: A call to renewal*. San Francisco: Jossey-Bass.

Pink, D. (2006). *A whole new mind: Why right brainers will rule the future*. New York: Penguin Group.

Rendon, L. (2009). *Sentipensante (sensing/thinking) pedagogy: Educating for wholeness, social justice and liberation*. Sterling, VA: Stylus Publishing.

Ward, D. (2007). Academic values, institutional management and public policies. *Higher Education Management and Policy, 19*(2), 9–20.

ABOUT THE CONTRIBUTORS

Editors

Kirsten Allen Bartels, PhD, is an honors faculty fellow at Grand Valley State University where she teaches a wide range of courses and is actively involved with service learning and community engagement and their advancement as pedagogical practices. Kirsten's work with sustainability and environmental issues has come full circle (so to speak) as she began her professional life as an environmental geologist before she returned to school to earn her MA in classics and begin teaching. In addition to teaching for the English Department, the Liberal Studies Department, the Environmental Studies Program, and the Honors College, Kirsten continues to pursue her research interests exploring controversial topics including ecocriticism and sustainability and multicultural perspectives and representation in contemporary works of fiction.

Kelly A. Parker, PhD, is a professor of philosophy at Grand Valley State University where he teaches courses in philosophy, liberal studies, and environmental studies. His research centers on American pragmatism and environmental philosophy. His publications include "Ecohumanities Pedagogy: An Experiment in Radical Service-Learning," *Contemporary Pragmatism* (2011); "Pragmatism and Environmental Thought," in *Environmental Pragmatism* (1996); and "Economics, Sustainable Growth, and Community," *Environmental Values* 2 (1993). He has served on the board of the West Michigan Environmental Action Council and was a founder of the Greater Grand Rapids Food System Council.

Contributors

P. Sven Arvidson, PhD, is director of liberal studies, visiting associate professor of philosophy, and senior faculty fellow in the Center for Excellence in Teaching and Learning, at Seattle University. His interdisciplinary research centers on attention, human nature, ethics, and pedagogy. His most recent books include *Teaching Nonmajors: Advice for Liberal Arts Professors* (SUNY 2008) and *The Sphere of Attention: Context and Margin* (Springer 2006). He received his MA and PhD in philosophy from Georgetown University, MA in psychology from Duquesne University, and BA in human development from St. Mary's College of Maryland.

Bart A. Bartels, a graduate of University of Wisconsin–LaCrosse, is the campus sustainability manager at Grand Valley State University. He is also a member of the GVSU Climate Action Committee and a LEED green associate. Prior to beginning his work at Grand Valley, Bart was the Entrepreneurship Champion at the University of Wales where he is currently pursuing his MBA with an emphasis in sustainability.

Kyle Bladow is a PhD student in the Literature & Environment program at the University of Nevada, Reno, where he teaches in the core writing and core humanities programs and has also served as the assistant book review editor for the journal *ISLE: Interdisciplinary Studies in Literature and Environment*. He received his BA and MA from Northern Michigan University, where he completed a thesis on bioregional literature of the southern shoreline of Lake Superior. In addition to bioregional literary criticism, his research interests include queer ecology, material feminisms, and contemporary literature on sustainability and environmental justice, the latter of which entwines with his work at food coops in Marquette, MI, and Reno, NV, and on several small-scale family farms.

George English Brooks teaches writing and humanities at the University of Nevada, Reno, where he recently completed his MA in the Literature & Environment program. He is also an editorial assistant for the journal *Interdisciplinary Studies in Literature and Environment* (ISLE). Before coming to Reno, he studied literature (English and Spanish/Latin American) and linguistics at the University of Utah, and spent several years teaching college writing, running countywide adult literacy and recycling programs, and working as a youth counselor in central Utah's Sanpete Valley. His research and teaching interests include ecocomposition, bioregionalism, inter-American literatures, border studies, postcolonialism, environmental justice, and globalization.

Sarah S. Brophy, MA, is a leadership in energy and environmental design accredited professional (LEEDAP), by the U.S. Green Building Council, and cochair on the American Association of Museums's Professional Interest Committee on Environmental Sustainability. She teaches the graduate level course The Green Museum in The George Washington University's museum studies program, and in the University of Delaware's museum certificate program. She is researching the practice of ecosystem design in natural and cultural facilities, and in developing regenerative practices as important aspects of nonprofit management. She is a strong supporter of collaborative greening practices among institutions and across sectors. She is coauthor with Elizabeth Wylie of *The Green Museum: A Primer on Environmental Practice* (AltaMira Press, 2008). She is a longtime independent professional with a practice in grants development for cultural, educational, and natural resource nonprofits nationally and internationally. She works with zoos, gardens, museums, aquariums, historical societies, and housing and education organizations interested in greening their properties, practices, and services.

John Cusick, PhD, coordinates the University of Hawai'i at Manoa (UHM) environmental studies undergraduate degree and certificate programs and is faculty advisor for the Ecology Club, which is supported by the Ecological Society of America Strategies for Ecology Education, Development, and Sustainability (SEED) program. His research interests in the area of human-environment relationships focus on places designated protected area status, with an emphasis on World Heritage sites, where the interests of residents, conservation research and tourism merge. As an East-West Center degree Fellow, he completed graduate research that compared protected areas on the islands of Maui and Yakushima, Japan. He is a member of the World Conservation Union (IUCN), World Commission on Protected Areas and Ecosystem Management, and of the UHM Center for Okinawan Studies. He has conducted fieldwork related to sustainable development in the Hawaiian Islands, Japan, New Zealand, North America, and Latin America. Since 2009, he assists the East-West Center with an environmental leadership program for international students.

Chris Doran, PhD, is assistant professor of religion at Pepperdine University. He earned a BA in biology, an MDiv from Pepperdine University, and a PhD in systematic and philosophical theology from Graduate Theological Union, where he focused on the various creative relationships between theology and the natural sciences. He regularly teaches an undergraduate course entitled "Christianity and Sustainability" and has taught environmental policy at Pepperdine's School of Public Policy. His current research focuses on Christianity's contribution to the global discussion about sustainability, particularly looking at Christian notions of hope and frugality. He was recently vice-chair of the task force that authored the definition of sustainability that will be used by Pepperdine's Center for Sustainability.

Christine Drewel, MA, is an instructor with the liberal studies department at Grand Valley State University, where she has taught for eleven years. She earned a BA in English and religious studies and a minor in Latin from Aquinas College, an MA in comparative religion from Western Michigan University, and is completing her PhD in American studies at Michigan State University. Her research interests include interdisciplinarity, religion in higher education, pedagogy, sustainability, and the intersectionality of institutional values into all of these areas.

Bruce I. Dvorak is a professor of civil engineering and biological systems engineering at the University of Nebraska. Dr. Dvorak has won numerous teaching awards, including the 2005 University of Nebraska University Holling Family Master Teacher Award/University-Wide Teaching Award. He is a registered professional Environmental Engineer and earned his BS in civil engineering from UNL and PhD in civil (environmental) engineering from the University of Texas at Austin. Dr. Dvorak's teaching and research focuses on environmental engineering (especially physical/chemical treatment processes) and applied environmental sustainability for industry. Since 1995, he has obtained grants with total expenditures of more than $5.8 million. He has published more than 25 refereed journal papers, 50 conference proceedings, and 30 extension publications. Among his key related publications include an evaluation of long-term impacts on workplace behavior of intensive environmental sustainability education published in 2010 in ASCE's *Journal of Professional Issues in Engineering Education and Practice*, and 2008 papers in the *Journal of Cleaner Production* related to impact assessment of pollution prevention programs, as well as quantifying the benefits and value to clients of indirect benefits often overlooked by traditional metric accounting.

Stacey A. Hawkey holds a BS in chemistry from the University of Nebraska–Omaha and an MS in industrial hygiene from Central Missouri University, and is certified in the comprehensive practice of industrial hygiene by the

American Board of Industrial Hygiene. She has served in the position of program coordinator of the Partners in Pollution Prevention (P3) internship program at the University of Nebraska–Lincoln since 2003. She has over 20 years' experience managing occupational safety, health, and environmental programs and projects in industry, academia, and the public sector. She has specialized in applying cutting-edge principles such as ISO 14000, EMS, performance metrics, and TQM to increase program successes and decrease environmental risks. She authored one of the first articles in the *American Industrial Hygiene Association Journal* (February 1992) on pollution prevention methodology, entitled "An Algorithm for Setting Priorities and Targeting Wastes for Minimization."

Tom Hertweck is a PhD candidate in the program for Literature & Environment at the University of Nevada, Reno, where he is completing a dissertation on post–World War II American consumerism and food narration, and teaches as a distinguished teaching assistant in the core humanities program and in the English department. He is also currently the managing editor of *ISLE: Interdisciplinary Studies in Literature and Environment*. Prior to coming to UNR, Tom received a BA in English and an MA in American studies from Purdue University. Tom lives in Reno with his partner Cassie and two cat-folk, Kiki and Panza; all are vegan.

Patrick Howard, PhD is an associate professor of education in the School of Professional Studies at Cape Breton University in Nova Scotia, Canada. His interest in sustainability studies began as a secondary school teacher on coastal Newfoundland and Labrador, Canada during the collapse of the northern cod stocks—once the greatest biomass on the planet. The devastating impact on coastal families and communities was swift and highlighted the tragic consequences that result from a blatant disregard for the ecosystems that sustain us. Patrick Howard continues to research the intersections between language, experience, and ecological literacy with the hope of learning how we may deepen our relationship with the living world. Patrick Howard's work has been published both nationally and internationally in *Diaspora, Minority and Indigenous Education, Phenomenology & Practice* (www.phandpr.org), and the *Canadian Journal of Environmental Education* among others. His most recent essay, "Living as Textual Animals: Curriculum, Sustainability and the Inherency of Language," was published in the *Journal of the Canadian Association for Curriculum Studies.*

Krista Jacobsen, PhD, is an assistant professor of sustainable agriculture in the department of horticulture at the University of Kentucky, and teaches several courses in UK's Sustainable Agriculture Program. Jacobsen is an agroecologist by training, earning her doctorate in 2008 from the University of Georgia's Odum School of Ecology, conducting research at the Spring Valley Ecofarm and working extensively with the local farming, academic and non-profit cooperative communities in the Athens, Georgia area. She was a postdoctoral researcher at Penn State University, and currently conducts organic farming systems research that seeks to balance environmental and economic productivity goals in horticultural crop production.

Evi Karathanasopoulou is a PhD candidate at the University of Sunderland. Her area of research is radio studies with a focus on aesthetics, radio art and the radio voice. She has a BA (First Class Hons) in media production (television and radio) from the University of Sunderland and an MA in radio from Goldsmiths College, University of London.

Douglas Klahr is an assistant professor within the School of Architecture at the University of Texas at Arlington. He has an MA from the University of Virginia and a PhD from Brown University. Both degrees are in architectural history, and although he is a scholar of nineteenth-century German architecture and urbanism, he questions the relevancy of such pursuits in an age of unprecedented global economic, environmental, and social crisis. He therefore increasingly defines himself as a scholar of "contemporary history," creating courses such as Sustainability for Everyone, Architecture and Politics, The Bright Green Movement, and Slum Housing in the Developing World to help his students address urgent current issues. Within these dual roles as traditional and contemporary historian, he has delivered papers at conferences in London, Paris, Berlin, Washington, Glasgow, Miami, Dallas, and San Diego. His work has been published in the *Journal of the Society of Architectural Historians*, the *Oxford Art Journal*, the *Zeitschrift für Kunstgeschichte*, and the journal *German History* (published by Oxford University Press). In March 2011, his essay "Becoming Builders again in an Age of Global Crisis" was published in *trans*, the half-yearly journal produced by the ETH in Zurich. The essay is a damning indictment of the failure of architectural pedagogy and practice to respond to the global slum housing crisis and can be accessed at http://issuu.com/kudamm/docs/klahr_article_in_trans_eth_zurich.

Danielle Lake, MA, is an affiliate faculty member in the liberal studies department at Grand Valley State University. She received a BS in liberal studies from Grand Valley State University and her MA in American philosophy from The University of Toledo. Her master's thesis, *Institutions and Process: Problems of Today, Misguided Answers From Yesterday*, was published by VDM in 2008. She is currently finishing her PhD in American philosophy and environmental studies at Michigan State University. Her current research interests include systems thinking, wicked problems, and democratic deliberation, especially as they relate to issues of healthcare rationing and sustainability.

Alex Lockwood, MA, is senior lecturer in journalism in the faculty of arts, design and media, where he is program leader for the master's programs in journalism. For ten years he was a practicing journalist where he worked in sustainable development settings, including training journalists in Zambia and the Balkans. His publications include chapters on environmental journalism in *Climate Change and The Media* (Peter Lang) and *Land and Identity* (Rodopi). He was cofounder of the Media, Communications and Cultural Studies Association (MeCCSA) Climate Change Network.

Gina Matkin, PhD, is an assistant professor of leadership studies at the University of Nebraska–Lincoln in the Department of Agricultural Leadership, Education, & Communication. She holds a BS in biology from Southeast Missouri State University, an MS in sociology, adult education, and women's studies from Iowa State University; and a PhD in human sciences/leadership from the University of Nebraska–Lincoln. She teaches graduate and undergraduate courses including environmental leadership, leadership theory, and leadership and diversity. Her research interests include: diversity and intercultural competence, multicultural teambuilding, critical thinking and cognitive development, and emerging models of sustainability leadership. She has served on the board of directors for her local natural foods cooperative, and enjoys organic gardening. Her recent publications include Quinn, C.E., Burbach, M.E., Matkin, G.S., & Flores, K.L., "Critical Thinking for Natural Resource, Agricultural, and Environmental Ethics Education" in the *Journal of Natural Resources and Life Sciences Education*, 38 (2009); and Matkin, G.S., and Burbach, M.E., "An Educational Model to Help Create Meaningful and Sustained Changes in Groundwater Management Practices," Proceedings of the 51st Annual Midwest Ground Water Conference, November 6–9, 2006, in Lincoln, NE.

Caroline Mitchell, MA, is a senior lecturer in radio in the faculty of arts, design and media at the University of Sunderland, U.K. and an independent community media researcher and trainer. She has devised, led, and taught on numerous radio training courses in the U.K. and Europe, particularly about enabling minorities to have a voice. She was cofounder of Fem FM, the first women's radio station in Britain. Her publications include *Women and Radio: Airing Differences* (ed. 2000 Routledge), "Organic Radio: The Role of Social Partnerships in Creating Community Voices" (2006 with A. Baxter) in Peter Lewis & Susan Jones (eds) *From the Margins to the Cutting Edge: Community Media and Empowerment* (Hampton Press), and "Praxis and participation in community radio training in Europe" in J. Gordon (ed.) *Community Radio in the 21st Century* (in press, Peter Lang).

Kimberly R. Moekle, PhD, teaches in the program in writing and rhetoric (PWR) at Stanford University and codirects the Stanford Undergraduate Sustainability Scholars (SUSS) program. She completed her PhD in comparative literature at the University of California, Irvine (UCI) in 2000, where she held a variety of teaching and administrative positions and served as an assistant course director for undergraduate writing. Kimberly's current writing and research interests include issues at the intersection of environmental rhetoric and environmental ethics, with a particular focus on sustainable energy, ecohumanities pedagogy, and the rhetoric of environmental politics in America. She has published both in edited volumes and in peer-reviewed journals on the critical role of rhetoric in environmental controversies, and also on the concept of writing studies as an ideal disciplinary arena for engaging undergraduates in conversations about sustainability. Kimberly teaches various undergraduate writing seminars on themes such as the rhetoric of sustainable energy, invasive species, and the discourse of places and spaces. She also mentors graduate students in a variety of disciplines, and has co-taught a graduate seminar sponsored by the School of Earth Sciences and the Interdisciplinary Graduate Program on the Environment and Resources (IPER), with support from the Hume Writing Center (HWC).

Michael D. Mullen, PhD, is a professor of soil science and associate provost for undergraduate education at the University of Kentucky (UK). Under his leadership as the associate dean for academic programs in the College of Agriculture (2004–09), the UK sustainable agriculture program was established. Mullen received his doctorate in soil science from North Carolina State University. His current research focuses on student success in higher education while he continues to pursue interests in soil biology and bio-chemistry with an emphasis on microbial ecology in agricultural soils. His teaching experiences have spanned the spectrum of university students, from agricultural and environmental issues courses at the freshman level to soil biochemistry courses at the doctoral level. Mullen has coauthored two publications related to teaching agricultural sustainability, including: "Engaging Agriculture and Non-Agriculture Students in an Interdisciplinary Curriculum for Sustainable Agriculture," *NACTA Journal,* 54(4): 24–29; and "The Soil Science Profession: Investment, Vestment and Validation," *Soil Science Society of America Journal,* 74(2).

Valdeen Nelsen received a BS in education from the University of Nebraska Lincoln and an MA in public administration from the University of Nebraska at Omaha. She has been an intern project associate with the Partners in Pollution Prevention (P3) program at the University of Nebraska Lincoln since 2006. Prior to joining the P3 program, she served as coordinator for the master of public health program at the University of Nebraska medical center. She has worked on behalf of the public's health and well-being for most of her professional career in a variety of public and nonprofit organizations.

Catherine O'Brien, PhD, is an associate professor in the education department of Cape Breton University, Nova Scotia, Canada. Her research and teaching have focused on sustainability and sustainable communities for the past twenty years. Some highlights of this work include a research project at the Barefoot College in Rajasthan, India to explore its education process for sustainable community development. She spearheaded research and policy development for child- and youth-friendly planning in Canada to create healthier communities for young people. Working with Dr. Richard Gilbert, Catherine has developed *Child and Youth Friendly Land Use and Transport Planning Guidelines* for every province. Her most recent innovation is the development of a groundbreaking concept called "sustainable happiness" which merges work from sustainability principles with research from happiness studies. She developed the world's first university course in sustainable happiness. Preliminary research evidence suggests that the sustainable happiness course has fostered healthy lifestyles that students have maintained for a year following the completion of the course. Sustainable happiness is being integrated into formal education at the elementary level with the *Sustainable*

Happiness and Health Teacher's Guide. More information is available at www.sustainablehappiness.ca

Justin Pettibone is a visiting professor in the liberal studies department at Grand Valley State University and is currently a doctoral candidate in American studies at Michigan State University. His interests include ethics, political ideology, cultural replication, and the relationship of these to issues of sustainability.

Courtney Quinn is a PhD candidate in leadership studies at the University of Nebraska–Lincoln. She holds a MS in natural resources from UNL and a BA in environmental policy from Drake University. She teaches environmental leadership and ethics in agriculture and natural resources. Her research interests include environmental leadership and leaders, environmental ethics, agricultural ethics, and critical thinking development in undergraduate students.

Carrie R. Rich, MS, serves as the director for vision translation at Inova Health System. Working alongside the executive leadership team, her role is to guide development and implementation of system wide strategic goals for Inova. Prior to joining Inova Health System, Ms. Rich served as the healthcare specialist at Perkins + Will, an international architecture firm known for sustainable healthcare facility design. Carrie developed and teaches a healthcare sustainability curriculum for higher education, piloted as an adjunct faculty member at Georgetown University. Today, Carrie partners with national and international organizations to disseminate the healthcare sustainability curriculum, including the Association of University Programs in Health Administration (AUPHA), the Institute for Healthcare Improvement (IHI), the Association for the Advancement of Sustainability in Higher Education (AASHE) and others. In the community, Carrie translates healthcare sustainability principles to develop tools for underserved populations. Carrie codeveloped a sustainability checklist for community health centers in partnership with the National Association of Community Health Centers (NACHC) and contributes probono to Ibasho, a nonprofit dedicated to creating socially integrated, sustainable communities for elderly underserved populations. Ms. Rich chairs the Board of Everybody Eats, a nonprofit café committed to sustainable, nutritious foods. She also serves on the Board of Directors of the National Capital Healthcare Executives (NCHE) and Teens for Technology, an international computer literacy nonprofit. Carrie received a master's degree in health systems administration from Georgetown University and completed her undergraduate degree at Lehigh University.

Tamara Savelyeva, PhD, studied education at Virginia Tech after receiving her training in sustainability and environmental education at Cornell University. Her teaching and research areas include sustainability education, sustainability curricular modeling, and design of global learning environments in higher education. Savelyeva has taught and coordinated multiple research and educational projects since 1992, when she directed her first sustainability education initiative supported by UNESCO. An active member of the European Academy of Natural Sciences, she serves an education task force for the *Earth Charter International*, Costa Rica. She also assists sustainability-related projects for other not-for-profit organizations, including *Sustainability*, Canada; *Noosphere Lab*, Russia; *Curricula Resource Center*, Hungary; and *We Value*, U.K. This work, which is international in scope, has resulted in a book entitled *Global Learning Environment: Innovative Concept and Interactive Model for Changing Academia and Academics* (VDM, 2009) and a more recent publication, entitled *Campus Sustainability: Emerging Curricula Models in Higher Education* (coauthored with Jim McKenna, International Journal for Sustainability in Higher Education, 2011). Currently, Savelyeva works as a research fellow in the Faculty of Education at the University of Hong Kong.

J. Knox Singleton, MHA, is CEO of Inova Health System, one of the nation's most integrated and most wired health care delivery systems and one of the largest in the metropolitan Washington region. Through Mr. Singleton's stewardship for the past 25 years, Inova Health System has pursued its not-for-profit mission of providing world-class health care to all members of its diverse northern Virginia community, regardless of ability to pay. Mr. Singleton was first named to lead the organization in 1984 when it was called the Fairfax Hospital Association. He joined the Fairfax Hospital Association as executive vice president for operations in 1983. Mr. Singleton is a director and officer of a variety of community organizations that address issues such as affordable housing and human services. He is a trustee of Maryville College in Tennessee, serves as president for the Community Coalition for Haiti, and is a ruling elder of Vienna Presbyterian Church. Mr. Singleton is one of 16 members appointed to George Mason University's Board of Visitors by the governor of Virginia. He was named 1990 Citizen of the Year by *The Washington Post* and received the 1993 Community Care Award for Health from the Northern Virginia Community Foundation. In 2000, he received the distinguished Regent's Award from the American College of Healthcare Executives (ACHE), and that year also received the Distinguished Leadership Award from the Washington Chapter of the American Jewish Committee. In 2004, he received the distinguished Governor's Award from Virginia Gov. Mark Warner, recognizing Mr. Singleton's outstanding leadership in business and education partnerships. In November 2009, he was inducted into the Washington Business Hall of Fame. Mr. Singleton is a graduate of the University of North Carolina and received his MA in health administration from Duke University.

Keiko Tanaka, PhD, is an associate professor of rural sociology and Dr. & Mrs. C. Milton Coughenour Sociology Professor in Agriculture & Natural Resources in the Department of Community & Leadership Development at the University of Kentucky. She received her doctorate in sociology from Michigan State University. Her research focuses on the role of agricultural science and technology in transforming the relationship between food production and consumption in the global context. Her work examines knowledge politics surrounding food safety, healthy food, agricultural sustainability, food localization, and food security. Dr. Tanaka teaches courses in the sociology department in the College of Arts & Sciences, the sustainable agriculture program in the College of Agriculture, and the university honor's program. She also directs the UK Asia Center that provides instructional and outreach programs on Asian societies and cultures for Kentuckians. Her publications on teaching sustainability include: "Public Sociology: Building Engaged Scholarship in Lexington—The Case of the University of Kentucky," *Agriculture and Economy* (2011 [Japanese]); "Public Scholarship and Community Engagement in Building Community Food Security: The Case of the University of Kentucky," *Rural Sociology*, 75(4); and the special issue on the Pedagogy of Rural Sociology in *Southern Rural Sociology*, 24(3).

Seema Wadhwa, LEED AP, is the director of sustainability at Urban Ltd. and serves as the sustainability engineer for Inova Health System. Ms. Wadhwa is responsible for the creation and adoption of sustainable management practices at Inova. Prior to her role with Inova, Ms. Wadhwa spent several years managing engineering design projects. She unites industry experience in the areas of project management and logistical planning with technical leadership in water management, urban design and environmental engineering. Ms. Wadhwa's industry experience extends to advising about best practices in green building as prescribed by her professional accreditation as a Leadership in Energy and Environmental Design (LEED AP), enabling a sustainable approach to the design and implementation of health-care projects. Ms. Wadhwa consistently aligns environmental and engineering best practices with business requirements, including cultural and process change throughout the healthcare system. Ms. Wadhwa's leadership in promoting healthcare sustainability initiatives include guest speaking at industry venues, content submissions for national healthcare symposiums and cofounding the National Capital Region Sustainable Healthcare Alliance with member hospitals, design professionals, and industry partners.

Mark Williams, PhD, is an associate professor of landscape horticulture and weed management in the Department of Horticulture at the University of Kentucky. He is the director of Undergraduate Studies for the UK sustainable agriculture program and the founder of the Organic Farming Research and Education Unit at the Horticulture Research Farm. Dr. Williams received his doctorate in developmental and cell biology from the University of California, Irvine. He teaches multiple courses in the sustainable agriculture curriculum, including classes in sustainable plant production systems, weed management, and the apprenticeship in sustainable agriculture. His research is focused on organic horticulture, with a particular interest in trying to understand plant microbe interactions in organically managed soils. Williams recently published an article on the UK program: Keating, Mark, Victoria Bhavsar, Herbert Strobel, Larry Grabau, Michael Mullen, and Mark Williams, "Engaging Agriculture and Non-Agriculture Students in an Interdisciplinary Curriculum for Sustainable Agriculture" *NACTA (North American Colleges and Teachers of Agriculture) Journal,* 54 (2010).

Also available from Stylus

Social Responsibility and Sustainability
Multidisciplinary Perspectives Through Service Learning
Edited by Tracy McDonald
Foreword by Robert A. Corrigan

Presents the work of faculty who have been moved to make sustainability the focus of their work, and to use service learning as one method of teaching sustainability to their students.

The chapters in the opening section of this book—Environmental Awareness—offer models for opening students to the awareness of the ecological aspects of sustainability, and of the interdependence of the ecosystem with human and with institutional decisions and behavior; and illustrate how they, in turn, can share that awareness with the community.

The second section—Increasing Civic Engagement—explores means for fostering commitment to community service and experiencing the capacity to effect change.

The concluding section—Sustainability Concepts in Business and Economics—addresses sustainability within the business context, with emphasis on the "triple bottom line"—the achievement of profitability through responsible environmental practice and respect for all stakeholders in the enterprise.

Pedagogy of the Earth
Education for a Sustainable Future
Edited by Carlos Hernandez, Rashmi Mayur

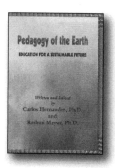

* Includes the writings of Rachel Carson, David W. Orr, Leonardo da Vinci, Paul and Ann Ehrlich, Pablo Neruda, and Herbert Marcuse

"If knowledge is power and power can change the world, then *Pedagogy of the Earth* serves the most significant purpose of educating common people about the environment."—**Noel Brown**, *Former Director, UNEP*

It is generally believed that in order to bring changes for a sustainable future, it is most important that all people are educated about the basic facts concerning ecology and development. *Pedagogy of the Earth* is a rare book of ideas, information, and inspiration from some of the world's finest ecologists, thinkers, scientists, poets, and philosophers. It is a book of learning, joy, and transformation for those who are endeavoring to build a sustainable and equitable world.

Kumarian Press

Sty/us

22883 Quicksilver Drive
Sterling, VA 20166-2102

Subscribe to our e-mail alerts: www.Styluspub.com